# FOR EACH OTHER

Also by Lonnie Barbach:

*For Yourself: The Fulfillment of Female Sexuality*
*Women Discover Orgasm: A Therapist's Guide to a*
    *New Treatment Approach*
*Shared Intimacies: Women's Sexual Experiences* (with Linda Levine)

# FOR EACH OTHER

*Sharing Sexual Intimacy*

## LONNIE BARBACH, Ph.D.

*Anchor Press/Doubleday, Garden City, New York*
*1982*

Copyright © 1982 by Lonnie Barbach

Library of Congress Cataloging in Publication Data

Barbach, Lonnie Garfield, 1946–
  For each other.

  Includes index.
  1. Women—Sexual behavior.  I.  Title.
HQ29.B319     306.7′088042     81–43538
ISBN 0–385–17296–6              AACR2

To all my clients who, in sharing themselves, were my greatest teachers.

# Acknowledgments

A book is never written alone. Without the support, love, and input from my family and friends this one might never have been completed. I would like particularly to acknowledge the assistance of Paul Aron, Carol Rinkleib Ellison, Caroline Fromm, Victoria Galland, Mark Glasser, Paul Goldsmith, René Van Dervere, Deborah Villa, Joan Levin, Jeri Marlowe, Beverly Whipple, and Bernie Zilbergeld, whose critical feedback has made the book a far better, more accurate contribution.

I am grateful to my typists: Jean Price, Tom Gartner, and especially Mickie Denig; to my editor, Loretta Barrett; my agent, Rhoda Weyr; and my assistant, Cherie Martin Franklin.

Most of all, I would like to thank my husband, Alberto Villoldo, without whom my life would be seriously diminished.

# Contents

# FOR EACH OTHER

# Introduction

Almost all American women face a sexual problem at some point in their lives. The most recent polls show that between 30 and 50 percent of women have problems with orgasm.[1] And a University of Pittsburgh study found that your relationship does not have to have serious problems for you to experience a sexual problem. Sixty-three percent of the female partners in couples who defined themselves as happily married reported arousal or orgasmic difficulties.[2]

Sexual problems have many causes. Some are the result of communication problems, stored-up resentment, and unresolved power struggles in a relationship. Others result from cultural attitudes which have taught women to be anything but sexually comfortable.

Recent changes have had an impact on a woman's expression of her sexuality. Never before have so many women been aware of orgasm, aware of their clitoris, aware of their right to pleasure. With effective contraception, sex is no longer inextricably tied to reproduction and women are freer to enjoy sexual fulfillment. More lesbians are willing to speak out about their sexual preference without guilt or shame. Still, many women cannot entirely shed the effects of religious and family backgrounds which taught them that sex is sinful or at least unbecoming.

As a result, many women have not developed the sexual aspects of their intimate relationships as fully as they have developed their roles as mother, homemaker, and co-supporter. While they may have intellectually rejected their negative attitudes toward sex, the ability to express sexual feeling has not always followed. Many women still worry about their partner loving them, respecting them, and staying with them if they become less inhibited. Ironically, most men long for female partners who are sexually responsive. Women who obviously enjoy sex not only make their partner feel adept as a lover, but increase their partner's sexual enjoyment by providing additional sexual energy and input.

Today both men and women express longing for greater satisfaction from their intimate relationships. As the technological society reduces the emotional fulfillment derived from work, and distance separates people from their extended families, more nurturing is required from intimate relationships. A satisfying and loving sexual relationship is one way to meet this need. This is not to say that sex cannot be enjoyed without love. But for most people, good sex is a part of a close and caring relationship.[3] The more trust a woman has in her partner, the more likely she is to be able to relax and fully enjoy sex. Problems in nonsexual areas of a couple's relationship can affect the sexual relationship and reduce the satisfaction experienced.

*For Each Other* has been conceived of as a guide to help negotiate the complex aspects of a relationship that can affect sexual satisfaction. It is based on nine years' experience working directly with hundreds of women in group, individual, and couple sex therapy, and supervising therapists counseling hundreds more. Originally I worked with women who had never experienced orgasm through any means. Out of this work came *For Yourself: The Fulfillment of Female Sexuality*, which taught women about their own bodies and orgasm largely through the process of self-stimulation. Since then I have broadened the program to include women who are orgasmic with masturbation but not with their partners, women who rarely desire sex, and women who find sex painful.

These sexual problems were discussed among small groups of six or seven women over a period of ten sessions. The women varied in age and background. They were involved in committed relationships—both long and short term—as well as in casual sexual relationships. They were largely heterosexual, but about 10 percent were in lesbian relationships. It was through leading these groups that I learned the necessary approaches and steps required for women to gain sexual satisfaction with a partner.*

The exercises the women carried out at home included both talking exercises that reduce anger and improve communication and physical touching homework assignments designed to break unsatisfying lovemaking patterns and pave the way for more fulfilling sexual experiences. As these women experimented with various homework assignments, I learned which exercises were most effective in helping women improve their sexual relationships.

Some of the women participating in the groups had partners who were aware of the problem and were willing to participate in homework. Others were involved in casual sexual relationships and preferred to carry out assignments without informing their partners about their sexual problem—particularly when it concerned orgasm. While it is most likely to be successful for women who have partners willing to participate actively in the exercises, the program outlined in this book can also be helpful for women who have a partner who is unaware of the problem or the process. However, this would mean that the entire responsibility would be placed on her shoulders to initiate and monitor the assignments. Obviously, the involvement and support of a partner improves the chances of success.

If you have a partner with whom you can talk openly and carry out the exercises, your partner should read this book before you begin. Sometimes couples read the chapters aloud together and sometimes they read them separately, underlining the sentences or paragraphs that seem to describe their particular concern or situation, as well as the exercises which seem relevant.

Exploring our sexuality is a journey that begins at birth and continues throughout life. Our ideas of sexual fulfillment change as we grow, opening different avenues of exploration. It is important to hold goals, not final destinations; reaching one goal simply frees us to move toward the next. Like an adventure in a new and exotic land, our sexual journey provides us with unending opportunities to add richness to our lives. The longer we explore

* If you are a therapist and interested in learning to run preorgasmic groups, please read *Women Discover Orgasm: A Therapist's Guide to a New Treatment Approach,* which I wrote specifically for this purpose.

and the deeper we delve, the more intimately we know the sexual terrain and the richer the experience becomes.

*For Each Other* explores some of the major factors that affect sexual fulfillment. Unraveling and reversing a sexual problem may not be entirely possible with only a self-help book. However, the chapters ahead should provide some direction. Although I cannot supply magical solutions, I can offer new ways of perceiving a sexual relationship so that it becomes less of an enigma, as well as exercises to break old patterns and create new ones.

While the examples in the book are heterosexually biased, most of the physiological and psychological factors that affect sexual relationships apply to heterosexual and lesbian relationships in the same way. There are some relationship issues which are unique to lesbian couples. Unfortunately, since the number of lesbian couples that I have worked with is small, I would prefer to leave those specific issues to a lesbian author who would be more experienced in this area and hence better equipped to address them. However, since so many interactional problems are similar, the large majority of the exercises in this book are as applicable to lesbian couples as they are to heterosexual ones. Certainly all of the communication exercises and self-sexuality exercises are equally useful to women in a relationship with a man and to women in a relationship with a woman. All oral and manual stimulation exercises are applicable to both. Even the vaginal-awareness exercises and exercises specifically dealing with intercourse can be relevant to lesbians who want to enjoy vaginal penetration. Although I have tried always to use "partner" to refer to a woman's lover, I have not been wholly successful. I apologize in advance, for I know this may alienate some of my lesbian readers.

The chapters in Section I address the three major areas which underlie sexual problems: role scripting, relationship dynamics, and the physiological and emotional components of sexual response.

The second section—which contains chapters on observation and risk taking, and communication—gives a method for analyzing the sexual problem, as well as the initial steps necessary for change.

The chapters in the third section address the difficulties in attaining orgasm with a partner. They discuss the causes of lack of orgasm and provide homework exercises to help women who are already orgasmic learn through masturbation to be orgasmic with a partner.†

Section IV is directed toward women who experience painful sex as a result of insufficient lubrication, clitoral tenderness, deep vaginal pain that occurs with penile thrusting, or vaginismus, a spasm of the vaginal opening that prevents intercourse.

The chapters in Section V explore sexual interest and delve into the causes of and solutions for lack of sexual interest and discrepancies in desire. In addition, some approaches are provided for enhancing sex when it has grown routine or boring. The final chapter explains what to expect from the exercises and what to do next if your goals have not been met.‡

Since the readers of this book will vary greatly, not every suggested exercise will be relevant for you. Each of you will have to individualize the exercise programs in much the same manner as each woman who participates in the women's sexual therapy groups individualizes her approach. Don't be afraid to experiment.

If you choose to make some changes in your sexual relationship, you should be prepared to experience a period of upheaval, both individually and as a couple. Focusing on a sexual interaction which has been a cause for distress may bring some negative and possibly long-held feelings of resentment out in the open. Your partner may become aware of feeling irritated over your sexual unresponsiveness. Or, your partner may worry about no longer satisfying you should you become more sexual. Almost every male partner of a woman with a sexual problem believes that at some level he is responsible. Female partners of women in lesbian relationships often experience the same reaction.

These fears are common and are to be expected. During this sexual-exploration time your partner may become moodier than usual or be easily offended. He may experience transient periods of

† Women who have never had an orgasm or who have had only a few in their lives should begin by first reading *For Yourself*, which provides detailed instruction on learning to experience orgasm first through masturbation.

‡ If you are experiencing no sexual problem but wish to enhance an already good sexual relationship, or if you have particular interests as to the effects of pregnancy, parenting or aging on your sex life you may be interested in reading the ideas and attitudes of women interviewed for *Shared Intimacies: Women's Sexual Experience*, which I co-authored with Linda Levine.

rapid ejaculation or erectile problems. You may have to face basic assumptions you had about yourself or sex. You may find that some of the premises your relationship was based on have become obsolete. Or you may have to challenge fears that inhibit the development of a satisfying sexual relationship. Both you and your partner may become discouraged and wonder if you will ever succeed. All of this is not said to discourage you from trying, but to prepare you for some of the hurdles that could lie ahead. Take care, during this period, not to make any hasty decisions. Our groups have shown that a few weeks after the exercises have been started, many of the aforementioned concerns fade away, as changes in the sexual relationship foster changes in other areas.

I wish you the best in your journey. Remember, you are not alone. There are many others working toward similar goals. Also, you need not hurry. Your sexuality will continue to unfold throughout the rest of your life. You have no time constraints and can feel free to move at your own pace. Most important, enjoy the process. There is a special kind of excitement that occurs when you learn something for the first time. So savor each step. The desired outcomes will arrive in due time and of their own accord. There is no need to sacrifice the journey to attain a goal. You can have the pleasure of both.

*Section I*

# BASIC PREMISES:
*Preparing for the Journey*

# Chapter 1

# THE WAY WE ARE:
## Role Scripting and
## Female Sexual Problems

Many of us have worried silently for years that we are neurotic or sexually abnormal. Sometimes our concerns are almost subliminal and sometimes they become full-blown anxiety attacks. How come I'm not sexually turned on as much as I should be? As much as the magazines say? As much as my partner wants? How come I don't have orgasms often enough? Every time? During intercourse? "Maybe I don't love my partner enough," comes one answer. "Maybe my partner really doesn't love me enough," is another. "Maybe I'm a latent lesbian," or "Maybe I was molested by my father or an uncle when I was young." A myriad of possibilities come to mind.

Unfortunately, there is rarely anyone to turn to for help. It is not easy to talk about the intimate details of our sex lives. We may be unable to talk about them to our women friends—what if talking about sex offends them and ruins the friendship? What if they pity us or think us inadequate? Or worse, what if they view our partner as inadequate? Although we may discuss our concerns somewhat with our partner, such conversations can result in anger and hurt feelings. If each person feels responsible and no one has a solution, the conversation may become especially difficult. Frequently, we can't talk with our physicians. Most of them don't have the time and even if we muster the courage to voice our questions, we may sense their disapproval (or perhaps their discomfort). So we keep our questions and concerns to ourselves and secretly wonder "What is wrong with me?" One minute we think we have the answer; the next minute we are quite sure we are fooling ourselves and the problem lies deeper.

Whatever your worries are, you are not alone. Sexual concerns are shared by millions of women. Women in happy relationships have sexual problems. As we would expect, however, the percentage of sexual problems is higher for women in unhappy relationships. But the point is that it is not only how we feel about our partner, but other issues, that can cause sexual dissatisfaction. Some of these issues stem from the negative way women have been conditioned to view sex.

Although sexual drive may be innate, what we consider right or wrong sexual behavior, what we think is decent or indecent, which actions or partners are considered appropriate or inappropriate, are all the result of learning. In this sense, sex is culture-bound; it can only be fully understood by looking at the values of the given culture. Even within our society, a variety of beliefs and attitudes are specific to individual religious and racial subcultures. Since it would be impossible for me to delineate the sexual attitudes of each of the major subcultures of this society, I will stick to the general attitudes that affect the majority of American women.

## CULTURAL ROLE SCRIPTS

Role scripting is a term used for behaviors individuals learn in order to fill certain functions. We learn to be girls and boys, women and men, mothers and fathers. For example, women learn to be nurturers, to be cooks, to provide emotional solace; men learn to be providers, to repair things, to exhibit logic. There is no doubt that the scripting is different for males and females, even though not *all* males and females precisely fit their scripts.

The scripts that males and females learn have changed over the years as social ideas and trends have changed. Thus, depending on our age, there are a number of different role scripts we may have learned. These scripts can have a powerful effect on our sexual functioning. The following are some of the more common ones.

## The Puritanical/Victorian Script

Our society has had very puritanical undertones, especially before 1940. Women, to be considered decent, were expected to be sexually pure and innocent. They were not supposed to like sex, at least not overtly. Activities were considered important or worthwhile only if they were productive, if they produced money or sustenance, or were done for the good of others. Activities that merely produced pleasure were considered selfish and hedonistic. Since it was not necessary to enjoy sex or to experience an orgasm in order to procreate, these aspects of sexual expression were given a low priority. Many parents believed that educating their children about sex would merely arouse their interest and lead them down the path of sin and destruction. In their attempt to assure innocence and purity, parents often assured sexual ignorance as well.

I call the way these women learned about sex the "nonmodel" of learning. They were taught nothing about it. Most of their mothers never mentioned the word "sex" and their fathers, heaven forbid, certainly didn't. If anything was mentioned, it was that girls who had sex were being used by their boyfriends and did not deserve respect. Those who became pregnant deserved what they got, and the neighborhood gossip about them served to entrench the determination of others not to end up the same way. So many buried their sexual feelings—some so deeply that they were no longer even aware of their existence. Yet, without any information, adult women were still expected to develop a satisfying sexual relationship once they married.

Young women who did engage in sex often felt cheap, loose, and like the tramps they were told they were. Yet many of them used sex, particularly during adolescent years, as a way to get some nurturing. As Barbara, a woman who joined a sexual therapy group, put it:

> I felt cheap and dirty, a real tramp because I was sleeping with my boyfriend. My mother and father didn't bring me up that way, but they were both alcoholics and very unhappy, and there was no love in our home. I needed love, and even though I always felt somewhat used, still there was some comfort in being held and having someone who would take me away from the fighting in our home.

My own experience in learning about sex is probably typical for women born in the forties and fifties. Although parents are becoming aware that sexual information is important for their children, their own upbringing gave them no experience in discussing the subject. Before I was twelve years old and in the sixth grade my mother and I never discussed sex. (Nor did my father and I, which was lucky for me, as I would have died of embarrassment.) However, one day that year, my mother and I saw a school film about the birds and the bees, sperm and egg. As we were walking home together, she asked if I understood it all. (I remember part of this conversation, and years later she filled me in on the rest.) I answered, "I understand about the egg and the sperm, but how does the sperm get to the egg?" My mother quickly thought to herself, "If she asks, it means she's ready to know, so I probably should tell her." She took a deep breath and explained to me about how the penis is put into the vagina and ejaculates the sperm—at which point I exclaimed, "You and Daddy don't do that, do you?" My mother was absolutely mortified by my response. I realized something was terribly wrong, but didn't know exactly what, as we both clammed up with embarrassment. We didn't have another discussion about sex until I was twenty-five, divorced, and had written my first book on sexuality.

## The "Sex Is Good/Bad" Script

Women have been given mixed messages about sex. We are told that sex is dirty—yet we are instructed to save it for someone we love. I've always wondered why we should want to save something that is dirty for someone we love. We are taught that being a virgin is virtuous and that keeping our genital area (considered by many to be a dirty and disgusting area that some even had to wash with a separate washcloth) untouched is the greatest gift we can give to our husband on our wedding night. Some religions teach that premarital sex leads to damnation, yet they never relate the pleasures of marital sex—except to say that producing children is a righteous act. Is it better to be a virgin and be pure or be a better lover by gaining sexual expertise? If you are faithful, are you normal or sexually restricted? If you're unfaithful, are you neurotic or a swinger? One way a woman secures her self-esteem is by attracting males. This is most easily accomplished by being seductive. Yet carrying through the seduction could result in a bad reputation and lowered self-esteem. Not carrying through the seduction means she is a tease. No wonder many of us walk around confused.

Women rarely see sex as being for their own enjoyment; instead they learn that it is a way to get a man. There is the joke about the woman who entered her neighbor's house obviously upset. "What's the matter?" her friend asked. "I just caught my husband making love," she replied, nearly hysterical. "So?" said her friend. "That's how I caught my husband!" The message is clear.

During adolescence young women have to learn to walk a tight-rope. This is as true today as it was in the past. We learn to go far enough to keep our boyfriends interested, but not so far that we lose their respect or become pregnant. The guy is supposed to try to get the girl to go as far as he can, and the girl is supposed to stop him. So, as our boyfriend's hand inches down toward our breast, we have to consider the pros and cons of taking this new step. We know the decision is irrevocable and we can't go backward the following Saturday night.

Carefully measuring the pace of our sexual progress teaches us how to be more in our heads controlling our feelings and less in the physical experience. Then, later on, when we get married or finally become old enough to make decisions for ourselves regarding sex, many of us find that it is not easy to let go of the control we have spent so many years developing. Some of us have learned to suppress our sexual urges so well that we are unable to recognize feeling sexually turned on.

Julia Heiman conducted some interesting research on this subject. She had women listen to tapes of erotic stories while a photo-plethysmograph was placed in their vagina. A photoplethysmograph is an instrument which measures vasocongestion and lubrication, two physiological signs of sexual arousal. She found that 42 percent of the women showing the largest blood volume increase said they did not feel any physical response.[1] This indicates that either the social scripting dictating that women should not be turned on by erotica is so strong that the women hesitated to report otherwise, or that some women are so out of touch with their bodies that they are not even aware of the physiological process of arousal.

A second unfortunate outcome of the double bind we felt while dating was that we inadvertently taught men not to listen to us. Instead, we taught them to persist in the face of our protests. Our bodies were turned on and our boyfriends knew it. So when we said no, they knew that if they kept pursuing their desires, more often than not, they would get their way. When we said, "No, no, no," they heard it as "Yes, yes, yes, but pretend you are making me do it." It reminds me of a traveling salesman joke. This traveling salesman was way out in the country when his car suddenly broke down. It was late at night, so he stopped at a nearby farmer's house and was invited to stay. However, because of space limitations, the farmer told the salesman he would have to share his daughter's bed. The traveling salesman could hardly complain. He went to the bedroom and got undressed, waiting for the farmer's daughter to arrive as he occupied himself with tantalizing fantasies of a sex-filled night. When she arrived, he couldn't believe his eyes, as she was far more beautiful than even his fantasies. But, as she got into bed, she placed three pillows between the two of them and told him not to cross over the pillows. He was disappointed at first, but being a guest in the farmer's home—and grateful for the hospitality—he decided to cherish his fantasies as he went to sleep. When the salesman awoke the next morning, the farmer's daughter had already gone. Once dressed, he thanked the farmer and was leaving the house, when he saw the daughter on the other side of the fence milking a cow. "Wait a minute," he said to her, "while I jump over this fence and kiss you good-bye." To which she replied, "Hell, if you can't make it over three pillows, you ain't never gonna make it over that fence."

The sexual conquest and resistance scenario, which had its seeds in our adolescence, has a strong impact on what images and activities we find sexually exciting. No wonder sexual fantasies of being forced to submit are so prevalent among women. They recapture the height of adolescent sexual energy. The tension produced by the interaction of the powerful dominating male and the demure resistant female creates images that tend to be highly erotic long after sex has been legitimized. Unfortunately, this image may have generated some harmful social consequences. As sex becomes more legitimized and female partners become more readily available, men will no longer be able to gain excitement from the tension created by the persist/resist battle between the sexes. Child molestation and incest already seem to be on the rise. More unconventional and even dangerous sexual practices may grow in popularity as a way to duplicate the sexual thrills created by adolescent sexual scripts.

## The "Don't Touch Down There" Script

While growing up, many of us received messages that caused us to develop negative attitudes about our genitals. We were taught not to look "down there" and certainly not to touch ourselves. Negative feelings about our genitals have resulted in many women being concerned that they might smell or taste bad, concerns which interfere with being able to relax and focus on the sexual feelings during cunnilingus. It is not surprising that one of the repercussions of these messages is that it takes young women longer to find cunnilingus pleasurable than it does for young men to relax and enjoy fellatio.[2]

At least little boys get some praise for touching their genitals. If they hold their penis and urinate in the right direction they are positively reinforced. Most boys masturbate. Masturbation, however, is much less frequent among girls. A teenage sexuality study found that 80 percent of eighteen-year-old boys said they masturbated, while only 59 percent of girls the same age said they did.[3] Some girls were required to sleep with their arms outside the covers. One mother even went so far as to smell her daughter's fingers to make certain she was not engaging in this "sinful" behavior between bed checks.

Masturbation or onanism is considered a sin by most orthodox religious groups although the three references in the Old Testament —Leviticus 15:16, Deuteronomy 23:9–11 and Genesis 38:8–10— provide no basis for condemning masturbation.[4] The first two refer to nocturnal emission (wet dreams) and not masturbation, and the third, the passage from Genesis which is primarily used to condemn masturbation, is really not about masturbation at all:

And Judah said unto Onan, Go in unto thy brother's wife, and marry her, and raise up seed to thy brother. And Onan knew that the seed should not be his; and it came to pass, when he went in unto his brother's wife, that he spilled *it* on the ground, lest that he should give seed to his brother. And the thing which he did displeased the Lord: wherefore he slew him also.[5]

The custom of the time indicated that if a man died without heirs, it was the duty of his living brother to provide an heir through sexual relations with the widow. The child of the union was considered to be that of the deceased. Apparently Onan did not like the idea and so practiced withdrawal and "wasted his seed" by ejaculating outside the vagina. The Lord's disapproval of Onan's refusal to carry out the duty of impregnating the deceased brother's wife has been misinterpreted as his disapproval of masturbation and, as a result, masturbation has been referred to as onanism. The story was misinterpreted to mean that male masturbation was sinful, and this idea was then applied to the female as well, although there is no reference whatsoever in the Old Testament pertaining to women and sexual self-stimulation.

Also, during the nineteenth century, physicians commonly ascribed unknown diseases to the act of masturbation. Everything from insanity to warts and even poor eyesight was attributed to self-stimulation. Many of these beliefs that masturbation was sinful or unhealthy have had far-reaching repercussions even today.

Since sexuality is learned, forbidding masturbation interferes with one of the most frequently used and safest ways for adolescents and young adults to learn about sex. Masturbation does not involve negotiating complex emotional relationships in the way that sex with a partner might entail. And there is no risk of pregnancy. Furthermore, research has shown that learning to have orgasms through masturbation actually facilitates learning to have orgasms with a partner. Kinsey found a marked correlation between the premarital experience of orgasm and the ability to experience orgasm during marital sex. Premarital experiences of orgasm included orgasm through masturbation, as well as orgasm through petting and premarital intercourse.[6] Research on the preorgasmic groups shows that 87 percent of the women who participated in the group treatment program learned to have orgasms with their partner after they learned to be orgasmic through masturbation.[7]

Those women who defied societal reprehensions and learned about sex through masturbation often felt guilty and abnormal about doing so. These negative feelings associated with the physical pleasure have done psychological harm. Kinsey puts it quite well: ". . . Some millions of American females in the United States, and larger numbers of males, have had their self-assurance, their social efficiency, and sometimes their sexual adjustments in marriage needlessly damaged—not by their masturbation, but by the conflict between the practice and moral codes. There is no other type of sexual activity which has worried so many women."[8]

Haas, in his recent study of teenage sexuality, adds: "The negative messages that teenagers have received about masturbation have caused them a lot of distress. The majority of adolescents who masturbated reported feeling guilty, ashamed, dirty, stupid, embarrassed, or abnormal."[9] Consequently, there seems to be agreement that masturbation does not cause the problems; it's the worrying about it that does. Many women believe that they don't have orgasms with a partner because they masturbated in the past or because they continue to masturbate. They therefore try to stop masturbating and then feel weak and inadequate when they cannot stop.

As a result of much of this negative training, plus the fact that the female's genitals are not as readily visible as the male's, many of us grew up knowing nothing about the anatomy of our genitals. If we had no permission to touch, and never looked, we remained ignorant.

## The "Sex Is for Men" Script

One of the major tenets of sexuality that has interfered with women's sexual development is the notion that sex is for men. Unmarried women are "used" sexually. Married women do it as a marital duty. No wonder one woman told her daughter on her wedding day to always tell her husband that it hurt when they had sex. At least this would ensure appreciation for her martyrdom.

Despite a so-called sexual revolution, the idea that sex is the privilege of men is very much with us. Many women still don't feel comfortable being assertive or direct about their sexual interests. For example, the following recently occurred at a social gathering. A young woman was attracted to a man she had just met that night. They spent some time talking and at the end of the evening she made it perfectly clear that she was interested in going home with him and spending the night. He was caught off guard, feeling flattered yet not particularly interested in a sexual relationship since he was seriously involved with a woman who was away on business.

To make a long story short, they went back to his apartment together and spent the night. Later, when he related the story to me, he said, with disbelief, "You know, I felt kind of used. All she was really interested in was my body, in having sex with me." The story is striking because of the role reversal. We expect the man to be delighted and the woman to feel used. We rarely encounter the opposite.

Growing up not feeling good about one's sexuality and seeing it as solely for a partner's enjoyment may account for the belief that women reach their sexual peak around the age of forty. It appears to take time for women to grow into and accept their sexuality. As women free themselves of their inhibitions, their sexual energy and appetite seem to increase. This lessened inhibition and growing ease allows women to claim their sexuality as their own, rather than see it as the property of their partner.

## The "Fantasy Model of Sex"[10] Script

The fantasy model of sex espoused by males in locker rooms or portrayed in popular novels, and especially pornographic books and magazines, is far from your typical sexual experience. For example, the following excerpt is taken from a popular modern novelist who has sold millions of copies of his books. Because of this wide distribution, Harold Robbins is probably one of the country's most influential sex educators.

> Gently her fingers opened his union suit and he sprang out at her like an angry lion from its cage. Carefully she peeled back his foreskin, exposing his red and angry glans, and took him in both hands, one behind the other as if she were grasping a baseball bat. She stared at it in wonder. "C'est formidable. Un vrai caon." . . . She almost fainted looking down at him. Slowly he began to lower her on him. His legs came up . . . as he began to enter her. . . . It was as if a giant of white-hot steel were penetrating her vitals. She began to moan as it opened her and climbed higher into her body, past her womb, past her stomach, under her heart, up into her throat. . . . She began to climax almost before he was fully inside her. Then she couldn't stop them, one coming rapidly after the other as he slammed into her with the force of the giant body press she had seen working in his factory. . . . Somehow she became confused, the man and the machine they were one and the same and the strength was something else she had never

known before. And finally, when orgasm after orgasm had racked her body into a searing sheet of flame and she could bear no more, she cried out to him in French.

"Take your pleasure with me! . . . Quick, before I die!"

A roar came from deep inside his throat and his hands tightened on her breasts. . . . Then all his weight seemed to fall in on her, crushing the breath from her body, and she felt the hot onrushing gusher of his semen turning her insides into viscous, flowing lava. She discovered herself climaxing again.[11]

It's much like learning to be a doctor by watching "General Hospital" or learning to be a lawyer by watching "Perry Mason." They more resemble fantasy than reality. Yet, this is the way most of us gain information about sex. Men learned that women like to have sex hard and fast. The fantasy model dictates that they are supposed to have gigantic and rock-hard penises, which they drive into women like powerful machines. No wonder men are concerned about penis size and the strength of their erections. No man in the fantasy model of sex ever had difficulty getting an erection and, once erect, never experienced a loss of rigidity until hours later after orgasm.

The fantasy model of sex dictates that a sexual experience must keep building in intensity until it peaks in the ultimate simultaneous orgasm. Since this model of sex only has ups, any decreases experienced in the level of arousal can cause concern. In one of my groups, there were three women who believed that once the process of sexual arousal begins, the excitement mounts ever faster in a constant and dramatic incline until it finally reaches the orgasmic crescendo that leaves them exhausted and breathless. If they noticed their level of arousal beginning to subside because their mind wandered to the telephone call they forgot to make or to the dishes that remained unwashed in the sink, or if the sensations decreased when they changed sexual positions—or especially if the baby coughed or cried—they felt all had been lost. Once having lost the sensations, they feared they would never return, and the anxiety generated by this fear may have actually blocked their return.

To many women, this loss of arousal signals that the current sexual encounter will end just like all the others: in frustration. So, in expectation of the worst, and in an attempt to protect themselves from further disappointment, they quite understandably turn their feelings off and try to get sex over with as quickly as possible. In effect, they give up, and in so doing preclude any possibility of becoming aroused again.

But a sexual event, like any other, has its ups and downs. Once we recognize that the waxing and waning of sexual feelings are normal, we can look at the times when feelings have subsided as just one natural part of the event and not a signal that all is over. Sensations will be lost and generated numerous times during the course of the lovemaking before they develop into an intensity sufficient for orgasm.

## The "Romance and Candlelight" Script

For women, the fantasy model of sex is represented by paperback romance novels. Some interesting research by Arvalea Nelson asserts that women fall along a realistic/romantic continuum. "Romantics" express an idealistic, mystified vision of romantic love, while "realists" show a rational understanding of conscious sexual cooperation. Nelson found that realistic women were discriminating about their sexual activity and able to tell their partners what they liked and did not like; they were active in initiating sex; they concentrated primarily on themselves during lovemaking, and tended to direct lovemaking overtly in order to get what they wanted. Romantic women, by contrast, did not talk about sex, rarely initiated sex, focused selflessly on the partner in an attempt to please him, and amiably followed their lover's direction during lovemaking.

What makes this research particularly interesting is that the romantic/realistic dichotomy correlated quite highly with the women's ability to experience orgasm. Of the romantic women, 22.7 percent were high-orgasmic, while 77.3 percent were low-orgasmic. The women in the realistic group had just the opposite response: 70 percent were high-orgasmic, while 30 percent were low-orgasmic.[12]

Clearly, in this society, women are trained to be romantics, to believe that candlelight dinners and roses result in orgasm. Unfortunately, many of the women who grew up with these notions and continue to believe them are still waiting, while those who treat sex more like other activities, and expect to have to learn and communicate about it, are far more responsive.

## The "Men Should Know" Script

The fantasy model of sex portrays the male as the sexual expert, in total control of the sexual event. He is responsible for sweeping the woman off her feet against her better judgment, and then thoroughly satisfying her sexually. The whole idea that women are supposed to remain pure, innocent, and unknowledgeable, while men are supposed to be totally responsible and sexually all-knowing, presents a number of problems. First of all, where are the men supposed to gain their knowledge? Most men receive little or no sex education at home and the fantasy model of sex certainly doesn't provide many useful pointers.

Since men are not born with the same genital anatomy as women, they have no idea what areas and what kinds of touching provide a woman with pleasure. Furthermore, since every woman is unique sexually, there is no feasible way that any man can know every individual woman's preferences. And yet, each man is expected to know. And if he does not know, he can't ask, for fear of appearing less masculine. The woman, on the other hand, is not able to provide him with any information. If she does, she might hurt his ego, because, after all, a real man should know. Furthermore, if she is really the pure, virginal woman she is supposed to be, she shouldn't have any information to give him. Knowing what feels good sexually and passing this information on reveals that she is sexually experienced, that she is not as pure as she should be. Finally, a strong underlying cultural myth dictates that if it were true love, he most certainly would know what she needs sexually. If he doesn't, maybe it is not real love—a conclusion which has terminated perfectly good relationships.

And so, many of us are stuck, colluding in this cultural conspiracy of silence. When in bed, we wish he would move his hand a little higher . . . just a little higher, or touch us a little more firmly, and yet we often don't say a word. It is similar to telling our partner there is something very special we want for a birthday gift, that we would be deeply pleased and eternally grateful if we got it, and very hurt and dissatisfied if we didn't. Yet we refuse to provide any clues. Odds are, we will not get exactly what we want. A simple request would make it all so much easier, but getting over the hurdle of years of training in the opposite direction is difficult.

## The "Women Can't Talk" Script

Many women are embarrassed to talk about sex; we've had little or no practice at it. Words relating to sex are awkward to say, especially since many of us have learned only too well that it is not ladylike to use them. In addition, the English language is woefully inadequate for describing sensations and feelings. Even if we could rid ourselves of some of the embarrassment and attempt to let our partners know the kinds of touching and activities that create pleasurable feelings for us, the task is complicated merely because there are so few acceptable words to describe such things.

Even as women become more comfortable with sex and less inhibited in their sexual activities and attitudes, they often remain inhibited when it comes to communicating their sexual preferences. Being able to communicate about sex, to communicate sexual needs and preferences, requires some assertiveness, and assertiveness is not something most young girls are taught, particularly when it comes to sex. In fact, young girls are generally taught just the opposite, to be seen and not heard, to be submissive and accepting. Asking for what we want conjures up such unattractive labels as "demanding" or "bitchy." As one woman said: "If something doesn't feel good, I don't say anything. I don't want to be seen as being 'bitchy' in bed."

In addition, for many of us, talking about our feelings is far more intimate than physically expressing ourselves in bed. In response to a questionnaire asking what would be necessary in order to gain more satisfaction from lovemaking, one woman replied, "I know that it is necessary to communicate my needs, but sometimes I don't feel that I know him well enough yet." An interesting comment on sexuality today: we know him well enough to have sex, but not well enough to talk about it.

Not talking about sex can be a form of protection. Since society has lifted many of its prohibitions against interacting sexually, many of us need to find other ways to maintain psychological distance when physical intimacy occurs early in a relationship. We may do this by sharing our bodies, but not our true selves. Enjoying sexual intimacy before sufficient emotional intimacy has developed can cause other problems. Many of us may find that despite the sexual revolution, we simply don't get much out of the "zipless fuck"; we require a relationship to enjoy sex fully. And with the rapid changes in sexual attitudes, many of us may worry that there is something wrong with us because of this.

## The Media Script

The media has thrown us a tough set of standards to live up to. The magazine covers dictate what is pretty and what is not. If we are not as endowed as the "Playmate of the Month," we worry about not being sexually desirable. If our hips are larger than the most recent *Vogue* model's, we feel we are too fat, even though what we consider overweight in this culture would be considered unattractively thin in most Arab and African cultures.

Because of these cultural pressures, most of us are self-conscious about our physical appearance. We forget that our beauty lies in our uniqueness. Instead of accepting ourselves as we are, we may spend outlandish amounts of money and energy buying cosmetics and clothes to enhance our image and mask the areas considered undesirable. Once in bed, with no clothes to hide our "flaws," many of us twist and turn to keep our partner's hands from noticing softness where we have been made to feel we should be rock-hard. This constant self-consciousness can have a negative effect on our sexuality. One woman, who never had any difficulty achieving orgasm when she was on top, rarely assumed this stance because she felt that her breasts sagged and looked unattractive in this position.

Regardless of how closely our appearance matches conventional standards for attractiveness, as women, we are sexual beings, and each and every one of us has a right to enjoy the pleasures of our body. Furthermore, many women find that after they spend time exploring their own bodies, a new appreciation for themselves develops; the areas they considered to be the least attractive, like a rounded stomach, or a padded thigh, may actually be the most pleasing to the touch. After all, softness is an attractive feature.

## The "Dependent and Helpless" Script

Women are basically trained to be dependent and helpless. And although this may be changing, most women are not taught to go out and conquer the world in the same way that men are. While this frees us as women from some of the pressures men feel to be successful, it can also leave us feeling powerless over our lives. Instead, many of us learn that our power lies in our sexuality. If we use our sexuality wisely, we will attract a husband who will confer on us his social and monetary status. As Merle Shain said, "Our society smiles on a man who marries for sex but disrespects him if he marries for money, yet encourages a woman to marry for money but considers it absurd if she marries for sex."[13] Sex is a woman's major asset—success is a man's.

A sense of powerlessness can affect a woman's sexual behavior. If we have been taught that sex is not for pleasure, but rather something to give a partner as a reward or a way to keep him interested, we are likely to withhold that "gift" when we feel angry or insufficiently cared for. If we do not perceive ourselves as having the power to gain directly what we want, we may get our partner to obtain those things for us through the use of our sexuality (and love). If our partner is not successful, or if he does not treat us the way we desire to be treated, we may feel that the only recourse we have is to withhold our sexuality as a way of getting even or getting what we want.

If we have been trained not to rock the boat, not to express our anger, not to threaten the only security we have, we may be afraid to confront our partner directly. If our partner were to leave us, we might be left helpless and alone in the world. Therefore, the only power we may feel we have is the power of withholding—particularly withholding our sexuality. Some of us get headaches when it comes time for lovemaking. Others of us, while submitting, may express our ire indirectly by not feeling excited, by not responding orgasmically, or by trying to get sex over with as quickly as possible.

This negative withholding is powerful. It can make a partner feel inadequate for being unable to turn us on or make us experience orgasm. Our lack of enthusiasm can also successfully ruin the sex experience for our partner as well. In addition, handling anger in this indirect way is fairly safe. It frees us of responsibility. We really can't help what we don't feel and therefore we can't be blamed.

None of this may be intentional. If we were conscious of our sexual withholding, we would recognize that we were depriving ourselves as well as our partner of sexual pleasure. We might also realize that it rarely even produces the desired results since the original problem remains unresolved.

## The "Nurturer" Script

As women, we are taught early on that we are the nurturers. We are responsible for the emotional sustenance of those around us. We are taught to put our husband's needs, our children's needs, our parents' needs, and the needs of our boss before our own. Everyone else's needs get met first, and we relegate ourselves to last place. If a piece of cake or pie is broken when being cut, we will always save that one for ourselves, making certain that everyone else gets a "good" piece. It is not uncommon for women who have spent the better part of their adult years primarily in the role of mother to feel lost when their children leave home. They have had no experience finding activities or concerns of interest to them. All of their training has revolved around responding to the needs of others.

Placing the needs of others before our own and barely considering our own at all can greatly interfere with attaining sexual satisfaction. Many of us expend our energy on making our partner happy during lovemaking. We may concentrate on being a good lover for our partner's enjoyment. However, while we may be good at pleasing our partner, we may not be obtaining sufficient pleasure for ourselves. If our attention is so totally riveted on another person, or on external events rather than on ourselves, it is impossible to experience the full pleasure and sensation of the sexual event.

To experience this for yourself, try the following experiment alone or with a friend. Place a piece of candy in your mouth. Close your eyes and concentrate on experiencing the flavor of the candy. Now open your eyes and carry on a conversation with the real or imagined person. After thirty seconds, stop talking, close your eyes, and focus on the candy once again. Open your eyes and continue the conversation. Finally, close your eyes once more and concentrate on the candy. Do you notice a difference in your awareness of the flavor of the candy when your eyes are closed and you are silent versus when your eyes are open and you are talking?

Most people notice that when they are talking, their awareness of the flavor of the candy is diminished, and sometimes they don't even taste it at all. The same is true of sex. To experience the full pleasure requires some concentration on ourselves, on our bodies, and on the physical stimulation we are receiving in addition to concentrating on our partner. However, if embarrassment, nervousness, insecurity, or obligation causes us to focus totally on stimulating our partner and proving ourselves competent lovers, orgasms often vanish.

Learning to accept pleasure as a positive attribute and not to feel selfish and self-centered about focusing on ourselves may take some practice. Most women's training has been in the opposite direction. We have been taught that "selfish" is a bad word and that if we feel too good we will be punished. Many women see life as a cosmic balance sheet, where joy and pain equal out in the end. One of the biggest lessons women in preorgasmic groups learn is that they have a right to pleasure, that they deserve to feel good without always having to wait for it to be bestowed upon them as payment for doing good for others.

### The "Sex Equals Intercourse" Script

When we talk about sex, we rarely refer to kissing, holding, touching, or oral sex. We consider the "real thing" to be intercourse—not so much because intercourse is necessary to preserve the species, but partly because intercourse was the act that was forbidden during adolescence, while various stages of kissing, petting, and even genital touching were considered acceptable. One woman talked about her adolescence and what a "good girl" she had been. Basically, she had been a "technical virgin," meaning that she had done everything conceivable, short of intercourse. She and her boyfriend would spend hours being sexual together. They would invariably have their pants off, stimulate the other's genitals manually as well as orally, and be fully orgasmic—but she never had *sex*. No wonder going "all the way" was a letdown for her, and for many other women brought up this way. Expectations of intercourse grow unrealistically high, and once the "real thing" becomes an acceptable part of sex, other activities are often abbreviated, if not omitted entirely.

The idea that "real sex" is intercourse creates problems for both men and women. Intercourse requires a man to attain an erection and to maintain it for a considerable period of time—which is not always easy. For the woman this means learning to have orgasms quickly, before her partner ejaculates. In stereotypical fashion, women I talk with wish to reach orgasm faster, to do it in three minutes or less, in the missionary position, at the same time as their partner, and without additional manual stimulation—just through the thrusting of the penis. This is what we call a "Look, Ma, no hands!" orgasm. Why we should desire to reach a climax more rapidly and shorten the experience of sexual pleasure has always been a mystery to me. If sex feels pleasurable, why not extend it as long as possible? My guess is that women are trying to adapt to what they see as a male sexual arousal and release pattern. Since men are considered the sexual authorities and orchestrators, we adapt to fit their style rather than asserting a more leisurely pattern that we might prefer. We let the man's erection designate the beginning of sex and his ejaculation mark its termination. We shy away from teaching our partner the delights of nonintercourse sex which, not requiring an erection, could reduce the pressure men often feel to perform and could extend sex beyond ejaculation.

## The "One Right Way" Script

Just as sex does not equal intercourse, it also does not equal orgasm. The idea that sex means intercourse promotes a goal orientation. As a result, many women become less focused on the pleasure of the moment and more concerned about how close they are to orgasm and whether or not their partner is going to come first. If he ejaculates and his penis gets flaccid, which happens to most men, then the woman may worry that she won't achieve orgasm in the "real" way—through the thrusting of the penis. While the attainment of release through oral or manual stimulation may be possible, many women believe that if they haven't attained orgasm during intercourse, they have not had the "mature vaginal orgasm" labeled by Freud. And even though the research of Masters and Johnson and others has made it absolutely clear that an orgasm is an orgasm, regardless of where the stimulation is taking place, many women still *feel* that, unless the penis produces it, it is not good enough.

Even though we now know that an orgasm produced by breast stimulation is not a breast orgasm, and one produced by fantasy alone with no physical stimulation whatsoever,* is not a fantasized orgasm, many women still somehow feel, *deep down inside,* that an orgasm produced through clitoral stimulation is a "clitoral orgasm" and is inferior to one produced by vaginal stimulation. Clitoral orgasms continue to carry the curse of the belief that they indicate psychological maladjustment, that they are evidence of a deep underlying problem, and that they justify being labeled immature and neurotic.

Why is it, given extensive scientific evidence to the contrary, that we hold on so strongly to this belief? The answer lies in the incredible impact Freud had upon our culture and in the impact males have in determining sexual matters.

Sex is a male's realm and intercourse is often preferable for men —it provides soft, smooth, and intense stimulation of their most sensitive organ. And Freud was a nineteenth-century Viennese male who was a product of a Victorian culture. Sex was considered to be solely for procreative purposes and not for pleasure.

Freud created the foundation of psychology and psychotherapy as we know it today. We know that our dreams have meaning and that what happens to us early in life will have repercussions later on. So we "know" just as strongly that the "right" way to have an orgasm is the "mature vaginal" orgasm. Freud's first two theories were correct, so we continue to believe the third. However, as a pioneer he was bound to make some errors—and this was one of them.

Recent, as yet inconclusive, research seems to indicate that there may be different nerve pathways that contribute to orgasm. Most women respond the majority of time through clitoral stimulation, others through vaginal stimulation. Some spinal-cord-injured women who have no sensations in their genital area whatsoever are capable of having orgasms through the stimulation of other parts of their body which have become eroticized. There is nothing

---

* About one percent of women can have orgasms this way.

wrong with a woman who requires clitoral stimulation to reach orgasm, nor is there anything abnormal about a woman who requires vaginal stimulation, breast stimulation, or fantasy. We are each different and have different requirements for reaching orgasm. One is not inherently superior to the others. Saying one type of orgasm is better than another is like saying that a painter is better than a musician. Both are equally good, each is just a different form of expression. In sex, as in other areas, it is important to accept our individuality and to cherish it.

## The "Lesbian" Script

You may wonder why I have not mentioned lesbian sexuality in the various scripts so far. This is because our society doesn't teach women how to be lesbians. It only teaches us how to be females. Lesbians learn the same sexual scripts as heterosexual women. Each lesbian's reason for preferring women, or a specific woman over a man, is a result of many and often complex factors. Sometimes a lesbian is reacting against negative sexual messages instilled while she was growing up, so she seeks more respectful and equal partners in the form of other women. Some women had sexual experiences with other women initially because intercourse was forbidden and then became comfortable relating to women. Sometimes a woman is attracted to a woman because she resembles someone from a past relationship. These factors are not very different from those which cause a heterosexual woman to prefer blond men, or dark-complexioned men, or men of a particular religion, social class, or temperament.

In addition to learning that women should not really be sexual, that they should not be sexually assertive, and that they should respond in certain prescribed sexual patterns, lesbians carry the additional burden of having sexual feelings that the larger society labels as unnatural. If a woman hasn't already received enough negative sexual input to make her sexually awkward and inhibited, the desire for a female partner can lead her to submerge her sexual feelings altogether. As a result, many women attempt to fit into a heterosexual model or suffer years of secret shame before they are able to come to terms with their sexual preference and have the kind of relationship that provides them satisfaction and pleasure.

## The "Let's Be Modern" Script

People born before the 1940s often say that while *they* received repressive messages about sex, things are much different today. They expect that women who are younger than themselves are all sexually liberated and free of conflict. Unfortunately, this is hardly the case. Children brought up in the sixties and later may, in some cases, have more conflicts.

Women born before 1940 were impressed with the importance of premarital virginity. Since divorce occurred rarely and extramarital sex even less often, most women of that era experienced only one sexual partner. Women born between 1940 and 1960 are very much a transition group. The majority of these women received the same sexual training from their parents that their parents received from their grandparents. At the same time, they received sexually permissive messages from the media and their peers. Women born after 1960 have grown up with even less sexual restriction. Premarital sex, living together before marriage, and the frequency of divorce have made multiple partners common. And the more permissive media have brought explicit sexual information and solutions to sexual problems to every newspaper, magazine article, and television program. Instead of pressure to remain virginal, there is often intense peer pressure to have sex. As a result, sexuality is being expressed at younger and younger ages.

The biggest change is occurring among females. While the age of a young man's first intercourse experience has remained fairly constant over the years, young women are becoming sexually active far earlier than in preceding generations. According to recent statistics, the number of females having had intercourse equals that of males by the age of seventeen. However, girls still tend to have fewer partners than boys and tend to remain in one sexual relationship over a period of time. Teenagers who have multiple partners are likely to be considered promiscuous by their peers. According to Haas, "Teenage sexual values are neither casual nor indiscriminate. For the most part, adolescent sexual expression is a vehicle for communicating caring and intimacy."[14]

All this sexual activity, however, does not seem to breed greater sexual satisfaction. Haas found that 27 percent of these sexually active teenage girls never had orgasms with intercourse, and another 40 percent had orgasms less than half of the time.[15] Girls may be having more sex, but how much they are getting out of it seems questionable. They still often have sex to keep from losing their partner rather than from their own desire, and they still experience a great deal of conflict: "Reflecting greater inner and social conflicts, girls were more likely to report having mixed emotions about the experience (of intercourse). 'It feels good, but it is wrong. Girls aren't supposed to have sex, but many are. What will they think of me if I do? What will they think of me if I don't?' "[16] This conflict is at least in part responsible for the tremendously high teenage pregnancy rate. Ambivalence about being sexually active has resulted in unwillingness to take birth-control pills or carry diaphragms because many young women don't want to look too prepared—or, in some cases, have their parents discover they are sexually active.

Conflict is as great for boys as for girls. Teenage boys used to be able to count on teenage girls to stop them from going too far. They could push safely. Now, however, boys as well as girls are experiencing pressure to have sex. Fears of parental rejection on one side and rejection by peers on the other make it difficult for teenagers to evaluate their own position clearly and to make decisions about sex that reflect their own values and attitudes.

The "Let's Be Modern" Script is affecting adults as well. With the sexual revolution, women who were not supposed to want or like sex in the past are now expected to be tigresses in the bedroom. Instead of feeling guilty about having sex, more women are experiencing guilt from not wanting sex often enough, from not having orgasms, or not having enough of them. The new media blitz that has replaced the eons of lack of information seems to be providing tremendous pressure to live up to certain sexual standards. Each new sexual discovery adds more pressure to perform: we are prudish and uptight if we are unwilling to swing, swap, or follow the ten easy steps to ultimate sexual joy. We worry that our orgasms are not long enough, intense enough, sufficiently multiple. If we require certain conditions for good sex, like a loving relationship, trust in our partner, or security from being heard or seen, we wonder if we are neurotic.

Just as the media have led us to believe that we should all look like the movie stars and models on magazine covers, we are led to believe that if we are not experiencing everything available sexually, we are missing out.

It used to be that only men were not allowed to require specific conditions in order to enjoy sex. According to the "Ready Teddy syndrome," if a woman was available, a man was expected to be turned on, regardless of whether he felt tired or under stress, or even whether he found the woman attractive. Now, in the name of liberation, some of these same restrictive and coercive regulations are beginning to apply to women as well. The rules for women have grown no less restricting, their form has just changed. Instead of being promiscuous if you "do," you're a prude if you "don't."

This whole concept of a sexual Olympics keeps us constantly feeling inadequate. If it is possible for some women to have orgasms through fantasy alone, to have orgasms through vaginal stimulation alone, to have multiple orgasms, to have orgasms accompanied by screaming and nail scratching, we may feel inferior because our patterns of response differ. There is no other area in which everyone expects to be an Olympic gold medal winner— and without hours of daily practice, no less.

The sexual revolution and the resultant notion of the sexual Olympics seem to be creating sexual problems for men as well. The culture prescribes that a "real man" is always ready for sex. Consequently, men don't feel they have permission to say no when a woman initiates. When women didn't initiate sex, a man could be guaranteed that no sex would occur unless he was turned on and made the appropriate advances. As women become more sexually assertive, men are experiencing more and more pressure and anxiety. If their partner initiates sex when they are not in the mood, an erection may not occur. If a man holds onto the belief that a "real man" is always ready for sex, he is likely to feel inadequate if he is unable to perform at his partner's request. In addition, the new rules dictate that a man must satisfy his partner sexually in order to be an adequate male. At least in the past, the man's role could be respectably performed with a quick "Wham, bam, thank you, ma'am." Now he must not only turn himself on, but produce an orgasm for her as well. Many men are finding that sexual performance on demand is more work than fun, and are beginning to question whether it is worth all the effort.

## SEX IS LEARNED

With all of the culturally based conflicts, it is easy to understand why sex often does not just happen naturally, as we have been led to believe it should. We can also see why most sexual problems are not necessarily the result of some terrible underlying neurosis or childhood trauma. They are the result of the ways we learned to behave sexually. But today's society is different from the Victorian one that set down many of the rules from which we currently suffer. Prohibiting sex before marriage was a way to stabilize society and to avoid family units without a male provider. With contraception, sexuality can now be separated from conception and childbearing. Also, with laborsaving devices and a society of people who no longer have to struggle for survival, there is more energy and leisure time to enjoy the pleasures of life, among which are sexual pleasures and enhancing our intimate relationships. However, even with a sexual revolution and the increasing availability of good written material on sexuality, it is not easy to undo feelings that have been instilled in us for years. But it is possible. Remember, sex is learned. It just takes sufficient motivation and practice to undo the negative training and learn new attitudes and approaches. This, of course, is the aim of this book.

Now that we have looked at our early learning and the development of sexual attitudes and scripts, it is time to continue on our journey and explore intimate relationships and the effect that the nonsexual aspects of the relationship have on sexual satisfaction.

*Chapter 2*

# LOVE IS NOT ENOUGH:
## *The Nature of Relationships*

In our journey through adolescence and adulthood, most of us naturally seek out intimate relationships. We want to find one special person with whom we can share our innermost thoughts and feelings. The physical and sexual expression of intimacy with this special person can be an important source of pleasure and satisfaction. When there are problems in the sexual relationship, they can negatively affect the intimacy and nonsexual caring. When we encounter a sexual problem, we may secretly wonder if the problem lies in insufficient love—either on our part, or on the part of our partner—but the answer is rarely that simple.

While love, trust, and the familiarity that comes from knowing someone well is often a prerequisite for good sex, it is not necessarily sufficient in and of itself. In addition to technique, many aspects of a relationship affect the sexual interaction. Power, dependence, independence, self-esteem, expressing feelings, and the responsibilities and expectations determined by the roles of partner and parent make the successful navigation of intimate relationships a veritable miracle.

As if this were not enough, the images set forth in the media create unrealistically high expectations. We know that more opportunities are available to us. We see them on television and in films. We read about them in newspapers, magazines, and books. We anticipate the excitement, happiness, and fulfillment portrayed in television serials. We are living in the Now generation. We want it *all*—and we want it *now*. We expect to keep growing, to have free-flowing and open communication with our partner. We expect never to fight, and to maintain a high level of excitement with wonderful and frequent sex. And when reality serves up something less, we become frustrated and disappointed. We're unwilling to settle for anything short of total satisfaction.

When a relationship is less than totally satisfying, we are willing to end it and seek out another, more satisfying one, with another, more satisfying partner. Rather than struggle through the difficult times and with the difficult issues, we believe that if the going is rough, it is our partner's fault and that changing partners will rejuvenate our life and provide less hassle, more love, and better sex. And indeed it does—for a short period of time, while the romantic state prevails. People often fail to recognize that good relationships take work and even the best of them go through periods of stress and near dissolution. The research of Brandy and Lewis Engle indicates that many successful and happy relationships of more than ten years' standing have weathered such a period.[1]

In the initial stages of a relationship, when there is a strong physical and emotional attraction and the prospect of a real bond developing, infatuation flourishes. The newness of the partner, the excitement of getting to know one another, and the risk of exposing oneself often totally dominate other aspects of relating—as if nothing exists outside of the two people involved. Boredom is unthinkable as hour after hour is spent looking into each other's eyes or talking of the past or of families or of work. Fantasies abound as an attempt is made to place the new lover in the position reserved for them. The play has long been written, patiently awaiting the arrival of the proper actor or actress. And when certain behaviors or attitudes of the newfound lover do not fit the part, the inconsistencies are often dismissed or overlooked in an attempt to maintain the fantasy image.

When reality inevitably creeps in, little by little, the natural and mundane problems that are endemic to intimate relationships must be faced. Small things our new lover does begin to anger us. We may start to feel competitive or become aware of certain needs or interests that are in conflict. It is at this point—when we are forced to work out a way of resolving differences in priorities, values, or expectations—that a power struggle often begins.

## THE POWER STRUGGLE

The greatest single issue to be worked out in an intimate relationship is power. Who is going to control whom, who is going to decide what, who will get whose way and who will have to compromise? Almost every relationship must negotiate the power-struggle stage which ensues when the romantic image begins to fade.

Feelings of power or powerlessness are tied up with our sense of control over the environment and the people around us. The more we can control our environment, the more powerful we feel. Ironically, the more powerful we feel, the less control we need to exert on those around us. If past experience has taught us that our needs will be met, we are more likely to be able to relax and trust that the future will bring the same results without needing to control others.

However, when two people are living together and each fears that his or her needs will be squelched by the other, the power struggle begins. The battle will continue until both partners have carved out, to their satisfaction, areas over which they experience control. In some relationships, feelings of mutual respect and consideration provide sufficient acknowledgment so that a separation of roles and duties is not necessary. In others, the struggle for power never ends.

### Positive and Negative Power

When two people are in a struggle to ensure that their needs are met by their partner, they can use two forms of power. One is a *forceful* power in which needs, wants, and desires are stated, asked for, or in the extreme, demanded. The second is *withholding* power, which consists of not expressing feelings or holding back love or nurturing. When withholding power is met by withholding power, stony silence ensues. When forceful power meets with withholding power, positions often polarize. The forceful person gets louder, while the withholder gets quieter. In these cases, the forceful person can generally push the withholder to the point where they get them to express their feelings. However, when forceful power is wielded by someone far stronger (whether armed more effectively with weapons, physical strength, or verbal strength), withholding power can be quite effective. For example, during some sit-ins and other peaceful demonstrations, the power of the policeman's billy club or attempted arrest was met by "going limp." This passive yet unyielding power required a number of policemen to remove one dead-weight person.

Not wanting anything, not wanting sex, not wanting to make the relationship work, not wanting to go to a particular restaurant, is often a position of great power. Even with physical force, it is difficult to make someone do something they don't want to do. And often, if someone succumbs as a result of physical force or psychological pressure, such as guilt or other forms of manipulation, that person may retaliate in other ways.

When it comes to intimate relationships, neither form of power —forceful or withholding—works well. Both engender resentment and further power struggles. Aiming for self-satisfaction and compromise rather than winning or changing one's partner is more effective in the long run. For example, most of us have experienced conflict over attending a particular social function. One partner may want to go, while the other finds the people there boring and would prefer to stay home. As a result of pressure (forceful power), the reluctant partner agrees to attend. Then he or she gets dressed slowly, is obviously in a bad mood, yawns a lot during the affair, replies curtly to conversational overtures, and keeps asking if it's time to go home (withholding power). Neither person has a good time and the power struggle continues in a fight afterward.

Both people in a relationship have their own needs and perceive the circumstances from their unique viewpoints. Consequently, there are neither villains nor victims in relationships. Rarely is one person right and the other wrong. Each merely acts according to his or her perception of the facts. Both the perceived villain and victim are gaining something from the interaction. The villain may be getting what he or she wants by causing the victim to succumb. The victim, by allowing himself or herself to be treated in such a way may be using a martyred stance as proof of his or her righteousness.

Power struggles can take numerous forms. A common saying among therapists is that couples come into therapy because of three major problems: sex, money, and power. In reality, sex and money are really just power issues in different disguises.

## Power and Money

There is power in earning money. Money buys services, goods, pleasures. When there is only a certain amount of money to go around, a struggle can develop over whose right it is to spend it. Since women generally earn less money than men, they often feel less powerful. These women feel less of a right to spend the family money, even if they are responsible for rearing the children and taking care of all the family's needs at home. Even though a woman may realize intellectually that her work in the home and with the children makes her an equal partner in the relationship, she may still feel that she has no right to her husband's earnings. This conflict can lead to the buildup of resentment, which then may find expression in the bedroom in the form of withholding sex or orgasm.

## Power and Sex

Where, when, and how often a couple has sex can be the source of a power struggle. Both the person who demands more sex and the person who withholds it are exercising power. Sometimes couples fight about whether or not they will have intercourse or whether sexual stimulation will continue after one person is satisfied. Often, these sexual battles are vehicles for expressing resentment and dissatisfaction with other areas of the relationship. When a need for closeness is not being met, it is not uncommon (particularly for men) to seek more sexual contact as a way to gratify those needs. Conversely, withholding sex can be a way of expressing dissatisfaction with other aspects of the relationship. While legitimate sexual differences—such as disparate sexual drives or distastes for particular activities—can be real issues in and of themselves, more often, sex becomes a battleground because other needs are not being met.

## Power and Individual Differences

Individual differences often form the basis for power struggles. Many partners differ in their needs and values. People are unique in the degree of closeness and distance that they can tolerate comfortably. They hold differing views on numerous issues: the most efficient way to wash dishes, which activities are considered fun and relaxing, as well as what level of sexual frequency and experimentation is desirable. These are not right or wrong positions, just different ways of approaching life's many opportunities. However, they can lead to conflict.

It is not surprising that people from separate backgrounds with two sets of parents and childhood and educational experiences—not to mention basic genetic and biological differences—will have diverse desires and varying approaches to the world. It sometimes seems amazing that two people ever have enough in common to live together harmoniously. The older we get, the more entrenched our idiosyncrasies become, making it even more difficult to adapt to the needs and habits of another.

Misunderstandings and anger can arise as the result of these differences. The meeting of one person's needs can be seen as a purposeful disregard of the other's. For example, the proverbial Sunday-afternoon football-watching and beer-drinking husband often needs this as a way of relaxing and enjoying his day off. It may provide him with some necessary mindless rest. His wife, on the other hand, may perceive his behavior as indicating a lack of interest in her (which may or may not be true). If she is a housewife who is raising children, sitting home in front of the television on Sunday may feel like an extension of her normal work week and not much of a treat. This does not suggest that he is wrong and she is right, or vice versa. It is simply a situation in which the couple has found no satisfactory way to work out their different individual needs.

Since we begin with the assumption that the needs of two people will differ and their values will not always coincide, the challenge for a healthy, functioning relationship is to negotiate a way for the needs of both people to be adequately met. For example, the couple might decide that the husband will watch football only until 4:00 P.M., after which time they will go out for a drive. They might agree that he will take care of the children while watching television, leaving her some free time to visit a friend. Any solution that meets the needs of both people can leave both of them feeling satisfied. Otherwise, the dissatisfied partner may end up expressing negative feelings in the bedroom by sabotaging sex. If the power struggle is rooted in sexual differences—for instance, when one person has a higher sex drive than the other, or one has a greater need for variety, or one requires a sense of safety and the other prefers risk—this too must be dealt with by compromise.

When there is no give and take in a relationship, resentment may build. For some couples, winning a point today becomes more important than having their deeper needs met. However, if two people are to be satisfied with their life together, they must aim at solutions in which both people are winners, rather than outcomes where one wins and the other loses.

## Power and Commitment

Power struggles that are reflected in the bedroom often occur when the two partners are committed to the relationship in different degrees. Emily and Sam had been living together for two years. Emily hoped that she and Sam would get married someday, but every time she mentioned the subject, Sam would insist that he was not the marrying type and he liked the relationship the way it was. While Emily thought she could live with this decision, she found her insecurity growing. When disagreements arose, Sam seemed to take an uncompromising position: if she did not accept his rules, she could move out. And because she loved Sam and didn't want to lose him, Emily stopped bringing up issues that might upset him or cause an argument between them. But she began to feel like she was walking on eggshells, and became less and less happy in the relationship.

If only one person is committed enough to compromise and delay gratification, the prognosis for a mutually gratifying relationship is poor. In some relationships, or at different points in a relationship, one person may be committed to working out issues at whatever cost, while the second person is more ambivalent about his or her desire to be in the relationship. The fact that one person already has a foot out the door often causes the more committed partner to continually compromise and cater to the other's needs. Unless both partners are equally involved in the relationship, there will inevitably be problems. Unless the less involved person grows more committed, the more involved partner will never be able to do enough to satisfy the less committed person. Eventually, the more involved partner will begin to compromise less or make greater demands for intimacy and commitment. And if these needs cannot be met, the relationship may end, leaving the committed partner feeling compromised and resentful.

People who feel extremely vulnerable or who have been hurt by a partner in the past may protect themselves by holding back both emotionally and sexually. Unfortunately, in holding back they inadvertently bring about the very situation they're trying to avoid. They distance themselves in order not to become too involved, dependent, or vulnerable. And their partner, reacting to the distance and feeling their lack of involvement, loses interest. Sadly, such an outcome all too often confirms the belief that the relationship would have ended anyway, and only reinforces the position of emotional distance and noninvolvement.

## INTERDEPENDENCY

Because of these innate differences and imbalances, most people find maintaining a solid, intimate, and satisfying relationship a struggle. It is difficult, if not impossible, for one person to satisfy all the needs of another. Yet having needs satisfied in other ways or through other people can lead to problems.

Negotiating time apart and time together is a common aspect of the power struggle. People immersed in a job find their attention divided between their partner and their work. Because of the

variety of activities available—sports, travel, art, hobbies, etc.—
there are often many activities that are not shared.

Most relationships go through an initial period of social isolation
as the two people get to know one another. The couple focuses on
getting acquainted and sharing common ground. Since the couple
rarely spends every day and night together, sufficient time is left to
maintain their independent interests, activities, and friendships
separately. Once the couple begins to live together, however, a
shift must take place.

If they successfully negotiate the power struggle, a well-rounded
relationship incorporating different interests as well as separate and
mutual friends can result. Otherwise, enjoying separate activities
with different people may be a partial solution. Having some needs
met by friends other than the partner can lead to jealousy, however. One's mate may fear that another person will be seen as more
attractive or exciting; or one may feel guilty because of a belief
that he or she *should* be able to satisfy all the partner's needs. These
feelings of jealousy or inadequacy can result in fighting which ruins
the potentially intimate time the couple does spend together. If
such fighting is frequent and uncomfortable enough, some friends
or interests may ultimately be abandoned in an attempt to pacify
the partner. The resulting resentment can turn out to be a very
high price to pay for momentary relief.

The opposite may also occur, with both partners tenaciously
guarding their own interests and becoming less willing to compromise and participate in activities that interest the other. As a
consequence, the two may become more and more polarized, sharing fewer and fewer activities. And, after a few years of being
together, some couples no longer seem to have anything in common.
The closeness which has faded in other areas is then difficult to
maintain in the bedroom.

## Jealousy

In most relationships, the issue of meeting sexual needs tends to
be distinct from the meeting of other needs. While it may be
possible to negotiate time apart to enjoy separate interests, most
relationships will not tolerate that degree of openness when it
comes to sexual activities. Monogamous relationships require much

compromise about where, when, and how sexual intimacy together will be expressed, and hence provide fertile ground for power struggles.

With the sexual liberation movement, living together or being married does not necessarily imply monogamy. If the relationship is sexually open, the sense of security offered by a monogamous agreement is often absent, leading to more anxiety and concern about a partner's outside social activities. In addition, outside sexual activity can be used as a weapon. An unhappy or dissatisfied partner can use an affair as a way to express negative feelings. This is not to say that it is impossible to maintain a strong, committed, and secure open relationship, but only to acknowledge that an open relationship is more difficult to negotiate. Most couples who have this type of relationship remark that the struggle is often an ongoing one.

The most successful open relationships are clearly based on the premise that the first priority is always given to the mate. If the partner is ill, or upset, and wants or needs care, outside plans are canceled. Also, outside plans are discussed together to ensure that both people feel good about them. When both partners experience some sense of control in setting the limits, when both feel they have some power in determining their partner's behavior, the use of outside sex as a weapon seems to be curtailed.

## SENSE OF ADEQUACY

Feelings of personal insecurity or inadequacy, on the part of either or both partners, can have a deleterious effect on a couple's sexual relationship. If people don't feel good about themselves, they are likely to assume that others also see them as inadequate. Thus, they often worry that others will discover that they are not as confident, skilled, intelligent, or good natured as they have led them to believe. Their fear is that, once their deficiencies are discovered, they will be abandoned or discounted.

How people learn to feel inadequate, insecure, helpless, or unlovable is far too complex an issue to explore in depth here. Somehow, whether because of early relationships with parents, peers, or teachers, events such as parental divorce or death, or anxiety-producing situations that were never completely understood or resolved, this self-image is created. The feelings generated then continue to be carried around and are never updated to form a self-image more appropriate to the reality of the person in the present. While these feelings of inadequacy may be unfounded, they can cause a person to relate to a partner in destructive ways.

## OVERLY ACCOMMODATING

Eleanor was the ugly duckling in her family. Her father clearly favored her older sister, and her mother doted on her younger brother. When it came to family disputes, Eleanor was always alone. As a result, she grew up believing that in order to win the love of others she had to constantly give to them. Her overwhelming generosity often made her friends and family uncomfortable. In an effort to maintain her husband's love, she would agree to everything he wanted, even sexual activities she found distasteful. Finally, after years of disproportionate giving, Eleanor developed migraine headaches which not only interfered with her availability to others, but severely curtailed the frequent sex her husband had become accustomed to.

If you have negative feelings about yourself, you may tend to compensate by being overly good natured and accommodating. Believing that you are inherently unlovable, you may think your partner cares for you only because of how giving you are. If you are not constantly giving, you may worry that your partner will leave you, even when there has been no evidence to substantiate the fear. In trying constantly to please your partner, you may submit to sex even when you don't want to, or may participate in certain sexual activities that are unappealing or frightening. In so doing, you may continually discount your own natural needs and desires.

By complying with the needs of your partner, you may be trying to ensure that your partner finds nothing in you or the relationship to criticize or be dissatisfied with. Inevitably, however, you are likely to feel shortchanged. Resentment is apt to build as your partner does not seem to respond with equal generosity and selflessness. You may find yourself feeling chronically angry and expressing these feelings by acting passive/aggressively: by forgetting to do things you promised to do, making sarcastic comments, or "accidentally" frustrating your partner. Eventually, enough indirectly expressed anger cannot only rock the boat but can cause it to capsize.

## OVERLY CRITICAL

Another typical way of handling feelings of unworthiness and undesirability is to treat people harshly. Rather than bending over backward to keep a partner happy, some people maintain control by finding fault with all their partner's actions, from dishwashing to lovemaking. They are as critical of others as they are of themselves. In the two years Bonnie and Alan had been married, Bonnie had grown increasingly intolerant. Alan seemed to be able to do nothing to suit her. Finally, Alan could no longer endure her constant criticism and asked for a separation. Although it appeared that Bonnie responded with anger and further insults, on the inside she felt totally inadequate and unlovable and saw Alan's rejection as proof of her unworthiness.

If you are overly critical, you may be compensating for feeling inadequate by setting yourself above others. Deep down, you may be testing your partner. You may feel that if your partner stays with you despite your difficult and uncompromising ways, you are really loved. However, in attempting to find reassurance and security in this way, you may alienate your partner. Harsh behavior can ultimately drive your partner away. When your partner finally leaves, there is a tendency to interpret it as a response to your unlovability rather than a natural reaction to your constant testing behavior.

## ALWAYS RIGHT

People who feel insecure and inadequate often get into the right/wrong battle. They try to raise their self-image by being "right." One way of proving oneself right is to make the other person wrong. However, being right or wrong generally has very little to do with working out a good relationship. As a matter of fact, having to be right creates serious problems. Making someone feel wrong has an alienating effect. Not liking the one-down position, people naturally retaliate as a way of maintaining their own sense of self-esteem and self-worth. When one person wins an argument and the other loses, both will inevitably lose. The loser will almost always, either consciously or unconsciously, try to even the score, sometimes by losing interest in sex.

## ROLE SCRIPTING AND RELATIONSHIPS

There are certain problems that affect relationships which result from the different ways males and females have been role-scripted in this culture. For example, males tend to be scripted to be rational and not emotional, while women are often scripted in reverse. As a result of this basic difference, heterosexual couples may find difficulty sharing common ground. Men frequently complain about a woman's illogical approach to life, while women complain about a man's lack of emotional sharing. The result can be an unsatisfying level of intimacy. These differences in role scripting can lead to misunderstandings or feelings of alienation, which can reduce the frequency of sexual activity and interfere with sexual enjoyment.

While growing up, women are generally trained to place a higher priority on nurturing than on sexual activity. Consequently, less frequent sexual relations are often more tolerable to a woman than to a man. As long as there is sufficient nurturing and intimacy within a relationship, women are less likely to see a decrease in sex as a great problem. In general, women seem to accept sexual interest waxing and waning more easily than do men—possibly because many women's level of sexual interest fluctuates with their menstrual cycle. Since men are trained by the culture to see their sexuality as a way of fulfilling their intimacy needs, sexual frequency often holds greater importance for them. A "real man" in this society is often depicted as a superstud. Hence, infrequent sexual activity may be very uncomfortable for a man who has his masculine self-image tied to his sexual activity.

Since men are not scripted to be physically affectionate outside of sex, men usually rely on sex to satisfy their intimacy and touching needs. When sexual frequency drops, a general lack of physical touching often occurs between the couple as well. As a result, couples who are having sexual problems may also experience serious secondary intimacy problems.

On the other hand, since men are used to being the sexual initiators and more active sexual partners, they will tend to re-establish sexual contact and sexual frequency after a period of disinterest. Whereas, if the man's interest in sex wanes, the woman is often likely to give up as well. Consequently, in lesbian couples, a lack of sexual interest is not uncommon. If both partners are women who have been trained not to be assertive sexually, neither may feel comfortable with the role of sexual initiator—and with no initiator, sexual activity can become less and less frequent.

## RESOLVING CONFLICT

It is unrealistic to enter a relationship expecting it to be problem-free. Each relationship has unique difficulties that result from the intermeshing of two individuals. Almost all couples experience a setback when reality doesn't measure up to the original fantasy. At this point, the power struggle must be worked through before a higher level of interaction can be achieved.[2] Working through differences in needs and values is a natural part of developing a long-term relationship that is satisfying to both people. Expecting that true love means never disappointing our partner, never being disappointed ourselves, never feeling anger or conflict, is unrealistic. Good relationships are based on accepting our own, as well as our partner's fallibility. Each of us is imperfect; each of us has idio-syncrasies; each of us has flaws. We can never do better than our best and no more than that can be expected of our partner. "They met, they fell in love, and then lived happily ever after" only occurs in fairy tales. Real people grow and change and fight as well as love.

Nothing exists without its opposite. In all relationships where there is love, there must also be hate. The more we love some-one the more vulnerable we are to that person and the more likely we are to be hurt by that person. A negative comment from the one we love can be devastating, while the same comment made by someone unknown to us is often easily dismissed.

Communication is the key. It is necessary to share both positive and negative feelings, hurt and anger as well as love and affection. We need to define clearly our own limits and then ask for what we want and say no to what we don't want. Fear of conflict as well as love for our partner often makes us hesitate to be clear about our limits. Instead of saying no to something we don't want to do, we say yes, but then sabotage ourselves by avoiding the issue, for-getting our agreement or carrying it out ungraciously. Often we sabotage ourselves by not asking for what we need, or by denying our pain. It is interesting that when a demanding partner's needs are met, he or she becomes less demanding. Demands by most people are pleas for attention and affection. And if needs are not met in one way, they are likely to try another. Human nature is such that our true desires and needs will always find expression, so instead of making these statements verbally, we may do it through sex, by not being sexually interested or responsive.

As a relationship successfully grows beyond the stage of disappointment and power struggle, there is less of a need to be overly demanding and absolute in staking territory. As both partners begin to realize that they will get what they need from the relationship in the long run and can start to relax, there is the realization that fighting to be right doesn't work, nor does trying to force a partner to be different. The only workable solution is to discover together the part that each person has contributed to the dispute. It is essential to recognize that we can never force another person to change and that no one else can force us to change—regardless of the ploys used. All we can do is change ourselves by being more conscious of the needs of our partner, more aware of our own needs, and more able to communicate these needs. A satisfying relationship requires time and attention. Like any other area of our lives, the more attention we devote to it, the more rewards we will reap from it. However, this does not mean that a relationship should necessarily be the major focus of our lives, although for many couples it certainly is.

Also required is the acceptance that some selfishness is necessary on the part of each person. Open and honest communication is essential. We must be willing to let our partner know when we are happy and when we need something more or something different. And we need the same from our partner.

Making a relationship work also entails taking risks—and taking risks means being vulnerable. Since there is no such thing as security—even the bestlaid plans can be waylaid by some unforeseen event—since we can count on nothing lasting forever, we have two choices. We can continually guard against the unknown by not taking risks, by operating under the myth that if we don't allow ourselves to get too close, we will be better able to survive a potential separation should it occur. Or, we can realize that there is risk and reward in everything we do and if we allow ourselves to be vulnerable to our partner, we will be able to enjoy more fully all the years that life gives us together. If for some reason the relationship is abruptly terminated, we have the benefit of having had that close time together. And if we have the good fortune to be able to remain together for a very long time, we will be twice blessed. In either case, the end of the relationship will have to be dealt with, if and when it occurs. Protecting ourselves against the inevitable does not necessarily make the inevitable any easier to handle. It only means that we have lost a significant amount of time that could have been spent being loving and caring for each other.

Some relationships are easier than others. Some relationships are less secure or less socially acceptable and are therefore more challenging. A relationship with a very exciting man, but one who frequently changes jobs, cities, or countries may be filled with adventure, as well as feelings of insecurity. Falling in love with a much older man, a much younger man, a man of another race, or with another woman, may present a greater challenge in terms of society's reaction, but may have the potential to be more satisfying than another relationship which conforms more closely to society's dictates.

Life is a series of challenges and rewards. Being in a relationship with a particular partner has its own particular challenge and concomitant reward. The partner we choose as a lover or mate, by presenting us with various challenges, stimulates our psychological and emotional growth. Very often, sex can act as a barometer. By watching the level of good sexual activity or lack thereof, we can get a better grasp of the issues which must still be worked through before a fully satisfying relationship can be attained. Frequently a sexual relationship is a microcosm of the whole relationship. By examining our sexual relationships carefully, we may also gain a better understanding of how we and our partners interact on other levels.

This, then, is the goal of the remainder of the book: to give you a basic understanding of how your sexual attitudes, role expectations, and individual personality characteristics interplay with those of your partner to create sexual problems. Once you determine some of the causes of those problems, appropriate exercises will be suggested. Carrying out these exercises may help to change unsatisfactory sexual patterns.

The next chapter is an important part of the journey of self-discovery. Knowing about ourselves is the foundation upon which to achieve a satisfying sexual relationship with a partner. Our partner is not omniscient and cannot know what is necessary for our sexual pleasure unless we provide the information; we cannot provide any information until we understand our own sexual functioning. Although some of the exercises in the next chapter are particularly useful for women who are not orgasmic, they have been found valuable for women with other sexual concerns as well. Getting a clearer understanding of our unique needs and responses and establishing a deeper level of comfort with ourselves as sexual beings can be beneficial goals for all of us no matter where we are in our lives.

# Chapter 3

# LEARNING ABOUT YOURSELF:
## *The Sexual Arousal Process*

If you don't become as sexually aroused as you would like, if you don't have orgasms, or if sex has been so unsatisfying that you find you are no longer interested, it may be that you have insufficient knowledge of your own sexual responses to enable you to enjoy sex. Self-knowledge is a fundamental key to satisfaction in many areas. Sex is no exception. However, due to our early training, many of us never developed expertise in this area.

Knowing the sensitive areas of our genitals is a crucial part of learning about our individual preferences. Many of us still consider physicians to be the experts on our bodies and therefore have little information regarding our own anatomy. Some of us have never even looked at our genitals carefully. We may have avoided learning about our genitals because we learned to feel that this part of our body was ugly. Some of us consider our inner lips too fleshy or too long, our pubic hair unattractive either because of the color or because it is too curly, too straight, too coarse, too thick, or too thin. And since most heterosexual women rarely get to look at other women's genitals, we may be left feeling that there is something terribly displeasing about our own.

We may not realize that genitals are like faces. Although we each have the same parts, we each look different. And the particular size and shape of the parts have no effect on their functioning. Just as a large nose is not necessarily more sensitive to smell, a large clitoris is not necessarily more sensitive to touch. These features merely represent our individuality. And at least in this area, we can set our own standards for beauty; there are no glamour-model genitals on the covers of magazines to give us the message that we are somehow lacking. We each have unique-looking genitals and we can consider them beautiful or we can label them ugly if we like. Beauty, in this case, is truly in the eyes of the beholder.[1]

## The Genital Drawing Exercise

If you feel uncomfortable with your genitals, concerned about the way they look, smell, or taste, if you worry that your partner finds them distasteful or if you are just unfamiliar with your genitals and don't really know the different structures and precise areas of sensitivity, the Genital Drawing Exercise should be helpful to you.

One way to be more accepting of the uniqueness of your genitals is to really observe them; leave prejudices aside and objectively look at the structures. One of the best ways of doing this is to draw them.[2] When asked to draw their genitals, many women worry about their artistic ability. However, your drawing skills have no bearing whatsoever on the usefulness of this exercise. The viewing rather than the drawing is the important aspect of this assignment. In order to draw something, it is necessary to focus very clearly and precisely on the details of what you are drawing in order to determine how the various parts actually attach together to form the whole. Looking without drawing does not require the same attention and rarely produces the same complete understanding. Therefore, although the logistics of this exercise can be awkward, bear with it. Many women have found that their negative feelings toward their genitals have substantially decreased once they were able to view them objectively by depicting them on paper.

First, find a hand mirror or, preferably, a mirror with a stand. Choose a comfortable location where you can lean back at an angle, supported by pillows. It should be warm enough to recline nude or seminude, and the light should be adequate to view your genitals. With a sturdy pad of paper or paper placed on a book or board, draw a picture of your genitals as they appear without spreading your outer lips.

After you have completed this drawing, use your nondrawing hand to hold open your outer lips, unfolding the hidden parts to view, as shown in the diagram, and draw what you see.

Notice that the inner lips join at the bottom to surround the lower part of the vaginal opening. At the top they attach to the clitoris. Pull the hood back over the clitoris as far as possible, exposing the tiny head of the clitoris so you can see it more clearly.

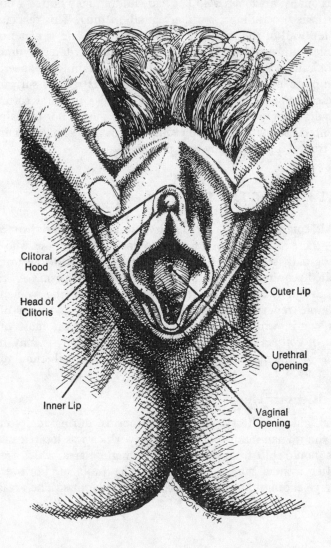

Not every woman's clitoris can be seen entirely, so don't worry if yours remains somewhat hidden beneath the hood. Look at the area between the inner lips to see if you can locate the small opening to the urethra from which urine is expelled. Sometimes this opening is found within the folds of the entrance to the vagina. Some women notice uneven tags of tissue, which are remnants of their hymen, surrounding the vaginal opening.

Occasionally, a woman who has had children may notice a bulge of soft tissue protruding from the vaginal opening. This relaxation of the top wall of the vagina is called a cystocele and is of no concern unless it protrudes so much that it becomes irritated by underpants or causes inadvertent urination upon coughing or sneezing.

Some postmenopausal women notice a distinct redness surrounding the opening to the urethra. This is called a urethral caruncle and results from decreased estrogen levels. It should not be painful and is no cause for alarm. If bleeding of this area should occur, it can be treated quite easily by your physician.

## GENITAL SENSITIVITY

When it comes to genital sensitivity, women fall into two categories—those who are more clitorally sensitive and those who are more vaginally sensitive. Hite found that 70 percent of the women she polled required some clitoral stimulation for orgasm.[3] A study by De Bruijn found similar results—35 percent of the women in her sample reported that they experienced orgasm more often during coitus, while 58 percent experienced orgasm most often outside of coitus.[4] The following physiological analysis may help explain why the majority of women respond to clitoral stimulation.

### Clitoral Sensitivity

Freud said that clitoral orgasms were normal during adolescence, but as the woman matures, the sensitivity which was located in the clitoris should shift from this area to the vaginal area, which would thereafter assume major importance. The problem, however, is that nerve endings don't just switch around like that. The areas of sensitivity that exist during childhood are likely to remain sensitive during adulthood.

Sometimes it is easier to understand female genital sensitivity when it is compared to the genital sensitivity of the male. It is interesting to note that both the male's and the female's genitals evolve from the same original tissue. A female fetus has two X chromosomes, while a male has an X and a Y. The X chromosome, basic to both, accounts for the natural form of the human as female. It is the male's sperm-carried Y chromosome that interferes with the development of what would have been a female by causing the production of the H-Y antigen that coats the developing gonads and the germ cells slated to become ovaries, and instead directs them to become testicles. During the first six weeks of pregnancy, before this H-Y antigen is produced, the tissue structure of the forthcoming male or female is exactly the same. At the sixth week, with the presence of the H-Y antigen, the embryo will develop into a male. If this antigen is not present, the tissue will continue to develop into a female.[5]

The point is that if both males and females develop from the same original tissue, our genitals must have also developed from the same tissue. Therefore, males' and females' genitals must have counterparts in the genitals of the opposite sex. By looking at which structures develop from the same tissue we can ascertain some similarities in sensitivities between male and female genitals.

Since every person is unique, these generalizations will not hold across the board, but ordinarily, the least sensitive tissue is that which forms the scrotum in the male and the outer lips in the female. Generally more sensitive than this tissue is the tissue that forms the shaft and foreskin of the penis in the male and shaft and hood of the clitoris in the female. Even more sensitive is the tissue that forms the midline on the underside of the penis that extends through the perineum and surrounds the anal opening. In the female, this same tissue becomes the inner lips and also forms the skin that encircles the vaginal and anal openings.

The most sensitive tissue in the male is that which makes up the head or glans of the penis and is equivalent to the tissue that makes up the head or glans of the clitoris. Consequently, during intercourse, the male's most sensitive tissue (the glans of the penis) is

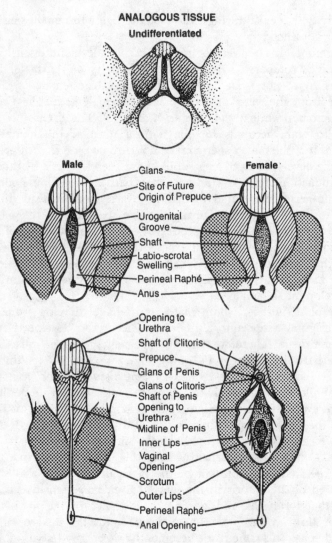

receiving direct stimulation by rubbing against the walls of the vagina while the female's most sensitive tissue (the glans of the clitoris) is often only being indirectly stimulated. As a result, direct clitoral stimulation during or separate from intercourse is sometimes more effective than intercourse alone for producing orgasm in the majority of women. This does not mean that intercourse is not pleasurable for these women, only that this form of stimulation by itself may be insufficient for attaining orgasm.

## Vaginal Sensitivity

A smaller number of women are more sensitive to vaginal stimulation than clitoral stimulation. The following may help to understand what may account for vaginal sensitivity in these women.

Vaginal sensitivity seems to be related to two known factors, the pubococcygeal (or PC) muscle: the muscle that surrounds the vaginal opening, and the Grafenberg spot (or G-spot): a small area of tissue in the anterior wall of the vagina. The Federation of Feminist Women's Health Centers calls what appears to be the same tissue the urethral sponge and considers it to be an underlying structure of the clitoris.[6] In all likelihood, other individual factors and areas of sensitivity also account for vaginal responsivity, but this complex subject is still not fully understood.

### THE PC MUSCLE

The relationship between pubococcygeal muscle tone and vaginal sensitivity was discovered when Dr. Arnold Kegel prescribed exercises to strengthen the pubococcygeal muscle for women who suffered from urinary incontinence.* These women would inadvertently expel urine when they coughed, sneezed, or in some cases, experienced orgasm. He found that when women carried out the exercises to strengthen the PC muscle they reported increased vaginal sensitivity during intercourse.[7] Others have since studied the correlation between PC muscle tone and orgasm.†

### THE G-SPOT

Recent research by Perry, Whipple, and Belzer has resulted in the rediscovery and naming of the Grafenberg spot, an area of sensitivity in the vagina midway between the cervix and the top of the pubic bone.[12] The G-spot is a mass of tissue that surrounds

---

* See pages 141–44 for a description of the Kegel exercises.

† While recent sex researchers, notably Graber, Klein-Graber,[8] Perry and Whipple,[9] have found direct correlations between anorgasmia and lack of PC muscle tone, others, such as Sultan, et al.[10] and Levitt, et al.[11] found no such correlations.

the urethra just below the neck of the bladder. However, for the sake of simplicity, Diagram 3 indicates the area that can be felt through the vaginal wall. The G-spot generally ranges between the size of a dime and the size of a quarter in the unaroused state. But since it seems to be composed of erectile tissue, it can double in size when a woman becomes sexually excited. Some women find that direct stimulation of the G-spot, once they are sexually aroused, can trigger orgasm.

Society has valued clitoral and vaginal responsivity differently, which has caused problems for clitorally responsive women. Women who are vaginally responsive and who experience orgasm in the traditional manner dictated by Freud and a male-oriented social structure are less likely to seek therapy for orgasm problems than women who respond clitorally. (Women who are vaginally sensitive but who have had their vagina excessively stretched as a result of childbirth may be one exception.) The fact that vaginal stimulation is more traditionally accepted does not make it inherently better. Classical music, while more traditional, is not necessarily

GRAFENBERG SPOT

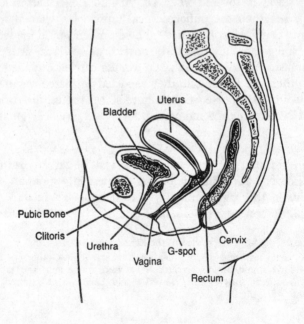

better or more enjoyable than rock music. People bored by a classical symphony might be ecstatic at a rock concert and vice versa. What's important is that each person has his or her musical needs met. The same is true of one's sexual needs.

## The Genital Touching Exercise

The Genital Touching Exercise is really a continuation of the Genital Drawing Exercise. It allows you to experience through touch what you have discovered visually. It is recommended for women who are uncomfortable with their genitals and for women who wish to become more knowledgeable about their areas of genital sensitivity. It is particularly recommended for women who have difficulty becoming aroused or reaching orgasm.

After you finish drawing your genitals in their open position, put your pencil down and gently examine the different structures with your fingertips. Explore the texture and the feelings generated when you touch your outer lips, inner lips, and clitoris. Then, place your finger inside your vagina. Can you feel the PC muscle contract around your finger if you squeeze the muscle as if trying to stop the flow of urine? Can you locate your G-spot?‡ You may require your partner's assistance to do this. Do you observe any differences in sensations as you press upward or downward at the vaginal opening or to the right, left, or the areas in between? The specific areas of sensitivity differ from woman to woman and also differ depending on whether or not you are feeling aroused. Don't worry if at first you feel self-conscious or uncomfortable while carrying out this exercise. Just take a deep breath and continue with the exploration. Feeling sexually aroused is not the object of the exercise, so relax and just observe what you feel; discover your own uniqueness.

## THE SEXUAL PROCESS

Once you have a better understanding of your genitals and their areas of sensitivity, it becomes important to understand what is known about the physiological process of sexual arousal and release.

‡ See discovering your G-spot exercise on page 144.

Understanding this complex process can help pinpoint where different sexual problems occur. Masters and Johnson, Kaplan, and others describe the sexual response process in various ways. But for our purposes, I have chosen to detail the process described by Zilbergeld and Ellison because it accounts for both physiologically and psychologically based problems.

Zilbergeld and Ellison divide the sexual arousal and response cycle into five parts: 1) desire, 2) arousal, 3) physiological readiness, 4) orgasm, and 5) satisfaction. A sexual problem can occur at any of these stages in the process.

## Desire

The initial stage, that of desire, accounts for how often a particular person is interested in or desires sex. Factors such as stress, fatigue, point in the menstrual cycle, change of routine, or even a slight change in one's sense of self-worth can affect one's level of sexual interest.

Since there is a tremendous range among individuals in terms of sexual interest, it is not possible to define a particular level of sexual desire as normal. Some couples have sex two or three times daily while others are very satisfied making love once or twice a month. The fact that the average couple makes love twice a week[13] does not indicate that someone who desires sex more or less frequently is abnormal. Determining the existence of a problem with sexual desire has more to do with one's personal assessment than some external criteria. Problems can arise, however, when one partner desires sex significantly more than the other.* Being dissatisfied with one's own frequency of sexual contact while lacking the motivation to initiate or even to positively respond to a partner's overtures, may also indicate a problem in this area.†

## Arousal

The second stage of the sexual process is the arousal stage. Arousal is defined by Zilbergeld and Ellison as the subjective experience of

---

* Discrepancies in sexual desire will be discussed in Chapter 11.

feeling turned on. A woman is aroused when she finds the love-making pleasurable and exciting. If she does not feel sexually excited while making love, she may consider this a problem.

Many factors can affect arousal. Focusing on outside noises or internal thoughts may distract one from the sexual experience. Concerns about oneself as a sexual woman—one's appearance, responsivity, or ability as a lover—can also affect arousal. Fear of looking ugly, losing control, releasing urine, or being angry at one's partner, concern over being abandoned, and chronic stress and fatigue, can effectively inhibit sexual arousal as well.

Although in most cases levels of arousal and desire go hand in hand, this is not always true. Some women have a frequent desire for sex, yet find that they have difficulty getting aroused. For example, a woman's fear that her partner may abandon her could cause her to cut off some of her sexual feelings. While still being interested in having sex, she may try to protect herself by not feeling aroused during lovemaking. However, continued experiences of sex without arousal are ultimately likely to affect her level of sexual interest as well.

It is also possible not to desire sex often and yet feel very much aroused when sexually involved. Some women feel overwhelmed by too much intimacy and may unconsciously avoid sex as a way of creating some emotional distance. Lack of interest may be a way to retaliate at a partner who is inconsiderate. Or, sex may simply be viewed as a distraction from other more important tasks, and therefore be given a low priority. Although women in these situations may not be desirous of sex, they may become very much aroused on those occasions when they do have it.

## Physiological Readiness

Basically, physiological readiness encompasses all of the physiological changes that occur before orgasm. There are two major components of physiological readiness: vasocongestion and myotonia.

### MYOTONIA

Myotonia is muscle tension. As sexual tension mounts, the body becomes more and more tense. Some women find that their legs begin to vibrate, their hands and feet may tense up, in some cases a woman's back may arch, her pelvic area or her whole body may begin to move up and down, back and forth, or in a circular motion. She might find that she is breathing heavily or panting. Meanwhile, sighs or moans may involuntarily escape her lips. Some women misinterpret this tension to mean that they are feeling anxious rather than recognizing it as an appropriate response to the buildup of sexual pleasure. While these signs of increased sexual tension are typical, all of them are rarely experienced by one woman.

### VASOCONGESTION

Vasocongestion refers to the retention of blood that flows into the pelvic area during sexual excitement. Comparable to erection in the male, the swelling of the outer lips, the inner lips, the clitoris, and the hood over the clitoris is the result of vasocongestion. Vasocongestion is also responsible for a general swelling of the breasts and nipple erection. (Some nipples invert when they become erect. Some women find that their nipple erection is masked when the areola, the dark area surrounding the nipple, swells as sexual arousal continues.)

As blood flows into the pelvic area, it causes lubrication by creating a "sweating"-like process along the walls of the vagina. Vaginal lubrication is an early physiological sign of sexual arousal. It does not necessarily indicate that the woman is ready to be entered. Also, a woman's subjective level of arousal does not necessarily match her physiological readiness. It is possible to feel aroused and yet not lubricate. Furthermore, a woman can feel very aroused and not experience orgasm.

### PREORGASM CHANGES

Finally, vasocongestion causes the swelling of the PC muscle that surrounds the vaginal opening. The swelling of this muscle forms what is called the orgasmic platform and occurs just prior to orgasm. Because of this swelling, the size of the vaginal opening may be reduced. At this point some women feel concerned that they are not turned on because they may be tight and hence difficult to enter. However, this tightness at the vaginal opening can be the result of being highly aroused rather than being unaroused.

In some women the clitoris retracts back under the hood at the point of high arousal, making direct stimulation of the glans difficult or impossible. However, most women still find the general area responsive to stimulation. The area in the vagina called the G-spot also swells and becomes more sensitive as the result of vasocongestion.

## PHYSIOLOGICAL READINESS PROBLEMS

A number of sexual problems can occur when there is insufficient physiological readiness. For example, a woman may not lubricate, or may not lubricate sufficiently to allow for intercourse to occur comfortably. Lack of lubrication can result from many things. Certain drugs, including birth-control pills, can affect the quantity or consistency of the lubrication. Also, women who are post-menopausal or who have had both of their ovaries removed may find that the resulting diminished estrogen causes a lack of lubrication and a thinning of the vaginal lining, thereby making penetration painful.

Fear or anxiety, which can inhibit the physiological process of lubrication, can also cause vaginismus, a spasm of the PC muscle. If this occurs, a woman may feel very sexually aroused and be able to enjoy manual and oral clitoral stimulation, and yet find penetration impossible.

Internally, women seem to undergo two different processes, depending on whether they are responding primarily to clitoral or to vaginal stimulation. The first process, described by Masters and Johnson, is called the ballooning or tent effect, and accompanies stimulation which is primarily clitoral.[14] With clitoral stimulation, the vagina balloons out and the uterus lifts up, creating a space in the vagina. The vaginal opening becomes tight with the formation of the orgasmic platform. With orgasm, the pelvic muscles, including those surrounding the vaginal and anal openings, generally contract. In some women there are also contractions of the uterus.

The second process, which has recently been observed by Whipple and Perry, is called, by comparison, the A-frame effect,[15] and results primarily from vaginal stimulation. With vaginal stimulation the walls of the vagina remain snug and the uterus does not lift up. The vaginal opening, rather than becoming very tight, becomes more lax. As orgasm approaches, a bearing down effect occurs, as if something is being pushed from the vagina. This is generally accompanied by rhythmical contractions of the uterus and pelvic muscles. Because of the bearing down effect and relaxed vaginal opening, it is not uncommon for the penis or other object providing the vaginal stimulation to be pushed out at the point of orgasm.

## Orgasm

Because some women reach orgasm through clitoral stimulation and some through vaginal stimulation, Whipple and Perry hypothesize that two separate neural pathways govern orgasm.[16] In fact, there are at least two separate nerves that go to the genitals. The pudendal nerve supplies the clitoris, PC muscle, inner lips, skin of the perineum, and skin surrounding the anus. The pelvic nerve goes to the vagina and the uterus. The fact that the pudendal nerve has considerably more sensory fibers than the pelvic nerve and contains the kind of nerve endings which are very sensitive to touch may be responsible for the higher percentage of women being more responsive to clitoral stimulation.

The two-nerve theory may account for more than differences between vaginally induced and clitorally induced orgasms. Because

**NERVES**

Pelvic Nerve — S1 — S2 — S3 — S4 — S5
Uterus
Vagina
Clitoris
Pudendal Nerve

[S1, S2, S3, S4 and S5 are Sacral Nerves.]

these two nerves partially overlap in the spinal cord, it may also account for blended orgasms which are both clitorally and vaginally induced. This theory is currently only speculative and does not take into account other nerves to the area or the powerful effect the brain has upon sexual response. There is still much unknown about the physiological basis for female sexual functioning, including how orgasms result from breast stimulation, stimulation of other parts of the body, or from fantasy without any physical stimulation.

In all likelihood, there are many different routes to orgasm. Singer has, in fact, already classified seven different types of orgasm.[17] The experience of orgasm differs from woman to woman, and even from one sexual or masturbation experience to another.

The process of orgasm is the reversal of the physiological process of the buildup of pleasure. As pleasure continues to build, it reaches a peak, and then, if nothing emotional or physical interferes to inhibit or block the process, it will naturally reverse itself. This reversal, or orgasm, entails a sudden release of the blood that has been accumulating, mainly in the pelvic area, so that it can flow back to the rest of the body. This release of blood often accounts for the feeling of warmth that often accompanies orgasm. As previously stated, the uterus and/or pelvic muscles may contract a number of times. However, many women either do not have or do not detect these contractions. Sometimes the clitoris becomes extremely sensitive immediately after orgasm, making it almost painful if touched.

The release of the muscle tension which also occurs with orgasm accounts for the feelings described by many women of being relaxed, exhausted, spent, or soft. A sense of well-being or a feeling of completion is often described. Other women continue to feel aroused afterward. Sometimes a woman remains aroused because she is multiply orgasmic and requires more than one orgasm to experience satisfaction.

Women have described orgasm as:

"A moment of ecstatic pleasure."

"A mint-flavored heat wave."

"A rush."

"Before [orgasm], I feel a tremendous surge of tension and a kind of delicious feeling I can't describe. Then orgasm is like the excitement and stimulation I have been feeling, increased, for an *instant*, a hundredfold."[18]

"Just before orgasm, the area around my clitoris suddenly comes alive and . . . seems to sparkle and send bright dancing sensations all around. Then it becomes focused like a point of intense light. Like a bright blip on a radar screen, and that's the orgasm."[19]

Some women feel that orgasms stemming from clitoral stimulation differ from those that result from vaginal stimulation and may prefer one over the other:

"During masturbation I experience a clitoral orgasm that approximates my idea of male orgasm—a buildup of over-all sensation in the general area of my clitoris, and a 'muscle spasm' feeling. A vaginal orgasm is a more pervasive sensation through the whole body, less concrete to describe—wider waves of feeling."[20]

"Clitoral orgasms are more intense and make me feel tingly all over. On the other hand, intercourse orgasm is a deeper, and more overwhelming, feeling."[21]

When orgasm does not occur, the muscle tension and vasocongestion will dissipate, but more slowly than if orgasm had occurred. It may require a period of a few hours or longer before the body returns completely to the normal unaroused state. Consequently, some women experience a feeling of irritation or fullness during this period of time. Other women, however, experience no discomfort whatsoever.

Sometimes a woman experiences an emission of fluid from the urethra at orgasm, and a recent chemical analysis of the ejaculatory fluid suggests that it is unlike either urine or vaginal lubrication, but rather is like male ejaculatory fluid in its high levels of glucose and acid phosphatase.[22] It is believed that the source of the fluid is a system of glands and ducts called the paraurethral glands (also known as the periurethral or urethral glands). These surround the female urethra and develop from the same embryologic tissue that develops into the prostate in the male. They may also contribute to the composition of the area called the urethral sponge or G-spot.

Bedwetting has deep-seated negative connotations. As a result, many women have reported that they were so embarrassed at emitting fluid upon orgasm that they inhibited their orgasms totally. Others underwent surgery for urinary incontinence even though the only time they reported any expulsion of fluid was at the point of orgasm and even though their PC muscle was very strong. (PC muscle weakness is often a cause of urinary incontinence.)

Some small percentage of women expels a small amount (generally less than a teaspoon) of fluid through the urethra at orgasm[23] and this appears to be another quite normal variation of the female orgasmic pattern. The amount of ejaculate emitted and even a woman's ability to ejaculate may be a function of the type or size of the glands in the G-spot. Clearly, further research is necessary before we can fully understand the female ejaculatory process.

What we do know is that each woman seems to have her own orgasmic pattern. This pattern is so individual that Hartman, Fithian, and Campbell, respected sex therapists and researchers, call this individuality "orgasmic fingerprinting."[24] Each woman's orgasmic pattern is as unique as her fingerprints. For example, some women have one very intense orgasm or one orgasm of a milder nature. Others may have a series of mild orgasms or what may be described as one long one. Still others have one intense orgasm followed by a few mild ones or a few mild ones terminated by a more intense one.

The way(s) in which a woman experiences orgasm is determined by a number of factors. Cultural expectations, individual learning patterns, and physiological differences all play their role in the range of female responsivity. Furthermore, each woman's experience of orgasm is likely to differ from situation to situation. The time of day, feelings about her partner, degree of relaxation, and preoccupation with other matters will all influence her orgasmic response.

While a variety of responses may be available to women, it is important not to use this information to create performance pressures. Unfortunately, many of us have used the readily available information on sex in the media to set our standards. And there is a tendency to expect everyone to fit the same sexual mold. If one woman can have orgasms through vaginal stimulation, we may feel pressure to have orgasms that way; if one woman is multiply orgasmic, we may consider ourselves inferior if we just have one; and now that we know some women ejaculate, we may feel concerned if we don't.

One kind of orgasm is not better than another; they are different. One may be more familiar and therefore preferred. Options may be there for those who wish to develop greater variety, but just as not every woman may wish to develop her skill at playing the piano, flute, drums, and violin, she should not feel pressured to develop all of the possible pathways to orgasm—some are more likely to fit her natural disposition than others.

ORGASM PROBLEMS

The most common sexual problems reported by women concern orgasm: inability to experience orgasm alone or with a partner, infrequent orgasm, an inordinate amount of stimulation required to produce orgasm. Nearly half of American women never or only rarely experience orgasm during intercourse.[25] In these cases, either something blocks or inhibits the process of arousal from going to completion, or the sexual technique used is not sufficient, or the necessary response pattern has yet to be learned. Sometimes lack of orgasm results from being overly concerned about a partner's pleasure or feeling judged by a partner. External factors such as a telephone ringing or thoughts of uncompleted chores inhibit some women from responding orgasmically. Frequently, lack of orgasm results from discomfort in accepting pleasure, sexual or otherwise.

## Satisfaction

Unfortunately, we often put too much attention and pressure on achieving orgasm, when sexual satisfaction should rightfully be the goal of a sexual encounter. Some women find that the process of being physically close to their partner, of holding and being held, can be fulfilling without their necessarily having an orgasm. One respondent to a questionnaire done by Gerda de Bruijn in the Netherlands wrote: "Often I prefer our togetherness and hugging above 'working' for an orgasm. I so much enjoy the warmth and aggressive about it. I don't mean to put it down, but it is a kind of trust which is within our lovemaking. An orgasm has something explosion which sort of blots out all the other small things—and I happen to enjoy those other things so much."[26]

Some women who are regularly orgasmic still rate the sexual encounter or their sexual relationship in general as unsatisfying. A woman may feel dissatisfied if, for example, a partner is too rough, not rough enough, does not indulge in sufficient foreplay before initiating intercourse, or if sex is too frequent or not frequent enough. If a woman's partner ejaculates too rapidly, he may not be able to last long enough for her to experience orgasm during intercourse.‡ Even though she may have no difficulty having orgasms during oral sex, she may miss experiencing the sensation of fullness that goes with her partner's erect penis being inside her at the point of her orgasm.

If warmth, trust, and affection are not present, the sexual experience, while physically satisfying, may be emotionally empty. Since a large majority of women feel that the most important element in a good sexual experience is the emotional relationship,[27] it is not surprising that these women feel sexually dissatisfied when that element of the sexual interaction is missing.

## MASTURBATION

Discovering your own areas of sensitivity and unique sexual arousal process through masturbation is a good way to learn what is necessary for attaining sexual satisfaction. Knowing what turns you on, what conditions provide for comfortable sex, and what physical and emotional factors are necessary for reaching orgasm will enable you to direct the lovemaking so that your needs can be satisfied. It will also enable you to provide relevant information to your partner so your lovemaking together can be more enjoyable.

The overwhelming majority of males have masturbated at some point in their lives.* A male therefore is likely to walk into his first

‡ See Bernie Zilbergeld, *Male Sexuality*. New York: Bantam, 1979. A self-help guide for the treatment of rapid ejaculation and erection problems.

* In 1948 Kinsey found that 92 percent of his sample had masturbated. In 1972 Hunt found the figure to be 94 percent, and in 1981 Hite's figures showed 99 percent of the male population she polled had masturbated.

sexual experience with some knowledge of the process. He then initiates those sexual activities and positions which he has found most pleasurable. The woman is trained to follow his lead whether or not he initiates the kind of touching, rhythm, and positions that are most arousing for her. For the woman to get as much pleasure out of the sexual experience as her partner, it seems obvious that she must also take some initiative. If she is totally ignorant of her body's requirements for pleasure and orgasm, she will have little to contribute. However, if she too has had experience learning her body's preferences and rhythms through masturbation, she will not only have some information to communicate verbally to her partner, but some basis from which to assert herself in the sexual encounter.

By observing your sexual experiences and responses while alone, you will also be better able to distinguish between problems that you can work on by yourself and those that are relationship oriented. If you can have orgasms on your own, you know you can function physiologically, and you only need to determine what is missing or occurs differently during sex with your partner. If you have pain with sex, you can help isolate the factors that cause the pain by carefully experimenting with masturbation. Stimulating yourself while inserting something in your vagina is also the most effective way to learn to overcome vaginismus. Observing your level of interest in masturbation and comparing it to your desire for sex with your partner can help you determine if a lack of interest is relationship based or just an indication of a general low physiological need.

## LACK OF ORGASM

Masturbation is an excellent way to determine whether or not you are orgasmic. Basically, there are two major categories of orgasm problems. The first are women who have never had an orgasm, and therefore may not be entirely certain what an orgasm actually is. The second are women who are not presently orgasmic but at some time in their life and through some type of stimulation have been able to experience orgasm. This second group of women may have experienced orgasm in dreams, with oral sex or masturbation, but feel that they do not have orgasms often enough, or with a partner, or through diverse enough stimulation. The first group will be referred to as "preorgasmic," since they are not yet orgasmic, and the second group will be referred to as "situationally orgasmic," since they are orgasmic in certain situations and not in others.

Women who have never had an orgasm by any means or who have had only a few orgasms in their lives are in many ways the easiest to treat and have the greatest expectation for success because they tend to be naïve about their sexuality. Once they thoroughly explore their bodies and experiment with various kinds of physical stimulation, they generally learn to be orgasmic on their own rather easily. Possibly because all the information is so new, these women are often readily able to incorporate their newfound learning into the techniques used while making love with their partner.

Some women who don't think they are orgasmic may actually have experienced orgasm. This has been true of nearly one out of every ten women who have joined one of my preorgasmic groups. Often these women do not label their response as orgasm simply because the experience differs from their expectations. Since so few women have had any experience actually talking to other women about their sexual response, they may not be aware of the wide range of responses that qualify as orgasm. Most women's initial experience of orgasm is mild, while their expectations reflect the proverbial fireworks. When, for example, they experience feeling relaxed, being satisfied, and not wanting to go on making love any longer, they may discount the experience and continue to wait for the earth to move.

Sometimes women discount their orgasm because it differs from the experience of another female friend. If one woman reports losing awareness of her surroundings, intense contractions in her stomach, and spasms of her hands and feet, another woman may consider her warm flush and very mellow afterglow to be something less than orgasmic.

Sometimes women don't feel they have orgasms because their partner or some other "authority" questions their response. One man was convinced that his lover was not orgasmic because she did not moan and scratch his back as had his previous lover. Another woman grew to question what she had always considered to be an orgasm when her psychiatrist asked if she experienced vaginal contractions. She did not have contractions (at least none she noticed), so he informed her that she was not having orgasms and sent her for sex therapy.

Women who don't feel good about themselves often discount their orgasms. When one woman who had considered herself anorgasmic was told that what she described occurring during her homework was probably an orgasm, she replied: "Really, I've been having these for years. I guess until now, I never felt good enough about myself to believe I was actually a complete orgasmic woman."

If you are uncertain as to whether or not you have orgasms, there are ways to find out. However, they require that you pay attention to the physical experience rather than to your expectation or mental image of orgasm. Because masturbation allows total self-concentration, it is the activity that can most easily enable you to determine if you have had an orgasm. Since numerous distractions are present while having sex with a partner, it is sometimes difficult to discern the occurrence of a mild orgasm. If you have your orgasm before your partner ejaculates, and intercourse continues, you may miss the feeling of relaxation and satisfaction that can occur immediately afterward. Instead, you may begin the arousal process a second time and find yourself heading toward another orgasm when your partner's orgasm brings an end to the lovemaking, leaving you feeling tense or unsatisfied. Finally, orgasms resulting from vaginal stimulation can be very mild and diffuse compared with orgasms occurring from direct clitoral stimulation which tend to be more clearly defined and recognizable.

Although masturbation is the easiest way to determine whether you are orgasmic as well as one of the best ways to learn to experience orgasm, many people carry negative feelings about masturbation as a result of early parental or religious messages. Some women worry that experiencing orgasm through masturbation will interfere with attaining orgasm through intercourse. This myth is thoroughly unfounded. In fact, Kinsey found just the opposite: "Much more important is the evidence that premarital experience in masturbation may actually contribute to the female's capacity to respond in her coital relations in marriage. . . . In any event, it was certain that the capacity to respond in orgasm in marital coitus had not been lessened by the premarital masturbatory experience of the females in the sample. . . . The type of premarital activity in which the female had acquired her experience of orgasm did not appear to have been as important as the fact that she had or had not experienced orgasm."[28]

Most children and adolescents naturally explore their own bodies. In the process of this body exploration, they often discover pleasurable feelings in their genitals.† If the negative societal messages about masturbation are not sufficiently strong to restrain a youngster, most will continue exploring their bodies and their sensations until orgasm is reached. Most males learn about orgasm this way, and the majority of females who are orgasmic also taught themselves to have orgasms by masturbating. Of the women Kinsey interviewed, 62 percent masturbated and only 4–6 percent of these women masturbated without reaching orgasm.[30] The ones who did experience orgasm were able to do so almost every time they wanted to.[31]

## The Masturbation Exercise

Masturbation allows you to take as much time as you need without having to worry about taking too long or your partner becoming tired or bored. Also, being alone, there is no need to be concerned with what you look like or if your body appears unattractive when sexually aroused. These factors make self-stimulation particularly good for learning.

To carry out the Masturbation Exercise, set aside an hour when you will be free from outside interruptions. Pick a place that affords privacy and is warm enough to enable you to be comfortable while nude.

Since the brain is the most powerful sex organ, the first order of priority is to get into the right erotic frame of mind. During sex with a partner, many of the cues for arousal are provided by a partner's physical presence—sight, smell, voice. However, when making love to yourself, it is often necessary to create the erotic mood on your own. You might want to remember some erotic and satisfying past sexual encounters as one way of setting the mood. Or you might want to spin a fantasy out of your own imagination. Reading erotic books or viewing erotic pictures is still another approach. All of these methods serve to start the arousal process and form a basis upon which the physical stimulation can build.

† Of the females Kinsey polled, 57 percent learned to masturbate through self-discovery.[29]

Once sexual arousal has begun, the second important component of enjoyable and orgasmic sex is the physical stimulation—general overall body stimulation and, specifically, genital stimulation.

Experiment with different touches and different positions. You might want to begin stroking your body all over before you touch your genitals. When you stimulate your genitals, you may find that using an oil enhances the pleasure of the touch.

Most women masturbate using some form of clitoral or labial stimulation in order to reach orgasm.‡ The exact type of clitoral stimulation preferred differs from woman to woman. You may like hard, direct stimulation of the glans of the clitoris, or you may prefer a lighter touch on the glans. You may find you are more responsive to stimulation of the shaft of the clitoris or stimulation along the sides of the shaft or the glans. Up-and-down strokes, side-to-side strokes, or a circular motion can make the difference between mere pleasurable sensations and the buildup of intense sexual feelings. However, the appropriate type of stroking totally depends upon your unique preferences and frequently changes as arousal builds.

Some women prefer vaginal over clitoral stimulation or feel the desire to be vaginally penetrated once they reach high levels of arousal.* If this is true for you, use your fingers or some sort of phallic-shaped object to supply the sensations of fullness or to stimulate the G-spot while you masturbate.

If you have never masturbated before, you may find masturbation boring and may feel like giving up when after five or ten minutes you feel no arousal. If this happens, negative feelings about masturbation might be rising to the fore. Or, arousal may not result because masturbation is different from sex with a partner and you may have to learn to tune into different erotic cues and experiment with a different kind of physical touching before you can expect to feel strong sensations of arousal. In either case, you may

‡ Kinsey found that 84 percent of his female sample depended primarily on labial and/or clitoral techniques.[32] Hite found that over 80 percent of the women responding to her questionnaire relied primarily upon clitoral stimulation.[33]

* Kinsey found that 20 percent of the women he interviewed had at some time used vaginal insertions in connection with masturbation.[34] Hite found that only 2 percent of the women she polled used vaginal stimulation exclusively, while approximately 20 percent used it occasionally or in conjunction with clitoral stimulation.[35]

require more time and experience before self-stimulation produces an orgasm.

Once you have become comfortable masturbating for periods of an hour or longer and are reaching higher levels of arousal, notice why you stop stimulating yourself. Do you stop masturbating because an hour is up? Or do you stop because you don't feel like going on anymore, because somehow you feel relaxed and satisfied? If you feel a rising in the intensity of sexual sensation, followed by a feeling of release or relaxation, you are probably having orgasms. If, at the point of intensity, you have a finger inside your vagina (you can continue to apply clitoral stimulation with your other hand), and you can feel the opening to your vagina mildly or strongly contract around your finger, you are almost certainly having orgasms. If your clitoris becames unbearably sensitive following sensations of warmth or release, unless this tenderness is the result of rubbing too hard, you are experiencing another sign of orgasm.

Pelvic muscle contractions, feelings of warmth, clitoral tenderness or ultrasensitivity, etc., may be helpful in defining the response, but a major determining factor is the physical and emotional feeling afterward. Do you feel relaxed, finished? Do you have some sense of satisfaction that terminates the desire to continue sexual stimulation? This is a subtle, yet important determinant of orgasm.

Don't expect to have all the signs; one or two are sufficient. Every woman's response is unique. If you have some of the signs of orgasm, but do not feel relaxed afterward and feel like masturbating more, it is possible that you may require more than one orgasm before you feel satisfied. Feel free to repeat the process.

If you are fairly certain that you are not orgasmic with masturbation, you may require further practice. Some women stop stimulating themselves just prior to the point when they would have an orgasm because they find the sensation irritating or uncomfortable. What they label as irritation or discomfort, however, is often intensity. And this intensity of sensation may be new and unfamiliar. A few weeks of practice may be necessary in order to become accustomed to the new feelings. For further information and direction, you may want to read *For Yourself: The Fulfillment of Female Sexuality*, a guide for women who have never experienced orgasm which contains numerous additional exercises that are pertinent to learning to have a first orgasm. If practicing alone is insufficient, you may require some assistance from a trained sex therapist or you may want to take part in a preorgasmic women's group.

Once you have become orgasmic with masturbation—or if you already are—the next step in the journey toward sexual fulfillment is to be able to describe precisely the sexual problem and better understand exactly when and how it occurs.

*Section II*

# THE FIRST STEP:
*Starting the Journey*

# Chapter 4

# OBSERVATION AND RISK TAKING

There are many causes for each of the different sexual problems. Lack of desire, lack of orgasm, and painful intercourse all can result from stress, fatigue, and unresolved anger at one's partner. They can also result from lack of information, faulty sexual technique, sexual inhibition, or unrealistic expectations.

A woman who is angry at her partner and who feels powerless to change the basic relationship may withhold sexually. She could have a lover who lacks the appropriate sexual technique for her needs, but since she believes the myth that "men should know," she may do nothing to change the situation. She could be conflicted about her sexual relationship with another woman and not having orgasms may protect her from having to face the question of whether she is really a lesbian.

The many possible causes of a sexual problem make it evident that each person's situation is unique, and close scrutiny is necessary to determine the specific causes and solutions. A woman who is withholding sexually from her partner because she is angry would have to work on interactional problems in the relationship in addition to the sexual problem. In the second situation, where no serious relationship problems exist, appropriate information might suffice to bring about change. In the third case, the woman might have to examine her feelings about having a sexual relationship with another woman before she could go on to remedy the lack of sexual response. Trying to find a solution before clearly defining the problem is like prescribing cod liver oil for every ailment. If you are lucky it might work, but the odds are stacked against you.

If you are not content with your sexual functioning or your sexual experience, and you are considering the possibility of changing the situation, the first and most important step is to pinpoint the exact difficulty. Too often, people entirely skip this step in their haste to find a solution.

## The Journal Exercise

To determine what may be inhibiting your sexual interest, enjoyment, or response, it is helpful to observe your sexuality for a period of two weeks. Memory sometimes has a tendency to trick us. We often remember what we want to remember and forget the details that do not coincide with our expectations. To ensure an objective picture, it would be beneficial to keep a daily diary (one that is small enough to carry around) during this two-week observation period.

Record your observations on the following three dimensions that tend to affect sexual satisfaction: feelings about yourself, feelings about your partner, and the explicit sexual contact that takes place. Some aspects of these dimensions may not be relevant to you, so pick those that you feel might have some bearing on your sexual satisfaction.

Record your feelings as soon as possible after they occur, and certainly before the end of that day. Include all feelings and don't avoid contradictions. This is not a time for value judgments. Be careful to avoid labeling the behavior and attitudes that you observe as either good or bad. Just observe them as objectively as possible. This is merely a time to become aware of your situation so that when you decide to take some action you can do so as directly as possible in the precise area that is really causing the problem.

### FEELINGS ABOUT YOURSELF

In your journal take the time to note how you felt about yourself that day. Did you feel physically attractive or fat or unkempt? Did you feel satisfied with yourself, or did your handling of a certain situation continue to bother you after it was over, leaving you

† Lack of sexual interest will be discussed in Chapters 12 and 13.

feeling inadequate or self-deprecating? Did you feel very tired or under particular stress from work or family problems? Were you aware of feeling turned on or of having any sexual thoughts or feelings during the day?

## FEELINGS ABOUT YOUR PARTNER

Did you feel close to or distant from your partner? Did you find yourself feeling loving toward your partner when you were apart? Did you look forward to your partner's return at the end of the day? Did you have an amicable evening or did you argue or fight with each other? If a fight occurred, when did it begin? Was it resolved? Some people use sex as a way to make up after a fight, whereas many others are not ready to be intimate so quickly and need more time before they feel like having sex.

## EXPLICIT SEXUAL CONTACT

Since the dimension of explicit sexual contact is so large, it has been divided into five subsections: interest and initiation, time and place, sexual activities, thoughts and fantasies, and arousal and satisfaction.

**Interest and Initiation**  Note what activities led up to sex and how you felt about them. Who initiated sex and how did you feel about the way it was initiated? Was it done when you were feeling close and affectionate or when you were preoccupied with cooking, work, or your children's activities? Were you in a sexual mood or were you automatically responding to your partner's initiation? Would you rather have said no, but for some reason didn't?

**Time and Place**  Note the time of day that you had sex. Was it late at night when you were tired? If it was in the early morning, did you worry that your child would walk in on you, or were you distracted by thoughts or anxieties about the coming day? Did you have sufficient time to relax and enjoy the arousal process or did you feel rushed? Where did you have sex? Did you make any special preparations like lighting a candle or wearing sexy lingerie?

**Sexual Activities**  During sexual interaction with your partner, which activities left you feeling more aroused? Less aroused? Was there enough foreplay, sufficient kissing, and nongenital touching? Was oral sex a part of the lovemaking? If you had intercourse, were you ready for penetration when it began? What intercourse position(s) did you use? Did you feel pain at any point? If so, exactly what were you doing and where was the pain felt? Did your partner stimulate your clitoris in a way that excited you or irritated you? Did you have sufficient lubrication for both clitoral stimulation and penetration? Did some pleasurable sensations which might have grown to orgasm seem to subside prematurely? If so, did the feelings subside because the stimulation changed or stopped too soon, or because your own thoughts caused the sensations to be squelched?

**Thoughts and Fantasies**  Monitor your thoughts as well as your physical sexual feelings. Did you find that you were worried about your partner's pleasure? Were you concerned that you were taking too long? Or were you worried about your ability as a lover? Were you preoccupied by thoughts of an ill child or of your unfinished work? Were you thinking about how angry you were at your partner? Were you concerned about whether or not you would have an orgasm? Were you more aroused when you incorporated some sexual fantasies into the lovemaking or when you focused on the physical feelings of pleasure?

**Arousal and Satisfaction**  Finally, rate your sexual arousal level during each lovemaking session as well as your overall satisfaction with the sexual experience. Rate each of these on a ten-point scale. On the arousal dimension, a 1 would indicate low arousal and a 10 high arousal. On the satisfaction dimension, a 1 would indicate dissatisfaction and a 10 would indicate high satisfaction. On both dimensions, the numbers between 1 and 10 would indicate gradations in between.

The following is an example of two entries in a journal:

*Tuesday January 25*

SELF—Feeling good about myself. Landed a business deal.

PARTNER—Spent all day together, felt close, had an intimate dinner together.

SEXUAL CONTACT—

Interest and Initiation—I was interested and I initiated sex.

Time and Place—In bed, late at night (midnight) but I wasn't tired and we spent lots of time (one hour).

Sexual Activities—I felt most aroused during oral sex, but the feelings subsided when intercourse began.

Thoughts and Fantasies—I had none of my usual worries except about having an orgasm. I forgot to fantasize.

Overall Arousal—8    Overall Satisfaction—8

*Saturday January 29*

SELF—Feeling OK, neither good nor bad. I was tired.

PARTNER—Angry at Bill. Had a fight last night.

SEXUAL CONTACT—

Interest and Initiation—I was somewhat interested in sex. He initiated.

Time and Place—In bed at 7 A.M. I was tired.

Sexual Activities—Practically no foreplay, just intercourse and it hurt because I wasn't even lubricated.

Thoughts and Fantasies—After the first few minutes, I just wanted to get it over with.

Overall Arousal—1    Overall Satisfaction—0

Once you have completed the Journal Exercise and observed your sexual feelings and activities for a two-week period, read over your journal to see if any patterns emerge. Through this self-monitoring process, you may discover some of the issues that are causing problems and be able to see changes that could be made in your lovemaking. You might find that you are orgasmic when you make love in the evening, but never in the morning. You may discover that orgasm is more likely if your foreplay has extended over thirty minutes before penetration. Or orgasm occurs only when you are in certain positions or if you spend an intimate evening with your partner beforehand. You might note that pain occurs with one intercourse position, but not with others, or that it occurs only during one point in your menstrual cycle. You might find that your interest in sex is higher on weekends when you are not burdened with job worries, or is tied directly to your partner's demonstration of affection or to his preoccupation with work or other matters.

Once the problem has been identified, taking the necessary steps to solve it may not be that simple. Change involves risk. And while many people intuitively know what action is needed, they often lack the confidence or strength to risk actually making the change. Consequently, before going into the specific suggestions and exercises for ameliorating the various sexual problems, we will first explore some factors that facilitate or inhibit the change-making process.

## RISK TAKING

How we feel about ourselves largely determines what we will or will not attempt to do. While our mental self-image may have little to do with reality, it can cause us to hold ourselves back or enable us to strike out into unknown territory.

There are two main factors that contribute to our holding back. The first has to do with self-expectations. What we believe we are capable of doing develops out of our early sex role training as well as the opinions others had of us during our formative years. The second factor is our fears: fear of the unknown, fear of loss, fear of being hurt or rejected, and fear of failing or being wrong. These expectations and fears often prevent us from taking risks, even when logic tells us that the outcome would probably be positive.

### Expectations

As discussed earlier, women learn to be sexually inhibited. It is difficult to be sexually assertive when we have been taught to believe that our partners expect us to be sexually retiring. Interestingly, most men prefer an assertive partner who is sexually responsive and clearly demonstrative of her sexual pleasure. Not only does this add variety and enthusiasm to the sexual encounter, but most men say that an active partner makes them feel like a competent lover.[1] Nonetheless, our training still causes most of us to hold back and see ourselves as less than lusty sexual women.

The opinions of others also color our sexual self-concept. If our parents or relatives always told us that we were not as pretty as our sister, as smart as our brother, or as likable as our cousin, then we might have a tendency to believe their assessments rather than to discover our own sense of self. This can particularly affect our sexuality if we have been taught that we are not physically attractive, not sensual, not romantic, or that we lack qualities we believe to be essential in a good sexual partner. Starting off with the feeling that we are somehow deficient can cause us to restrain ourselves when it comes to taking risks. We may shy away from sexually assertive behavior and procrastinate when it comes to making important changes. Rather than seeking what we really want, we may find ourselves settling for less, believing that we are not the kind of person who could attain such a goal.

Not being able to imagine oneself as a sexual, sensual woman makes it very difficult to be one. This is not to say that we should swing too far in the other direction and expect more from ourselves than we are capable of, but neither should we accept the past as the sole determinant of the future. Taking the time to create a new self-image that reflects how we would like to see ourselves, rather than how others may have seen us in the past, is an important first step.

## Fear of the Unknown

Our fears, even more than our expectations, prevent us from making positive changes. The biggest fear that inhibits most of us is the fear of the unknown. While we may be dissatisfied with the present, we may fear that things could be even worse—especially if we *expect* not to be able to create the changes we desire. For example, we may find our sexual relationship boring, or feel that our partner is satisfied while we are not. We might fear that if we were to attempt a change, our partner might get angry or uncover feelings of sexual dissatisfaction, thereby causing the relationship to deteriorate even further. There are no guarantees, and the outcome of any risk is uncertain. Thus, some people seek safety by maintaining the status quo which, of course, precludes making any positive changes.

## Fear of Loss

Frequently, fear of the unknown takes the form of fear of losing our partner totally. Maybe if we try to change things we will discover that our partner doesn't love us after all; that our partner doesn't want to do things that would give us sexual pleasure; maybe if we make things uncomfortable by trying to make ourselves happier and more sexually fulfilled, our partner will ultimately leave us and we will lose everything.

## Fear of Rejection

If we are single, we may hesitate to express ourselves for fear of being rejected. What if we ask a potential partner out and we get turned down? Worse yet, what if we show our sexual interest and get rebuffed? We may interpret the refusal as a personal rejection. One woman had to call a man up three times before she finally got him on the phone. Each time she left a message, but he never returned her calls. When I asked her what enabled her to persist in view of his clear lack of response, she replied: "He didn't know me well enough yet not to like me." Getting sufficient distance from our fears to realize that another person's lack of desire for us does not make us undesirable takes time. What each of us finds attractive is personal and idiosyncratic. Because men's social role dictates that they be the aggressors, they ultimately have to learn this lesson in order to socially survive. Women, too, could benefit from learning this.

## Fear of Failure

Fear of failure prevents many of us from taking even the first step toward change. What if we ask our partner for exactly the kind of stimulation that we like—and we still don't have an orgasm? If we never ask we can't ever really fail. We search for the money-back guarantee and, finding none, we either don't try at all or only half try. After all, if we don't *really* try we can delude ourselves into believing that if we just tried harder we could succeed. While this may protect our ego, it is really the basis of a self-fulfilling prophecy: we predict that it won't work, so we don't put forth our full efforts and, as a result, it doesn't work.

## Fear of Being Wrong

Akin to fear of failure is the fear of being wrong. Most people like to be right, but no change can ever be undertaken with full certainty as to the outcome. Trying something new is always risky. The only thing that we can be right about 100 percent of the time is failing. We can always work it out so that we ultimately fail. And those who constantly fear being wrong often prove how right they are by never succeeding.

## TAKING THE FIRST STEP

How can you tell if you are letting your fears and expectations prevent you from taking control of your life and receiving the pleasure to which you are entitled? You can check your feelings for the answer. If you find yourself feeling generally angry or resentful, depressed or hopeless, victimized or buffeted about by the powers that be, it is likely that you are subjugating your needs to those of your partner or others in your life. These are the ideal circumstances under which to take the risk, to reach out despite the fears and expectations that tell you that you might fail or lose in the end, or that you are being too selfish by desiring so much pleasure.

When asked, most people remember with great clarity the risks that transformed their lives: the day they quit their job of ten years without another in sight, the times they moved to a different city or decided to go back to school or have a child. They barely recall those changes that didn't work out. Thus, either most risks turn out for the best, or more likely, we make the best of the risks we take. And in hindsight, those that didn't work weren't that important. We assimilate the experiences into our lives and carry on.

If your fears and expectations block your progress, you can sometimes fool yourself into taking the first step. There are a number of games you can play to make the risk taking seem less dire. Here are a few of them.

## Comparing Yourself with Others

One way to counter negative expectations is to compare yourself to those around you. However, be careful not to do so in the usual way, by only comparing yourself to those you feel are better than you are at whatever you're comparing. If you are feeling overweight, you are likely to compare your body to that of the most physically fit of your friends. Then you might compare yourself in intelligence to your smartest relative, and in creative ability to a professional artist. The point is, we never compare all of our attributes with those of one person. And we rarely compare ourselves to those who are less competent. Do you ever compare your figure to that of an overweight professional chef, or your artistic ability to that of someone who can't draw a straight line?

Comparing yourself to friends who are less capable in a particular area is one way to trick yourself into taking risks. After all, if Mary, who is forty pounds overweight, can have a great sexual relationship with her partner, why can't we? Or if Ginger, who never lets us get a word in edgewise and probably talks constantly during sex anyway, can go away for an intimate weekend to some small romantic resort, what about us?

## Getting Help

There is no reason why you should have to make all the changes by yourself. You might want to compare notes with others. For example, you might ask a friend how she communicates her likes and dislikes to her partner.* Or you might read a book on the subject. And if things really go wrong, you can always call on a marriage counselor or a sex therapist to assist you.

## You're Not Responsible

If you are very clever, you can disclaim any responsibility for the changes you want to make. If you run into trouble, for instance, you could blame the whole thing on me and on this book. You could just claim you were brainwashed in a moment of weakness. Glenda, a woman in a preorgasmic group, made tremendous changes in her sexuality as a result of getting involved with a woman partner she assumed was very sexually sophisticated and experienced. This perception freed Glenda to try all sorts of sexual activities

* A chapter in Barbach and Levine's *Shared Intimacies* is devoted to the words women use to communicate about sex to their partner.

that she had been far too inhibited to experiment with in prioi relationships with less experienced partners. She was very pleased with her progress. Months later, to her surprise, she learned from her partner that she was by far the most adventurous woman her partner had ever been involved with and that she had never before tried many of the activities Glenda had initiated. By making her partner responsible in her mind, Glenda was able to take risks she could not otherwise have imagined taking.

## The Worst Possible Outcome

It is sometimes liberating to imagine the worst possible outcome of your actions. You might envision your partner leaving you were you to voice your sexual needs. Then you could foresee yourself divorced and penniless with your three children. You could consider welfare, or selling your body on street corners as your sole means of livelihood. Possibly you could imagine an even worse outcome. Once you have spun this fantasy, compare it to reality. If the results seem unlikely, you might just dive in and trust the fact that you are too intelligent to pick a partner who if slightly threatened would leave you.

When one woman carried this fantasy out she concluded that the two worst outcomes would be welfare and suicide. After thinking about it for a while longer, she realized that she was too proud to go on welfare and too much of a chicken to commit suicide. She knew she was too intelligent not to be able to find a job, so she took a deep breath and started to make some important changes in her life.

## It's Only an Experiment

Looking at changes as an experimental process can free you to try new things. Experiments are never right or wrong, they are merely unbiased tests, the outcome of which proves a point. For example, you could experiment at initiating certain sexual activities during lovemaking. If the role of initiator doesn't feel comfortable, or if the activities you initiate are not enjoyable, you could conclude that the experiment is a bust and go back to having your partner initiate all sexual encounters and activities. No decision is forever.

Once you realize that you can always change your mind and go back to the way things were, it is easier to go ahead and try something new.

Life is always changing. For a relationship to survive intact, it must be sufficiently flexible to withstand the impact of lost jobs, new jobs, the first child, more children, children leaving home, illness, a recession, and innumerable other changes. As a matter of fact, some people even feel that it is precisely these kinds of changes that keep a relationship vital and protect it from becoming sedentary and boring.

Unfortunately, most people wait too long—until they are desperate—before they are able to take steps toward initiating change. Many relationships that could be saved deteriorate irreparably as anger and unresolved negative feelings accumulate while the perfect moment is awaited. While some moments are better than others, there is no perfect moment. We *create* the perfect time.

It also helps to be aware that there really is no security. Even the best-laid plans can go awry as a result of some unforeseen event. Jobs can be lost, employers can go bankrupt, a tree can fall on our house. Similarly, no matter how good and fulfilling a relationship may be, some unexpected disaster, such as an illness or accident, could terminate the relationship or change it drastically.

Our security lies only in our own hands and in our ability to live our lives in a creative and satisfying manner. I think that a story from *Illusions* by Richard Bach creates an image well worth repeating here.

Once there lived a village of creatures along the bottom of a great crystal river. The current of the river swept silently over them all— young and old, rich and poor, good and evil, the current going its own way, knowing only its own crystal self. Each creature in its own manner clung tightly to the twigs and rocks of the river bottom, for clinging was their way of life, and resisting the current what each had learned from birth. But one creature said at last, "I am tired of clinging. Though I cannot see it with my eyes, I trust that the current knows where it is going. I shall let go, and let it take me where it will. Clinging, I shall die of boredom." The other creatures laughed and said, "Fool! Let go and that current you worship will throw you tumbled and smashed across the rocks and you will die quicker than from boredom." But the one heeded them not, and taking a breath did let go, and at once was tumbled and smashed by the current across the rocks. Yet in time, as the creature refused to cling again, the current lifted him free from the bottom, and he was bruised and hurt no more. And the creatures downstream, to whom he was a stranger, cried, "See a miracle! A creature like ourselves, yet he flies! See the Messiah, come to save us all!" And the one carried in the current said, "I am no more a Messiah than you. The river delights to lift us free, if only we dare let go. Our true work is this voyage, this adventure." But they cried the more, "Savior!" All the while clinging to the rocks, and when they looked again he was gone, and they were left alone making legends of a Savior.[2]

Maybe we too can release our tight grips—just enough to experiment. Enhancing our sexual enjoyment will require us to try new ways of doing things. The first risk that must be taken is opening up communication: letting our partners know what is important to us sexually and why.

*Chapter 5*

# COMMUNICATION

A recent survey by Philip and Lorna Sarrel, sex therapists at Yale University, concluded that good communication is one of the most important factors in a satisfying sexual relationship. "Among women who have told their partners exactly how they like to be touched, seven out of ten indicated they have orgasms 'every time' or 'almost every time' they make love." They also found that only 54 percent of the women who put up with discomfort during sex without saying anything are happy with their sex lives. The Sarrels concluded that ". . . the ability to share thoughts and feelings about sex with your partner is the single factor most highly correlated with a good sexual relationship . . . the good communicators had intercourse oftener and were likelier to be satisfied with its frequency."[1]

## SHOW AND TELL

There are two basic methods you can use to communicate sexual information to your partner. You can do it nonverbally through the use of body movements during lovemaking. Or you can do it verbally, by talking with your lover either during lovemaking or at some other time. Verbal and nonverbal communication both have assets and liabilities.

The main drawback to nonverbal communication is that it can be misunderstood. For example, one woman attempted to communicate her preference for being kissed on the ears by kissing her partner's ears. Doing to our partner what we would like our partner to do to us is common. However, this woman found that the more she kissed her partner's ears, the less he seemed to kiss hers. Over a period of time her kissing of his ears continued to increase while his kissing of her ears stopped altogether. Finally she asked him why he never kissed her ears anymore, only to discover that he *hated* having his ears kissed and was trying to communicate this by not kissing hers. After their discussion, he began to kiss her ears, she stopped kissing his, and both were happier for the exchange. In this case, verbal communication was necessary to straighten out confusion created by nonverbal communication.

In other cases, however, nonverbal communication can be more specific than verbal communication. One woman I worked with required very precise clitoral stimulation in order to reach orgasm. She attempted to describe to her partner her needs in specific detail, but he was unable to touch her exactly the way she liked no matter how specifically she verbally guided him. This frustrated them both. Consequently, she resolved to overcome her discomfort with touching herself in front of him and, supported by his insistence, she showed him precisely the way she liked to have her clitoris stimulated. In this instance, the necessary information could not be transmitted through words alone and nonverbal assistance was required.

You may find that talking during lovemaking spoils the mood and prefer to rely on body movements and sighs of pleasure. Or, you may find that talking about sex while you are making love enhances the experience. Talking about what you would like to do to one another can act as a form of erotic stimulation. What's essential is to develop some comfortable means of communicating sexual preferences, whether it be verbal or nonverbal. At the same time, it is important to realize that the first few attempts at communication, no matter what method is used, are likely to be somewhat awkward.

## NEW RELATIONSHIPS

In the initial stages of a relationship, women find it particularly difficult to discuss their intimate preferences. Many women feel too vulnerable, too open to ridicule or rejection. A feeling of safety takes time to build. And with the new sexual freedom, it is often less intimate to interact sexually than it is to talk about it.

However, opening up the communication early in a relationship can only bring positive results. Lack of familiarity with each other makes it even more important to share specific information early on. This is true regardless of whether or not the relationship turns out to be ongoing. If it does not progress beyond a number of dates or evenings together, at least both of you will have experienced pleasurable times together. If it does continue for months or years, you will have learned the kind of communication necessary to maintain a mutually satisfying sexual relationship.

Also, letting your partner know early in a relationship what you like and don't like sexually helps to prevent negative patterns from developing. What frequently occurs in new relationships is that people make love to a new partner by doing what turns *them* on or by doing what pleased a previous partner or what they have read women or men like. During the honeymoon stages of a relationship everything tends to feel good, but people become more discriminating after a while. At that point, if you don't let your partner know what turns you on or off, you will only reinforce the belief that what is being done is fine, thus leading to more of the same behavior. This is particularly true if you have been faking orgasm. By faking, you are training your partner to do precisely what *doesn't* work for you. Then, when you finally discuss your lovemaking, your partner may feel deceived and may not trust you in the future. Your partner may also feel hurt or angry or foolish for thinking you were pleased when just the opposite was true. While your partner may balk at first when you try to provide helpful information, the memories of those initial awkward moments are likely to fade quickly once you begin to respond more positively.

One woman said, "I have always been direct in telling my husband what I like and don't like sexually. In the beginning this bothered him. He would rather I'd do it in some other way, or preferably, not do it at all. What he really wanted was that whatever he did would be perfect for me, and that wasn't how it was. But finally, after listening to his complaints, I have learned to be more gentle and positive in the way I communicate, and now he doesn't seem to mind at all."[2] There are obviously more and less tactful ways to give a partner sexual information, especially early in a relationship. Also, it is important to keep in mind that your partner is as unique as you are, and what would be tactful for one partner would not be well received by another. The best you can do is gently assert your needs and be sensitive to your partner's response. If talking during lovemaking causes a negative response, consider a discussion afterward or beforehand, over dinner or at the breakfast table. One woman developed the idea of an instant replay early in the relationship with her husband. They would go over the highlights of their sexual encounters just as a touchdown pass is replayed during a football game. After making love they would talk about how each of them felt, whether a particular intercourse position was comfortable, or if, when she was kissing his penis, she was doing it to get him to kiss her genitals, or just because it was something she wanted to do.[3]

Asking your partner directly about ways to communicate that would be most comfortable avoids having to guess. Your partner may have distinct preferences about how you should relate certain information. Merely asking could circumvent potential problems. When communication is done with caring and with the desire to better know and please one another, it is almost always well received. The more you get out of sex, the more you will desire sex, and the more active and interested you will be in the lovemaking. All of this will ultimately add to your partner's sexual enjoyment as well. A bored or frustrated sexual partner can severely dampen sexual pleasure, and anything that helps to prevent misunderstandings is bound to have a positive effect.

Many men I've talked with have confessed that they learned to talk about sex from a female lover and remain indebted to her. Some of these men said that if it hadn't been for a particular woman they might never have known what a woman liked sexually. These men were often too shy or too afraid of their lover's response to ask her directly, and they appreciated her willingness to take the lead.[4] Hence, a partner who is not initially comfortable discussing sexual topics should not be automatically written off as hopeless. Try not to let your partner's awkwardness or discomfort intimidate you. Don't give up because you feel self-conscious, just continue to experiment with different approaches. Sometimes comfort takes time to develop. The initial awkwardness is natural when trying anything new, like riding a bicycle for the first time or asking someone out for a date. With practice, things get easier. And in the end, the ongoing satisfaction is worth the initial strain and discomfort.

However, if you feel too uncomfortable to initiate a conversation about sex, you can still get some of your feelings and needs across to your partner nonverbally. You can assert yourself by initiating oral sex, by positioning yourself appropriately for a particular sexual activity, by stimulating your clitoris manually yourself, and by making pleasurable sounds whenever your partner does something that really turns you on.

It is important to keep in mind that when emotions are intense, and you think you might be in love, the worst of the awkwardness and the greatest of the fears seem to arise. There is little to be done in this situation except to enjoy it. Falling in love doesn't happen very often for most people and, as the realities of life impose themselves, subsides only too quickly. Trying to communicate at this point can be excruciatingly difficult. All you can expect to do is your best.

## OLD RELATIONSHIPS

Initiating sexual communication for the first time midway into a long-term relationship is not necessarily easier than starting from scratch in a new relationship. Although a level of trust and commitment may be established, many ingrained negative patterns may also exist.

Altering a longstanding relationship often requires considerable time and patience. Changes are unlikely to happen overnight, and they are even more unlikely to take hold after only one or two attempts. It requires constant attention to break sexual habits that have been established over a period of years.

The first challenge is to recognize the problem behaviors. Some are so natural and familiar, and have become so much a part of the lovemaking, that they are not readily noticed. It's similar to people who say, "Don't you think?" or "You know what I mean?" with every sentence—they're usually unaware of repeating these phrases until it is pointed out to them.

While becoming aware of the problem is the first step in making a change, awareness alone is insufficient. The next step is actually to inhibit the old behavior—to stop saying the repetitive phrase or stop sexually interacting in the programmed manner. Once the old behavior has been inhibited, it becomes possible to experiment with new behaviors or responses.

## COMMUNICATION SKILLS

Although we take all sorts of courses in school, we are never really taught how to communicate and work out disagreements with the person we love, or how to express our love sensitively in a physical way. The following principles are intended to assist in the development of positive and clear communication so that misunderstandings and defensive responses are kept to a minimum. These two principles should facilitate conversations not only about sex, but about other areas as well. The first principle entails the use of "I" statements; the second involves the statement of fears or concerns ahead of time.

### "I" Statements

Those of you who have read *For Yourself* and *Shared Intimacies* are probably already aware of "I" statements. However, since this is such an essential concept, you may wish to review it. "I" statements consist of saying the word "I" rather than "you" when talking about feelings, attitudes, and actions. Using "I" statements can be one of the most effective ways of clarifying communication.

For example, let's say you have already told your partner that he touches you too roughly and you would appreciate it if he could touch you more gently. When he again touches you roughly (which is bound to happen in the beginning), rather than saying, "You didn't listen to me when I told you what I wanted," it would be more effective to say, "I don't feel important when I ask you to do something and it doesn't get done." The former statement, "*You* didn't listen . . ." will in all likelihood elicit a defensive reaction from your partner. He may feel accused, blamed, and possibly even inadequate or guilty. To alleviate these feelings, he may become defensive and reply, "I did too listen; you're just never satisfied. All you ever do is criticize me." And you are off on an argument that is only apt to generate angrier and angrier feelings. If instead you say: "I don't feel important when . . ." your partner is not being attacked and therefore is less likely to react defensively. You are simply reporting your feelings. This leaves your partner free to ask for further guidance.

The following are *not* "I" statements: "I really think *you're* being selfish and inconsiderate when you do that." Or: "I felt *you* purposefully tried to hurt me when you said that." In both these statements the "I" is used only to open an attack. They are really analyses of your partner's behavior rather than statements of how your partner's actions made you feel.

Observe the difference between the following "I" statements and "you" statements:

| | |
|---|---|
| I feel unimportant or discounted when you make decisions without consulting me first. | You always make decisions without considering me and my feelings. |
| I feel like a sex object when you don't kiss and touch me for a while before going for my crotch. | Whenever we start to make love you always go straight for my crotch. |
| I feel deprived of those intimate moments just after we make love when you immediately roll over and fall asleep. | If you loved me you wouldn't roll over and go to sleep immediately after we make love. |

Since each person has his or her own perspective, it is more important to work together to discover what each contributed to a dispute so that it can be resolved than it is to prove one right and the other wrong. This can best be accomplished through the use of "I" statements.

## Stating Concerns

A second way to facilitate the communication of uncomfortable emotions is to state how you feel about what you are going to say before you actually say it. For example, if you are afraid that your partner will become angry with you if you tell him that he is still touching you too hard, it would be important to begin the conversation with something like this: "I have something terribly important to tell you, but *I'm afraid that it might make you angry.*" Explaining this in advance allows your partner to be aware of your concerns so he can monitor *his* feelings. If he does feel anger, he is less likely to just fly off the handle.

Also, if you are afraid of your partner's response but don't say so directly, you may unconsciously brace yourself for a negative reaction and inadvertently deliver your message in a harsh or critical tone. Your partner may then interpret the harshness as anger or disapproval rather than fear, and retaliate accordingly.

The following are some common concerns that, if stated beforehand, might facilitate communication:

1) I'm worried that you won't like me if I tell you this.

2) I'm afraid that you will misunderstand what I'm trying to say.

3) I'm confused about how I feel and I hope you won't be critical if I muddle through it with you out loud.

As you embark upon the following two communication exercises, keep the principles of "I" statements and stating your concerns in mind. Carrying out the second exercise may entail taking your first big risk.

## The Fantasy Rehearsal Exercise

If the prospect of talking to your partner about your sexual relationship seems very uncomfortable or frightening, you may find it useful to carry out the conversation mentally ahead of time. Before initiating any potentially awkward conversation—asking a boss for a raise, convincing someone to do something that he or she may have reservations about, sharing angry or hurt feelings with the person who "caused" them—it is common to rehearse the words that will be used and even to fantasize the entire dialogue. The fantasized interaction may be repeated a number of different ways in order to figure out what phrase or approach is most likely to elicit the desired response. This rehearsal can help develop confidence and reduce anxiety when the actual confrontation occurs and can also help determine the approach that is most likely to bring success.

To carry out the Fantasy Rehearsal Exercise, mentally rehearse having a conversation with your partner about sex. Imagine where the conversation would take place, how you would initiate it, what you would talk about, and how your partner would respond. Replay the fantasy rehearsal a few times using different approaches. After you have become comfortable with the fantasy communication, open the subject in reality.

## The Communication Exercise

Set aside a time to discuss with your partner the patterns you have observed in your sexual relationship. You might want to begin the conversation at a special restaurant where the atmosphere is quiet and where there is sufficient privacy. You might want to talk during a long drive together or at a favorite spot at the beach, on a trail, or in the privacy of your own home. Just make sure you will have sufficient time and won't be interrupted. If you are at home, you might wait until the children are sleeping or entertained elsewhere for the day. You may want to take the phone off the hook or just agree not to answer it. Another good time to broach the subject is after making love. However, it is important to make it clear that the conversation is not meant as criticism of the recent lovemaking, but as a way to enhance the next time.

You might want to use a book, magazine article, or television program to initiate the discussion. Or you might prefer to prepare your partner ahead of time by setting up a specific time to talk. Be careful not to bring the subject up when you are disagreeing or fighting about something else. Also, take care not to have the discussion after a particularly frustrating day—when you or your partner arrive home exhausted, overwhelmed, or just in a grumpy mood. While picking such a time can be a way of proving that your partner doesn't care or isn't really interested, it is unlikely to lead to progress. Choosing a time when you feel good about each other and are fairly relaxed will enhance the possibility of good communication.

There is probably no way to avoid all of the awkwardness of the first few minutes of the conversation. Every conversation about a problem of an interpersonal nature is bound to be uncomfortable at the beginning. So bear with it.

Open the conversation by expressing your love and assuring your partner that you have no intention of reassessing your commitment to the relationship. You can say that you recognize that you have not adequately communicated your needs, or reassure your partner in some other way that no one is to blame. Then you can discuss your concerns about your sexual relationship, your needs which are not being met, and changes you would like to see. Share with your partner what you have discovered from observing yourself through the Journal Exercise.* Suggest some of the conclusions you have drawn. Be certain also to include those aspects of your relationship which are satisfying and which you enjoy. Finally, encourage your partner to share any suggestions that might make the lovemaking more satisfying for both of you.

All information is useful. For example, if you feel you would be more likely to have orgasms if he could hold his erection longer before ejaculating, let him know. In all likelihood, he is already aware of this, but has had difficulty broaching the subject. Once it's out in the open, he may have some suggestions as to what you can do to help him maintain his erection.

Your partner may be unaware of some of your unique needs: that you need more intimate time together, that you worry about being a lousy lover, that not enough time is devoted to sex. Even if this is your first conversation on the subject, be as specific as you can be. Describe your feelings precisely and give examples from recent lovemaking experiences. And most important, express your desire to work on your sexual concerns together until you achieve some resolution.

This discussion should not be the only one you expect to have. It is a beginning. It is designed to open up your communication about sex. It may take a few conversations before you can fully express your sexual feelings and desires.

* See pages 80–84.

## THE NATURE OF CHANGE

After a conversation has taken place or a request has been made, don't be disappointed if your partner does not respond the very next time the appropriate situation arises. Or, if the next time you make love everything is different, expect a slipup the following time. Even given the best of intentions, most people won't catch a situation every time it presents itself. For example you may have requested that your partner spend more time kissing you and touching you all over your body before gravitating to your genitals. Your partner may remember to do this the next time you make love, but may fall back into the old pattern of grabbing right for the crotch the time after that. When this happens, some women deem the situation hopeless and immediately give up. Remember, however, that changing old habits is difficult, and your partner may have to be reminded a number of times before a real change can be made.

To expect perfection, particularly at the outset, is to set yourself up for failure. No one breaks a habit immediately after they become aware of it. It takes time to switch gears and permanently change an ingrained pattern. By throwing in the towel prematurely, you will have created the perfect opportunity to be the martyr. Being patient and clarifying your own needs during this period is more likely to pay off in the end.

The nature of relationships is such that making changes is always difficult. There is a tendency for both partners to seek homeostasis— to continue doing things in the established manner. When either partner attempts to interact differently, the other partner often resists these changes automatically. Change seems to be traumatic— even when it is for the better. Consequently, patience and understanding are of paramount importance.

Once you have opened the door to communicating about sex, you can begin to work on the specific problem. The remainder of this book is organized by the different sexual problem areas. The next section is designed for women having problems with orgasm. This is followed by a section that addresses problems of pain with sex. Finally, the last section is written for women who feel they lack sexual desire.

If chronic anger or other problems in the relationship seem to be at the basis of your sexual problem, it would be advisable to begin with the exercises in Chapter 13 (designed to rectify communication problems and relieve negative feelings) before trying any of the physical touching exercises that precede it. Going through the exercises aimed at enhancing arousal and sexual excitement before straightening out the nonsexual issues would be a disservice to yourself and your partner. When relationship problems underlie a sexual problem, unresolved feelings tend to block progress in the sexual area. Releasing and letting go of the negative feelings generally frees positive sexual feelings. Once some positive feelings have been restored and some of the negative ones allayed, the physical touching exercises have a much greater chance of succeeding.

Sometimes it is difficult to know which came first, the chicken or the egg—the relationship problems or the sexual problem. A sexual problem that creates frustration can have ramifications in other areas of the relationship. However, a sexual problem can also grow out of a relationship that is troubled. Constant power struggles, misunderstandings, and inadequate communication of feelings and needs can breed sufficient resentment to affect the desire to be sexually close. If the sexual problem was not present in the beginning of your relationship, if you were once sexually interested in your partner, had orgasms or experienced sex without pain, the cause of the sexual problem may lie in unresolved relationship issues. If you have had this problem with other partners or if it has been present since the very beginning of your sexual relationship with your current partner, there is a high probability that the sexual problem is not a reflection of your nonsexual relationship but has been caused by something else. The following chapters on the causes of the various sexual problems should help you clarify your particular situation.

*Section III*

# LACK OF ORGASM

*Chapter 6*

# BLOCKS TO ORGASM

If you have found that you are orgasmic with masturbation, you can feel secure that your body is physiologically capable of responding to the appropriate stimulation. Now you will have to compare carefully your sexual experiences while alone, with those you have with your partner, to determine why you have orgasms under one set of conditions but not under the other. This chapter will explore more common physical and emotional reasons why women have difficulty attaining orgasm with a partner. Due to its complexity, the subject has been divided into four categories: women who are orgasmic with masturbation but have never experienced an orgasm with a partner; women who have been orgasmic with a previous partner but not with their current partner; women who used to be orgasmic with their current partner; and women who are inconsistently orgasmic with their partner.

## WOMEN WHO ARE ORGASMIC WITH MASTURBATION BUT NEVER WITH A PARTNER

There are a wide variety of reasons why women are orgasmic when they masturbate but are unable to have orgasms with a partner. Some of these reasons are purely mechanical, while others are tied to feelings about one's self or one's partner.

## The Physical Component

Some women have difficulty responding orgasmically to partner stimulation because their own method of masturbation is quite different from what takes place during lovemaking with a partner. Since many of us learned to masturbate as young children, we may have stumbled upon ways to physically stimulate ourselves that bear no resemblance to sexual activities with a partner. Because the method worked, we repeated it and through repeating it established a pattern to which we became accustomed.

If we accidentally discovered a technique for producing pleasurable feelings in our genital area at a very young age, we may have had absolutely no idea that the feelings we were experiencing had anything to do with sex. Darlene mentioned that she had learned to masturbate when she was around four years old. One night in bed she was scratching her vagina because it itched. The scratching felt good so she continued doing it and after a while she had this good, warm feeling. Darlene remembered being surprised by this response, but since it felt good, she tried to make it happen again. Soon she could rub herself and have this good feeling whenever she wanted. However, Darlene did not know that she was masturbating and did not know that she was having orgasms. As a matter of fact, she had no idea that what she was doing had anything whatsoever to do with sex. Furthermore, she thought that she was the only person in the world with such feelings since she never talked to anyone else about it. In her adolescent years she discovered that if she pressed herself up against her boyfriend while kissing she could have the same feelings. So no one would know about her strange response, she learned to have orgasms without showing any outward physical signs. It wasn't until Darlene married that she realized she had been having orgasms, and not only did she not have to hide them but she was *supposed* to have them.

The way Darlene learned to have orgasms happened to transfer very nicely to sex with a partner. However, this is not always the case. For example, it is not unusual for girls to experience their first orgasm during gym or physical education class. Often, hanging from monkey bars or climbing on jungle gyms provides the kind of muscle tension that creates an orgasm. Some girls discover pleasurable feelings by rubbing against a pillow or a teddy bear, by hanging from doors, by rubbing back and forth on the edge of their chair at school, or by squeezing their thighs rhythmically together. Since some of these methods of reaching orgasm do not adapt well to partner sex, it is often necessary for women to learn new ways of reaching orgasm that are more like the activities that occur during sex with a partner.

Some women learn to have orgasms with stimulation from running water. Brenda discovered her first orgasm at age fifteen when she lathered her pubic hair and then placed it under the tap in an effort to rinse the soap out. Since that was the way her mother had rinsed the hair on her head this seemed like a normal procedure for her to use. Brenda discovered that it felt good to have the water running over her genitals this way and repeated the process a number of times, when to her total surprise a wonderful, pleasurable feeling resulted. She continued to reproduce these feelings the same way for years.

With all the information in the media about vibrators, more and more women are learning to have their first orgasm with the help of an electric or battery-operated body massager or vibrator. Although many women find that a vibrator is very helpful in learning to discover orgasms, they become frustrated when orgasm does not occur as easily from more subtle, nonmechanical stimulation. If this describes your situation, you may need to learn to respond to other forms of stimulation before you can experience orgasm from stimulation provided by a partner.

Even if you did not learn to masturbate in an idiosyncratic way, the probabilities are high that you always masturbate in the same position, either on your back, side, stomach, or possibly sitting or kneeling. And you probably always stimulate yourself with the same hand or with the same object.

Learning to have orgasms in your special way has created a well-worn path. Learning to respond in a different way is akin to blazing a new trail. It may be harder work and require more time and effort than the familiar method. However, with continued practice response to the new way will become easier and easier.

## The Masturbation Observation Exercise

To observe your masturbation pattern more carefully, set up a sensual atmosphere and prolong the stimulation. Even if it usually takes you just a couple of minutes to masturbate to orgasm, allow a half hour to an hour and slow down the experience so that you can pay close attention to the process. Many women, because of psychological discomfort with masturbation, masturbate as quickly as possible to achieve the physical release. The problem with masturbating quickly is that the experience is so rapid and automatic that it is sometimes difficult to determine precisely what produces the orgasm.

After paying close attention to what works for you when you masturbate, compare the positions and techniques you use during masturbation to those employed while you are making love with your partner. If you masturbate on your stomach, see if you are generally on your back during partner sex. If you use hard direct clitoral stimulation with masturbation, notice if the clitoral stimulation you receive from your partner is lighter or less direct. If you create a lot of leg tension by holding your thighs close together with masturbation, notice if you spend most of your lovemaking time with your legs wide apart.

Research by Gerda de Bruijn in the Netherlands found that women who masturbate by lying passively while stimulating their genitals with their hand or some other object reach orgasm more easily when their partner actively applies the stimulation. Women who masturbate while lying passively and inserting something in their vagina experience orgasm more easily during coitus where the male is the active partner. Women who masturbate by creating a stimulating friction through the use of their lower body muscles by rubbing against something are more likely to have orgasms when they rub their genitals against their partner's thigh, buttocks, or their partner's pubic bone during intercourse. De Bruijn concludes that "women who want to orgasm during lovemaking with their partner may have a better chance to achieve this orgasm if they engage in a type of sex play which corresponds with the woman's masturbation technique."[1] Consequently, enlarging one's masturbation pattern as well as employing masturbation techniques during lovemaking are two fundamental approaches to learning to be orgasmic with a partner.

## The Mental Component

The mental/emotional component of lovemaking is as important as the physical one. A woman could rub her clitoris all day, but if she is very uncomfortable doing so, if she is distracted by non-sexual thoughts, if she is angry at her partner, or if she doesn't feel good about herself as a sexual person, it is doubtful she will become aroused sufficiently to experience orgasm.

### SELF-WORTH

Your feelings about yourself contribute to your sexual comfort and satisfaction. If you have a sense of your personal value, you are more apt to feel that you deserve pleasure, including sexual pleasure. If you feel self-assured, you will be better able to let your partner know about your unique sexual needs. If you feel sexually attractive, you will feel less anxious and less inhibited when you are making love to your partner.

Some women have been taught that sex is dirty and bad. Even when intellectually these women know otherwise, such negative feelings can persist on a subtle level and cause sufficient anxiety and discomfort during sex to inhibit the orgasmic response. Connie found herself not enjoying sex without really understanding why. During our interview, she realized that she had received the message from both her parents that only bad women derive pleasure from sex. As a child, her father had witnessed his mother having extra-marital affairs, and he had grown up believing all women were sexually depraved. Not surprisingly, he chose a wife who was very puritanical in her sexual attitudes. Consequently, both of Connie's parents gave her negative messages about being a sexual woman. Through our discussion, Connie realized that she no longer wanted to allow her parents to dictate her sexual attitudes and responses. To overcome some of her negative training, she began to tell herself that sex is positive. While making love she affirms that sexual enjoyment is a sign of a mature woman. And with these positive messages has come increased sexual pleasure.

## NEGATIVE REPERCUSSIONS

Fears that something undesirable may accompany the attainment of orgasm can block orgasm from occurring. Can you imagine how the situation might be *worse* if you began to have orgasms? Although your immediate response may be, "Of course not. Everything would be better," don't gloss over this question too quickly. Could there be some negative repercussions? Any change entails risk. The status quo, although not terribly satisfying, is at least predictable. Some women fear that if they become orgasmic they will want sex too frequently, which might anger or annoy their partner. Some fear they will look ugly and turn off their partner. Possibly the lack of orgasm is a cover-up for other relationship problems which would become evident once the problem of orgasm were resolved. In some cases, a woman's orgasm problem provides a cover for her partner's feelings of sexual inadequacy.

Many women are afraid to make changes in their sexual relationship even though they would like to believe otherwise. Consequently, at this point in the process it would be helpful to think about how willing you are to risk doing things differently. If your answer is, "I'd like to see a change, but I'm not willing to go to any great lengths or to make myself or my partner at all uncomfortable," the prognosis for change is poor. However, if you are willing to experience some growth pangs, the prospect for success is far more hopeful.

## FEAR OF MERGING

Many women experience a vague, amorphous fear of losing themselves or of merging with their partner as they approach the somewhat egoless or diffused state of orgasm. This is a very subtle and complex issue. Do you anticipate a sense of merging with your partner that makes you anxious? Or do you fear becoming totally dependent if you have an orgasm with him? Do you feel as if your partner has power over you, that your partner "gives" you your orgasm through manual stimulation, oral stimulation, or intercourse? Or do you feel that your partner could overwhelm you with pleasure, leaving you helpless and vulnerable? If so, you may be forgetting that you are the one in control.

To overcome these feelings, it is necessary to be completely certain that you are in control. Your ability to block your orgasm all these years represents real strength. You will never lose the power to block it if you choose. You are the only one who can decide when and if you are going to have the orgasm. Once you realize this, you should find it less necessary to prove that you have control by withholding. And allowing yourself to have a few experiences of orgasm with your partner will also help you to realize that there is really nothing to fear.

## FANTASY

Your thoughts during sex can have a powerful effect on your sexual response. Do you fantasize while you masturbate? If you do, do you also fantasize while making love with your partner? Many women use fantasy as a way to keep their thoughts focused on sex and off their self-consciousness or worries. For some women, mental erotic images are absolutely necessary to experience orgasm.

Amanda could have orgasms through fantasy alone, without any additional physical stimulation. However, she never had orgasms with her partner. When I asked her if she ever fantasized while making love with a partner, she told me that she would never allow herself to fantasize with another person present because she felt that it wasn't normal. Her partner's physical presence should be enough. However, after finally accepting the idea that it was perfectly normal to fantasize, she decided to try fantasizing during partner sex and, to her surprise, had no difficulty attaining orgasm.

Even if the need for fantasy is acceptable, some women worry about the fantasy themes or actors that turn them on. If they respond to a fantasy which includes sex with a certain person, they become concerned that it means they would like to have that experience in real life. When that person is a forbidden sexual partner, like a parent, child, spouse of a best friend, or another woman (or man for a lesbian), they try to squelch their fantasy. Some women are afraid they might act on their fantasy, so they try not to think about it. This same fear of losing control affects women who fantasize about activities that they consider forbidden or abnormal. Many people don't realize that what is arousing in fantasy may in no way indicate what would turn them on in real life. A woman who finds a rape fantasy erotic is very unlikely to have the same response were she to be actually raped. Sometimes it is the safety of exploring the illicit without fear, harm, or repercussion that holds the sexual allure.

The research of Hariton and Singer shows that women have a wide range of fantasies and that these fantasies indicate nothing about a woman's mental stability. "In a sample of reasonably normal married women, the occurrence of daydreams during sexual relations is quite common and not generally related to interpersonal disturbances, adjustment problems, or lack of fulfillment in the sexual area. It seems likely that fantasy is a general phenomenon, accepted and indulged in more by some women than others. Its occurrence during the sex act probably reflects a stylistic variation rather than a withdrawal, defense, or alienation."[2]

Also, many fantasies have their basis in incidents occurring in early childhood or adolescence when sexual feelings were high and a real understanding of sexuality was very limited. An early spanking that was coupled with sexual feelings might persist in fantasy many years later. Peeking in a half-opened door and watching a couple make love might reappear in later life as voyeuristic fantasies. Feeling turned on by fantasies of being forced to have sex could stem from our adolescent years when, in order to maintain our reputation, we had to fight our boyfriends at each step of the highly sexually charged exploration. This may have trained us that it was all right to feel turned on as long as we weren't responsible, if we were being forced to continue. These early images and feelings of being forced to have sex may have then remained connected to feelings of high eroticism. However, no matter what kind of fantasies, thoughts, or images we find arousing, an erotic mental set, free of worry and excessive self-consciousness, is as necessary as the proper physical stimulation for sex to be exciting and orgasmic.

## The Communication Component

Even if we are fully aware of our requirements for orgasm, we may remain unresponsive because we are unable to communicate the necessary information to our partner. A study of over a thousand women in the Netherlands, who are mostly young, educated, and have rather liberal values in a country which is already quite liberal in its sexual customs, showed that at least 30 percent shied away from initiating certain types of sexual stimulation they considered exciting. The activities they particularly refrained from initiating were oral stimulation, rubbing against their partner's thighs or buttocks, or stimulating themselves manually during coitus.[3]

There is no question that as a result of female role scripting, many women are embarrassed to talk about sex or assert their desires. Women refrain from expressing their sexual needs—especially if it means interrupting "normal" intercourse to include concomitant clitoral stimulation, or to assume a position that would enable them to be more sexually active.

Thirty-nine-year-old Alicia admitted that she had never asked for what she wanted sexually or in any way asserted her sexual needs. Alicia had also never had an orgasm with a partner although she had had sexual experiences with about fifteen different men. She was quite easily orgasmic with masturbation and could masturbate in a variety of positions using diverse stimulation. Finally she confronted her role scripting, took a deep breath, told her current boyfriend that she had difficulty achieving orgasm, and asked if he would be willing to spend an extended period of time just touching and massaging her. He agreed, and during the massage, she told him exactly how she liked her neck stroked, her stomach stroked, and after much hesitation, she was able to tell him how to stroke her genitals. Because of the massage, she was very relaxed and as he manually stimulated her, she realized that an orgasm was building. She almost squelched it out of fear, but consciously decided to relax and enjoy the sensations for however long they lasted. She told her partner not to stop, that what he was doing was very pleasurable, and within a few moments, to the delight of them both, she had an orgasm.

Contrary to common belief, our partners are not mind readers. The communication of sexual information is often essential before two people can meet each other's sexual needs and before a woman can experience orgasm.

## WOMEN WHO HAVE BEEN ORGASMIC WITH A PREVIOUS PARTNER BUT ARE NOT WITH THEIR CURRENT PARTNER

Women who know they can be orgasmic with a partner because they have been regularly orgasmic with partners in the past, but who have never had an orgasm with their current partner, often feel confused. They wonder why their orgasms have suddenly disappeared.

### Technique

The most common cause for women not having orgasms with a new partner when they have been orgasmic in the past has to do with lovemaking style or sexual technique. Most couples don't automatically "click." If you are hesitant to let a new partner know your sexual needs, he is likely to use those techniques that work for him—which may not necessarily be right for you. People's approaches to sex are as individual as their approaches to other areas of life. You may find that a new partner has a sexual style that is very different from your own or from that of previous partners. For example, Betty and Phillip seemed to have sexual problems right from the beginning of their relationship together, even though neither had experienced sexual difficulties in any of their previous long-term relationships. Although they were very close friends and very physically affectionate, their styles of lovemaking were very different. Phillip liked to laugh and play in bed. His best sexual times consisted of flopping around like a puppy dog and laughing and playing with his lover. Betty, on the other hand, liked her sexual encounters to be serious and dramatic. Understandably, the two styles clashed. Working out such a serious discrepancy required considerable communication and willingness to compromise.

### Fear of Intimacy

Some women find that withholding their orgasm is a way to protect themselves from becoming too intimate too quickly. To prevent the emotional relationship with our partner from deepening too rapidly, we may hold back sexually. In so doing, we create an emotional distance that offsets the sexual intimacy.

Elaine was regularly orgasmic with her first husband and with most of her lovers after her divorce. But when she found herself, for the first time since her divorce, in a relationship which she felt could really develop into something, she was unable to have an orgasm. No matter how hard she tried or how much information she provided Peter, every lovemaking experience ended in frustration. Since Elaine was used to regular orgasmic release, and since she and Peter were making love almost every day, their frustration was intense by the time they came for therapy.

Like many other women who have weathered a divorce, Elaine was wary of becoming emotionally involved again. She thought she might be falling in love with Peter and felt very vulnerable. Although she was drawn to the excitement of a future life together, she was afraid of being hurt if the relationship did not work out. Her concern about the sexual problem only exacerbated this fear. As a result, she and Peter focused most of their lovemaking on trying to produce her orgasm which further increased her anxiety. Finally, in order to reduce some of the performance pressure she felt, Elaine decided to put a ban on orgasm for herself. At the same time, she did a lot of thinking about her relationship with Peter and realized that it was very important to her. Deciding to take the risk of fully exploring the relationship with Peter, plus removing the pressure she felt to perform, allowed her to relax sufficiently so that her orgasms returned.

While some women find that withholding their orgasm is a way to protect themselves from becoming too involved and intimate too quickly, others, who are very attracted to their partner and would like the relationship to develop into something deeper, inadvertently withhold orgasm because they distrust their partner's involvement. Some women feel particularly vulnerable when being sexually intimate. And if they sense a lack of commitment from their partner, they may hold back their feelings as well as their orgasm in order to protect themselves. In such cases, if a sense of safety can be created, it may be unnecessary to withhold orgasm.

If you are not sure whether or not commitment may be an issue in your relationship, take a few minutes to consider how you feel about your partner and how you think your partner feels toward you. Assess whether you think your partner foresees the relationship as a short and carefree fling or a more involved and possibly committed involvement. If the messages you get are ambiguous, this may be at the root of your problem and you may have to discuss the issue with your partner to know for certain where you stand.

## WOMEN WHO USED TO BE ORGASMIC WITH THEIR CURRENT PARTNER

Women who were at one time able to have orgasms with their current partner rarely lose that ability without a good reason. Generally, when women no longer experience orgasm with their partner, some kind of trauma or relationship problem has blocked the orgasmic response. In these cases, careful detective work can frequently pinpoint the precipitating cause.

### The Sleuthing Exercise

Try to remember back to the time when you stopped having orgasms. Do you remember if they declined in number gradually or if they disappeared suddenly? If you can't place the date, try to retrace the years by remembering the different surroundings in which you commonly had sex. If you redecorated your bedroom or if you moved from one house to another, use the different physical surroundings to help you recall some sexual experiences that took place during the period in question. Which of these experiences ended in orgasm and which did not?

Since even couples who are having sexual problems tend to be more sexual on vacation, and since vacations tend to stand out in one's mind, go back over your vacations during the approximate period when your orgasms stopped. If you took your last vacation in Cape Cod and the summer before you went to San Francisco, review in your memory the hotels or cottages in which you stayed. Try to visualize your surroundings and relive in your mind the sexual experiences which took place there. Once you can identify approximately when your sexual response changed, you will be better able to zero in on the cause. In all likelihood, some particular event or emotional upset occurred during that period.

EMOTIONAL UPSET

Gloria had been involved with Tom for four years. He was the first man with whom she had ever experienced an orgasm, and she had been regularly orgasmic during sex after the first few months of their relationship. However, by the time Gloria came for therapy, she had not had an orgasm with Tom for quite a while. She was not exactly sure when her orgasms stopped, so together we began sleuthing.

"Where did you make love during the initial part of your relationship?" I asked.

"In his apartment in Chicago," she answered.

"Did you have orgasms then?"

"Yes," she responded.

"Where did you live after that?" I asked.

"We moved in together in a different apartment in Chicago."

"Remember what sex was like there. Did you have orgasms then?"

After a moment of silence as Gloria recalled some sexual experiences which had taken place in that apartment, she again answered, "Yes."

"Where did you move after that?" I questioned.

"Well, after that, Tom went to California to go to graduate school. The plan was that he would go first and I was to follow if he liked it there. So we didn't have much sex during that time except for a few vacations when he came back to Chicago or when we met somewhere in between. Actually, he didn't write as often as I would have liked. I remember that. Now that I think about it, I rarely had orgasms during those brief two- or three-day periods we spent together over that year we were separated."

Gloria had pinpointed the period of time during which the change had occurred. After talking about it awhile longer, she also realized what had probably accounted for the change. Gloria had felt abandoned by Tom, particularly when he did not write regularly. Although he said he wanted her to come to California to live with him, she was afraid to let her hopes rise. When she did join him in Los Angeles after the year was over, the fear that he might abandon her still remained in the back of her mind and continued to interfere with her orgasmic response. Gloria defended herself against possible future hurt by holding back during sex.

One woman stopped having orgasms when she learned that her husband had been having an affair with his secretary. Another realized that her orgasms had stopped after she had a serious medical operation. During the period of her operation and convalescence she felt very dependent upon her husband, but found that he was not available to meet her needs because he was away on business trips almost constantly.

Sometimes orgasms stop at a decisive point in the relationship. Brenda and her boyfriend had been living together for four years and her parents began to seriously pressure her to get married. Although happy in the relationship, Brenda was not certain that this was the man she wanted to marry. She had grave concerns about his ability to be a parent. It was at this point that she suddenly stopped having orgasms.

Sylvia was thirty-five years old and had had sexual relationships with a number of men. When she joined our preorgasmic therapy group, she had for the previous two years been deeply involved and living with a woman. During the course of the group she learned to have orgasms. After she had been experiencing orgasms with her partner for a short period of time, they suddenly disappeared. Because she had been able to respond sexually with her partner, Sylvia found herself confronting the issue of whether or not this relationship was a permanent one, and whether she considered herself homosexual.

Sometimes women find that the emotional trauma which precipitated the lack of orgasm had nothing to do with their partner. In one case, Helen noted that her orgasms abated about the time her teenage son had a psychotic breakdown. Her husband was more than supportive, but the stress and anguish created by their son's illness resulted in a marked decrease in their sexual activity and interfered with her ability to experience orgasm. Another woman stopped having orgasms during the intensely stressful period of her father's illness and death.

If a traumatic incident originally caused your lack of orgasm, you may find the sexual problem persisting long after the incident has been resolved. Sometimes this is because the original problem created a habit that now needs to be changed. On the other hand, if trust in your partner has been violated, you may unconsciously fear that the event will recur. In this case you may have to directly discuss the problem with your partner before you can relax and allow yourself to be responsive—and perhaps vulnerable—during lovemaking.

## RELATIONSHIP PROBLEMS

Sometimes orgasmic responsivity declines gradually. More often than not, this indicates the deterioration of other aspects of an intimate relationship. As we discussed in the first chapter, if we do not feel powerful enough to make the changes necessary in our relationship, we may express our frustration by withholding. Those of us who learned to see sex, not as something for ourselves but as a commodity to be used to interest and capture a sexual partner, may use sex as a tool. If we give ourselves sexually to reward our partner, we may withhold sexually when we are not getting what we want. Most women tend to do this either by not feeling turned on or by not having orgasms. Withholding our own sexual enjoyment, rather than refraining from sexual participation altogether, may occur because we have been indoctrinated with the belief that a man's sexual rights are inviolable. Or, we may fear that if we withhold sex completely, our partner will find his sexual satisfaction outside the relationship. Withholding our enjoyment and pleasure gets the point across, it spoils our partner's enjoyment of the sexual experience, and often makes our partner feel inadequate at the same time.

Fran was fifty-five years old and had been married for thirty years. Her husband, Bill, was still as interested in sex and as sexually active as ever. Fran had never once denied Bill sex. However, over the past ten years, she had stopped having orgasms. Her inability to have orgasms frustrated Bill no end and it was he, and not Fran, who called for a sex-therapy appointment. During the interview it became quite clear that Fran could not care less about recovering her lost orgasms. Bill, on the other hand, would do anything necessary to bring her orgasms back since he considered their absence a failure on his part and an indication of a decline in his masculine prowess. Bill demanded his own way about everything while Fran was quiet, demure, and acquiescent—up to a point, and her point seemed to be orgasm. Although Fran never said it in so many words, it was apparent that she had found her way to get even after years of giving in.

When the absence of orgasm is a carry-over from a relationship problem that has already been resolved, recovering the orgasm through experimenting with the exercises in the following chapters should not be difficult. However, if the sexual problem is a response to a current relationship issue, it will probably be necessary to work on these problematic aspects of the relationship as well as the sexual problem itself. If the negative interactions have gone on for too long and the animosity and hurt feelings run too deep, it may not be possible to repair the relationship adequately without the assistance of a therapist.

## WOMEN WHO ARE INCONSISTENTLY ORGASMIC WITH THEIR PARTNER

Many women are orgasmic only irregularly. While they do have orgasms with a partner, they can't count on them. The occurrence or absence of their orgasms seems to have no rhyme or reason.

In fact, however, random orgasmic inconsistency is highly unusual. We respond sexually when our needs are met and we don't respond when they're not met. Our bodies are capable of making subtle distinctions that we may not even be aware of intellectually. For example, we may feel our partner is not really emotionally present, even though he claims he is. A stressful conversation that preceded sex can follow us into the bedroom even when we were sure we could leave it behind. Subtle distractions such as unconsciously waiting for an important phone call or hearing music we hadn't even noticed can interfere with experiencing orgasm.

This is not to say that if you were able to tune out all the distractions you would ever be orgasmic 100 percent of the time that you engage in sex. That is simply not a realistic goal. There are always going to be times when you feel like having the physical and emotional intimacy of a sexual experience but are too tired or just not in the mood to exert the amount of energy or concentration that would be required to attain orgasm. But if you know the conditions you require for good sex, you should be able to direct the lovemaking in such a way that your needs are met and orgasm occurs most of the time.

## Sexual Requirements

If you feel that you have realistic expectations but are dissatisfied with your frequency of orgasm, you may be unaware of your unique requirements for good sex. The Journal Exercise in Chapter 4 is the best way to determine these requirements. Most of us don't take the time or expend the necessary energy to monitor our lives, so we remain puzzled by occurrences that seem haphazard. If we monitor our actions and feelings carefully, we will notice patterns. They may be complex patterns, but they are patterns nonetheless.

Remember to include the following categories as you review each sexual experience in your journal: feelings about yourself, feelings about your partner, your interest in sex, when and where sex occurred, your thoughts and fantasies, the various sexual activities participated in, your sexual-arousal level and overall satisfaction with the sexual experience. Record your feelings and sexual activities in your journal at least once a day.*

After twenty years of marriage, Margaret was still inconsistently orgasmic. She claimed that she could never anticipate whether sex would end in orgasm or not. So she started keeping a journal. After writing in her journal after every sexual encounter for a period of three weeks, Margaret began to notice a pattern. When she and her husband spent time talking together about work or intellectual topics before making love, whether it was over a quiet dinner or just in bed before turning the lights out, she was almost always orgasmic. However, if they had sex without any intellectual communication, if they talked only about the children and household affairs, or if they didn't have time to talk, she would not be orgasmic. What Margaret realized from keeping her journal was that she needed to feel important as an intellectual person, not just as a mother or sex object, in order to be orgasmic. Consequently, she

* See pages 80–84 to review the Journal Exercise.

began setting aside short periods of time every evening to have an intellectual discussion with her husband. For Margaret, feeling like an intellectual equal was a necessary condition for good sex.

Karen discovered that she was much more turned on and far more likely to have an orgasm if she made love in dim light rather than in total darkness. Consequently, she keeps a candle by the side of the bed because she knows this will enhance her pleasure.

Debbie realized that although she was sometimes orgasmic during vaginal stimulation, this wasn't always the case. For her, the amount of time between sexual encounters made the difference. If three or four days had gone by without sex, she seemed to be readily orgasmic with vaginal stimulation. If only one or two days had passed, she required more clitoral stimulation. With this information, Debbie could be more clear about asking her partner for more clitoral stimulation on those days she anticipated being less vaginally responsive.

Once you discover your conditions for good sex, you can take an active part in making sure they are met. By avoiding what you know interferes with your sexual enjoyment, and including what you know arouses you, you will be more likely to experience orgasm. This does not mean that you must be limited to these conditions. Whenever you like, you can expand your range to include activities that you don't now use or that don't necessarily work for you today.

Meeting your conditions for good sex may require you to assert yourself, to say no when you don't want sex, to ask for more kissing and touching before intercourse, or to ask your partner to continue oral stimulation until you climax. Even if you don't assert yourself in the beginning, at least you will know why you are not orgasmic, rather than just feeling vaguely inadequate or abnormal.

Creating the necessary conditions for good sex sometimes entails planning. Some people who believe that sex is better if it is spontaneous may complain that their lovemaking is routine and boring, yet are averse to preparing for a sexual encounter in any way. Certainly, sex that occurs on the spur of the moment, when passion is high, can create memorable experiences. But day-to-day meat-and-potatoes sex can be far more enjoyable and will be far more likely to end in orgasm if you take the time and effort to lay the groundwork for making the sexual experience a good one.

## WOMEN WHO ARE DISSATISFIED
## WITH THEIR ORGASM

Although I addressed this issue in the first chapter, the myth of the superiority of the vaginal orgasm is so strongly rooted and the notion of the sexual Olympics so firmly entrenched that it seems worthy of further discussion here. The important factor in evaluating orgasms is not number or intensity, but how good they *feel*. Are they pleasurable? Do you enjoy sex? Check your expectations against reality. The one mind-blowing orgasm you had in 1972 may have been a unique experience, a rare combination of the atmosphere, your partner, and the chemistry the two of you created at that particular moment. Deprecating every orgasm after that as you strive to recreate that one event will only perpetuate your dissatisfaction. Focusing on what *isn't* there rather than what *is* there is a sure way to miss what is happening at the moment—something which may be different from, but just as good as, some past experience.

If you enjoy your orgasms but feel you could enjoy them even more, it might be more appropriate to emphasize what already works for you rather than search for what some friend or magazine article touts as the greatest. If oral sex pleases you most, do more of that. Spend more time at it and intensify the process by experimenting and guiding your partner. If quickies are the ultimate for you, forget about sex experts who prescribe long, drawn-out lovemaking episodes. We are each unique. Therefore we must look to ourselves for our preferences, not to the opinions of others.

Kathy was convinced that she was missing out on sexual enjoyment because she couldn't have orgasms through the thrusting of her partner's penis. She wanted to have orgasms the "right" way. She said she was willing to expend whatever energy was necessary to attain her ends, so I instructed her to assume the woman-on-top position during intercourse while her partner remained relatively passive. He was to relax and enjoy the sexual sensations but not increase his own intensity sufficiently to reach orgasm. Kathy was to take full control of the thrusting in order to enhance her own pleasure and to continue intercourse for as long as it took to have an orgasm—but to expect it to require a minimum of two hours. Kathy and her partner carried out the homework assignment, and Kathy had an orgasm after one hour of thrusting. One would have thought she would have been elated. Instead, she was just fatigued. Now that she knew that she could have orgasms that way she decided that it wasn't worth all the effort and, quite satisfied, she returned to her previous patterns of lovemaking, which included oral sex and manual manipulation of the clitoris.

*If* she had wanted to, Kathy could have continued having intercourse in the woman-superior position. In all likelihood, with more practice it would have taken less time. Once she had achieved it, however, Kathy ceased to find it important. Oftentimes, what we *don't* experience seems attractive. If we don't have multiple orgasms or orgasms through intercourse alone, we *think* that these experiences would be superior to our own. So we strive for them, and our unsuccessful attempts to reach the greener grass on the other side of the fence only result in dissatisfaction.

## CONTINUING THE JOURNEY

It does not have to be difficult to have an orgasm with a partner. Physiologically, if you are capable of having an orgasm alone, you are capable of sharing the experience. Part of the difficulty lies in disconnecting the sexual response from the emotional issues: "I'm a bad girl if I'm sexual"; "I can get even with my partner by not having orgasms"; "My orgasms define me as worthy, as feminine"; and other issues that can block the natural physiological process. Another part of the problem can be solved by ensuring that your requirements for good sex are met. When you are not feeling loving, it is usually a good idea not to have sex. If you are communicating your anger rather than your love, orgasm is an unlikely outcome. If you are tired, under stress, or distracted, you won't be able to put your full attention into sex and hence are not likely to get much out of it. If you are ambivalent about being sexual or about a particular relationship, don't have sex. If you do, orgasm is not a probable result. If you are unsure of your self-worth, look to your accomplishments—not to your orgasms. Remember, the whole object of sex is to feel good—to feel good about yourself, to feel good about your partner, to feel the good, pleasurable sensations.

To increase the pleasurable sexual feelings, we will focus on the specifics of orgasm as we continue our journey of sexual exploration. The exercises in the next chapter should enable you to better understand how your body responds, thereby allowing you to expand your natural sensitivities and patterns of response.

# Chapter 7

# EXPANDING ORGASMIC POTENTIAL

Experience running women's sexuality groups has taught me that success at becoming orgasmic with a partner begins with gaining comfort with our own bodies and responses before attempting any partner exercises. Therefore, we will start with exercises designed to increase body acceptance and knowledge and then move on to partner exercises in Chapters 8 and 9.

## BODY ACCEPTANCE

The media reinforces images of beauty that inevitably leave some of us feeling less than attractive. Comparing ourselves to magazine models, we find our breasts too large or too small, our buttocks too flat or too full, our scars too conspicuous—and we imagine that our partner sees only these "defects." As a result, many of us focus more on our appearance and our partner's reaction to our body than on our own sensations.

In order to enjoy the sexual experience with a partner more fully and to realize that the horrible faults we perceive are really not so terrible, we must be more accepting of our bodies. All too often, we are far more critical of ourselves than our partner ever is. In fact, the areas that embarrass us—a scar, bony knees, a large nose, tiny breasts, or ears that stick out—frequently are considered special by our partner. Our idiosyncrasies often call forth a teasingly affectionate response—an intimate reaction that a model's perfection rarely elicits. While perfection may be admired, it is rarely loved in the same way.

I always felt that my long nose was a terrible flaw. As a teenager I even considered a nose job, which my mother would have been only too happy to accommodate. (She lived by the same standards of beauty as the magazine editors.) And yet, now I find that what could be considered a major flaw is, to my husband, one of my most endearing physical attributes, because it is so uniquely me. He doesn't love me because of my nose, he loves my nose too. And to think I wasted all those years worrying about it.

Coming to terms with your own body, accepting and appreciating it not in spite of its uniqueness but because of it, is a worthwhile endeavor. The following body-looking and -touching exercises have proved to be an excellent method of creating a more positive body image.

## The Body-Looking Exercise

Set up a full-length mirror in the privacy of your room. Lock your door and undress in front of the mirror. As you stand there, make sure that the room is sufficiently warm to be comfortable in the nude. Then carefully examine your body. You might talk to yourself while you're looking, describing aloud exactly what you see. For example, "My hair is dark and curly and surrounds my neck. My forehead has a few wrinkles. My eyes are large and attractive. My lips are sensual. . . ." And on down to your toes.

Look at your body from all angles: standing, kneeling, sitting with your legs apart, with your legs together, as you move about. Look at yourself for a minimum of fifteen minutes. Seeing what your lover sees when looking at you might make you less embarrassed and inhibited. The object of this exercise is to gain a neutral perspective. Therefore, do not criticize what you see. Carry out the exercise with a curious attitude.

Repeat the exercise a day or so later. Most women need to complete this exercise on at least two or three different occasions before they notice any change in their attitude toward their body.

## The Body-Exploration Exercise

After you've examined yourself carefully in the mirror for at least fifteen minutes, begin to explore your body with your hands. Again, you might describe aloud what your hands are feeling. Pretend you're from another planet, landing on this unknown body for the first time. Your assignment is to explore this new body completely. Run your fingers over your arms, legs, stomach, etc.: feel the muscles, the bones, the fat, and the varied texture of your skin. Compare the skin on your inner thigh to that on the soles of your feet, to that on your lips, ears, chest, shins, buttocks. Enjoy the feelings of your hands touching your skin as well as your skin being touched. See if you can discover something you didn't know before—some area of unusual sensitivity, or a particularly pleasing type of touch. You may find that your fingers, your toes, your ears, or the tiny hairs on the small of your back are particularly sensitive. Do you like any areas better than you thought you would? Can you begin to accept the fact that it's OK to look the way you do? As with the last exercise, this one will probably have to be carried out two or three times before any change in attitude can be expected.

## The Self-Stimulation Exercise

Most women consider masturbation a purely genital experience. They rarely include stimulation of other parts of their body—their neck, their breasts, their inner thighs, or other areas that are pleasurable when touched by their partner. One way to make masturbation more like sex with a partner is to include your whole body. Take the time to make love to yourself rather than merely striving for the orgasm. You might consider building up to the masturbation experience slowly by massaging and touching your body in ways that turn you on. You might want to stroke your stomach with a light, feathery touch or massage your breasts or squeeze your nipples or pleasure other parts of your body in various ways before attending to your clitoris or vagina.

### MENTAL AROUSAL

To increase your masturbation pleasure, don't forget to also pay attention to your mental arousal. The mental component of sexual arousal is as important as the physical component. Getting into a sexual mood is sometimes more difficult when a partner is not present. A partner's very presence provides us with sexual cues. When we are masturbating, we must supply all of the mental erotic components ourselves. Some women do this simply by focusing on the pleasurable sensations experienced in their body. Others are more apt to fantasize, to have sexual daydreams about some real or imagined sexual experience. For some women, reading erotica or looking at nude pictures of men or women supplies the missing erotic cues. Whatever your method of keeping mental stimulation high, continue to use it when making the various physical changes suggested in the following exercise.

## The Slowing-Down Exercise

Even though you are orgasmic with masturbation, you may feel uncomfortable about the process—especially if it is something you were taught not to do. To offset the overt or covert messages that labeled masturbation harmful or sinful, you may have learned to achieve the release as quickly as possible. Although able to reach orgasm in a few minutes or even seconds, you may not experience masturbation as a process of making love to yourself. If you merely try to get the experience over with as rapidly as possible, it will be difficult to observe the process your body undergoes. Without slowing down the arousal sequence sufficiently to attend to the details, the masturbation experience may feel like a mystery, something far different and separate from making love with a partner.

Also, it takes most women longer to have orgasms with a partner than it does with masturbation. If you are accustomed to quick orgasms with masturbation, you may give up prematurely when you make love with a partner. Learning to simmer sexual feelings during masturbation is a good exercise for women who stimulate themselves to orgasm quickly.

To slow down the masturbation process, imagine a ladder with ten rungs, where the bottom rung represents the beginning feelings of sexual arousal and the top rung orgasm. As you masturbate, imagine stopping at each rung of the ladder. Let your sexual arousal simmer while you savor the feelings at each step for a few minutes before moving up to the next rung. For example, you could stroke your clitoris more lightly, or move from stimulating the head of the clitoris to stimulating the shaft, the inner lips, or the vaginal opening. Even changing the motion from an up and down motion to a circular one could slow the process down.

In all likelihood you will find that you are unable to proceed from one arousal rung to the next without having the sensations diminish and drop down a rung or two from time to time. This is not a problem. In fact, masturbating this way can help teach you not to worry when you find, during sex with a partner, that you have suddenly lost some or all of your sexual sensations. During partner sex, sensations ebb and flow depending not only on the type of stimulation or intercourse position used, but on the sudden appearance of extraneous thoughts that can divert attention from the sexual experience. Realizing that you can lose the sensations and still regain them later on can help prevent you from prematurely giving up when you're with a partner and the sexual sensations begin to diminish. Also, learning to increase the sensations once they have disappeared or subsided will make you more aware of the exact kinds of stimulation that are most effective.

Claudia learned to masturbate while standing up and could reach orgasm in less than two minutes. She would commonly masturbate once or twice a day in this way, especially if she was under a lot of pressure. However, Claudia never experienced orgasm while with a partner. While observing her masturbation pattern carefully, she realized that not only had she grown accustomed to having orgasms in a very brief period of time, but during masturbation her level of arousal never dipped or decreased. It simply kept increasing until orgasm was attained. Claudia realized that with a partner her arousal progressed quite differently. While making love with her boyfriend, she would be quite turned on initially, but after the first few minutes, her feelings of excitement would decrease. Since she was not accustomed to experiencing any decrease in her level of arousal before she reached orgasm, she would unconsciously give up when this happened. Consequently, before concentrating on experiencing orgasm with a partner, Claudia taught herself to masturbate more slowly. Once she could experience ups and downs with masturbation and still reach orgasm, she found that she was more relaxed with her boyfriend during sex and less concerned about dips in her arousal level and how long it took her to reach orgasm. The final result was that she was able to experience orgasms with him, first during oral sex and later in other ways.

## WIDENING YOUR HORIZONS

As mentioned in the previous chapter, some women who have masturbated over a long period of time may have developed a particularly rigid and idiosyncratic method of masturbating. Whenever we do anything over and over again, we train our body to respond in a particular way. Take driving, for example. Initially, learning to drive requires all of our attention. We need to remember to stop at stop signs, look behind us as we pull out, judge the speed of oncoming cars. But after months of attention and practice we begin to respond automatically. After years of experience we sometimes find that we have driven miles without even noticing. Our mind was elsewhere while our body, which had been programmed, carried on. If we initially developed a particularly idiosyncratic driving style, we would now probably find this difficult to change. For example, if we learned to drive an automatic car and if for some reason, we learned to brake with our left foot, we might find it very difficult to learn to drive a stick shift. For a period of time we would probably continue to brake with our left foot and forget to throw in the clutch, thereby causing the car to stall each time we stopped. In order to learn to drive a stick shift, we would have to unlearn the habit of using the left foot to brake.

Women who have learned to masturbate in a way that is very different from what occurs during sex with a partner—such as masturbating while standing up, with legs tightly crossed, or by using a vibrator—may need to retrain their bodies to respond in another way. In order to make the masturbation experience more transferable to lovemaking with a partner, it is helpful to vary the masturbation pattern so that it more closely resembles patterns occurring during partner sex. In this way, the body can be trained to respond to new types of stimulation.* The following exercises are designed for women who feel that their response pattern is rather narrow and wish to expand it.

* It is also helpful to make sex with a partner more like masturbation in order to make use of the years of training the body has already received. Exercises for this purpose will be covered in Chapter 9.

## The Enlarging Options Exercise

Begin by making subtle changes in your masturbation pattern so that it resembles the types of positions, stimulation techniques, rhythms, and pressures that occur during sex with your partner. Spend thirty to sixty minutes masturbating in a new way. Begin with small changes, not major ones. For example, if you masturbate with your legs tightly crossed, don't immediately try to masturbate with your legs wide apart. Begin by masturbating with your legs still crossed since the leg tension this provides is probably an important factor in your arousal pattern. When you become aroused with your legs somewhat tightly crossed, reduce the crossing a bit while still maintaining the leg tension.

Women who have learned to masturbate without using their hands, either by squeezing their thighs together, hanging from doors, or rubbing against a chair, pillow, or some other object, might first masturbate in their usual position whether it be sitting down, standing, or lying on their back or stomach, and simply add to the usual method of masturbation, manual stimulation of their clitoral or vaginal area.

Women who have been conditioned to a vibrator can practice laying a hand over their genitals and pressing the vibrator against the hand rather than contacting their genitals directly with the vibrator. This serves to subdue the stimulation. Or they can alternate vibrator and manual stimulation by using the vibrator until they begin feeling aroused and then substituting their hand for the vibrator. This process provides one way of learning to become more responsive to nonmechanical stimulation.

The important factor to keep in mind when changing masturbation position or technique is to first discover what it is about the current position or technique that brings about the orgasm. It may be leg tension, firm clitoral pressure, a feeling of safety, or the use of fantasy—to name a few. Then change the masturbation pattern in some way while trying to preserve the aspect of the pattern that is necessary for orgasm.

For example, Susan always masturbated on her stomach. When she tried to turn over and masturbate on her back, she realized that she felt exposed and vulnerable in this position. To maintain a feeling of safety and protection while on her back, Susan masturbated with a large comforter covering her body. This way, she could relax because if someone suddenly entered her room they would not be able to see what she was doing.

When varying your masturbation technique, remember not to change more than one factor at a time and to make changes gradually. For example, change the position of your body from standing to kneeling, from kneeling to lying on your stomach, from lying on your stomach to lying on your side, from lying on your side to lying on your back—or add direct manual stimulation of your genitals if you don't usually use your hands. Change one small aspect at a time and once that becomes comfortable, then make another small change.

Use your creativity. Experiment. There is no one right way to carry out the exercise. You are trying to expand your pattern, not develop an equally rigid new one. Simply experiment with different techniques to see which ones prove to be the most arousing. Remember that breaking old habits is difficult. For the first few attempts, nothing may work. Rather than trying something for five minutes, deciding it's hopeless when it doesn't immediately produce results, trying something else, and then giving up on that as well, pick one innovation in your masturbation pattern and stick with it. Spend thirty to sixty minutes over two or three masturbation sessions before discarding a new technique.

Don't forget to use appropriate mental stimulation both to get yourself in the mood and to help maintain your feelings of arousal. While you are changing your masturbation pattern you may find it even more important than usual to fantasize or read erotica. These techniques can sometimes help to create arousal while you're learning to respond to new and different—and therefore initially less exciting—physical stimulation.

If you are feeling frustrated or if no arousal is produced with the new technique, even after fifteen or twenty minutes of stimulation, revert back to your usual technique. After you begin to feel somewhat turned on using the old method, change your masturbation technique or position again. At this point you will probably lose some of the feelings of arousal. This is normal. Just continue with the new mode for awhile to see if the feelings return. If they do not, try your usual method again. Then, when you begin to become aroused, switch back to the new technique. In this way, you will teach your body to associate feelings of being turned on with these new positions or stimulation techniques.

Remember that whatever works should be maintained. We never want to repress or eliminate anything that produces feelings of sexual arousal. We are merely trying to *add* options, trying to *expand* the repertoire to include additional positions and types of genital touching. Because of this, you never have to worry about masturbating in the old way. For example, utilizing the vibrator even directly against the genitals outside of the practice sessions will not interfere with your efforts to masturbate without it. There is nothing wrong with maintaining the old tried-and-true method—especially for those times when you want to experience a quick release.

## EXPANDING SENSITIVITY

Women who are comfortable stimulating themselves manually often know their bodies so well that they can provide the exact stimulation they need. While this is an asset during masturbation, it can be a liability during sex with a partner. During masturbation there is immediate feedback. If you move your hand a little to the right, a little to the left, or if the touch is too hard or too soft, you are able to correct the motion within seconds. All the communication is internal. You are relieved from having to explain the details of what area you would like stimulated, what stroke or pressure you prefer. However, because there is not the same immediate feedback when making love with another person, a partner's stimulation can never be as precise as your own. One way to learn to be more responsive to less precise stimulation is to practice arousing yourself using different kinds of touches while masturbating. The following three exercises can help attain this goal.

### The Breaking-the-Pattern Exercise

The first exercise involves masturbating with the hand you don't ordinarily use (assuming that you masturbate using your hand or have learned to use your hand as a result of the last exercise). If you generally masturbate with your right hand, it is amazing how uncoordinated you can feel using your left hand. Even though your right hand has become an expert, your left hand can remain quite untrained. Masturbating with your untrained hand can provide the experience of imprecise stimulation while at the same time leaving you in control of the experience.

Don't think about orgasm the first few times you attempt this exercise. Just set aside thirty minutes or so to experience the new sensations. If orgasm results, fine. If it does not, revert back to your usual hand to attain orgasm if you desire. Carry out this exercise at least two or three different times so that you become more responsive to less precise stimulation.

## The Subtle Sensations Exercise

The second exercise is to masturbate with a very light, teasing touch. Many women respond to direct hard clitoral stimulation simply because that was the kind of stimulation they learned to masturbate with. The stimulation received from a partner and particularly the stimulation resulting from intercourse is often less forceful and less direct. The following exercise has taught women to be more sensitive to soft or indirect clitoral stimulation. Again, we are attempting to change masturbation in order to make it more like the stimulation that occurs during sex with a partner.

To complete this exercise, set aside thirty to forty minutes. The goal of the exercise will simply be to appreciate subtle sexual sensations. Remember to utilize fantasy or erotica if you normally do so. Begin by masturbating in your usual manner until you have attained some feelings of arousal. This doesn't necessarily mean that you should be close to orgasm, but just that you feel turned on and your genitals feel sensitive. At this point, continue the stimulation using soft, feathery touches. Experiment with different gentle movements. If your feelings of arousal begin to disappear, occasionally interject a firmer touch.

Relax and enjoy the subtle nuances of sexual feelings. After thirty or forty minutes, you can revert to your usual manner of stimulation if you desire an orgasm. Repeat this exercise at least two or three times until you are able to maintain some feelings of arousal with the lighter touch.

Remember, the object of this exercise is not to experience orgasm through this touch, but to help you appreciate the more subtle sexual sensations, those that don't necessarily bowl you over, but just ever so gently make you sigh. Concentrating on these less intense sensations will help you maintain your sexual interest when the sensations provided by your partner are more delicate. There is much pleasure to be gained from subtle nuances. Although the powerful scent of wisteria is beautiful, the more delicate fragrance of a rose is a delight to the senses.

## The Body-Movement Exercise

The majority of women masturbate by stimulating their clitoris with their hand. Often, these women do not move their bodies at all. They lie quite still and passively receive the stimulation of their fingertips and hands. During lovemaking with a partner, the tendency is to be more active. During penetration, pelvic thrusting movements ofter occur. If a woman has learned to reach orgasm by lying very still, she might find it difficult to concentrate on the sensations while being more physically vigorous.

If this is true in your case, you may want to broaden your responsiveness by moving your body against your hand when you masturbate, rather than moving your hand against your body. Again, set aside thirty to forty minutes to masturbate. After stimulating yourself in your usual manner to the point where you begin to feel somewhat aroused, begin moving your body. Firmly place the side of your hand, your palm, fingers, or fist against the area of your genitals that you usually stimulate. Then, without moving your hand, concentrate on using your hips and pelvic area to bring about the desired sensations. As with the previous exercises, remember to create the necessary erotic mental set. If you lose the sexual sensations and are unable to regain them after a few minutes, revert back to your usual method of masturbating until the feelings of arousal have returned. Then continue with the body movements. Practice this exercise on at least two or three different occasions until you are able to maintain and even build arousal through the movement of your body. Again, the initial goal is not to reach orgasm by this method. This is likely to take considerable practice. The exercise is simply designed to expand your masturbation repertoire and, in so doing, make you more responsive to the kinds of stimulation that take place when you are making love with a partner.

## INTENSIFYING ORGASM

Some women who are orgasmic complain that their experience of orgasm is so mild that it is almost disappointing. If we believe in the fantasy model of sex, we may expect fireworks and bells ringing. We may be disappointed when reality produces only pleasurable sexual feelings. Or we may be quite realistic and somehow know that our sensations could be stronger. In the second case, there are masturbation exercises which can be used to intensify orgasm.

We have found that most women who have very mild orgasms bring themselves to orgasm too quickly. A longer period of sexual tension before release creates more vasocongestion and muscle tension, which generally results in a more intense response. A balloon half-filled with air will not have nearly as intense an explosion when punctured as one that is filled to the limit. The same is true of an orgasm.

For many women the sensations experienced immediately before orgasm are of paramount enjoyment. They find the orgasm itself anticlimactic because it signals the end of those exquisite peak feelings. Consequently, prolonging the sexual sensations just prior to orgasm can increase the pleasure derived from the entire sexual encounter.

### The Intensifying Orgasm Exercise[1]

To prolong the sexual intensity prior to orgasm, focus on the buildup of the sexual sensations and not on the orgasm itself. In fact, the object of this exercise is to withhold the orgasm for as long as possible.

Masturbate using any technique that produces strong feelings of sexual arousal. As you get close to the point of orgasm, find a way to reduce the sensations so that you do not go over the top. In other words, maintain the level of arousal at the edge of orgasm. To do this, you might want to slow the stimulation down somewhat; use a lighter, more teasing touch; stimulate another area that is not quite as sensitive; actually stop the stimulation for a moment; change your fantasies to ones that are less intensely arousing. You may want to experiment using one or all of these techniques. Then after you lower the arousal somewhat, use techniques that you know will intensify the sexual feelings until you again are close to the point of orgasm. Then allow the sensations to subside once more. Each time you build on the sensations you will find that you can reach a slightly higher level of intensity. After you have raised and lowered your level of arousal three or four times, build the intensity while simultaneously holding back the orgasm for as long as possible until the orgasm finally takes over.

In the beginning you will probably misjudge your level of arousal and experience orgasm when you are really trying to back off. Many women feel disappointed if this happens because they get neither the full enjoyment of the prolonged feelings nor the intensity of their usual orgasm. Instead, the orgasm is experienced as a sort of blip. However, as you practice, you will more precisely be able to determine the point just prior to orgasm so that you can reduce the stimulation in time.

## INCREASING VAGINAL SENSITIVITY

Most women masturbate by stimulating their clitoris; far fewer use vaginal stimulation. Kinsey found that while 20 percent of the women he interviewed had masturbated on occasion by inserting their fingers or other objects into the vagina, only a small portion did so regularly.[2] Hite's data showed the same results.[3] Most of us have learned to focus on and build clitoral stimulation, so once vaginal stimulation begins, many of us lose the sexual sensations we were feeling prior to penetration. However, some of us may not be as vaginally sensitive as we could be. Sometimes the muscle surrounding the vaginal opening needs to be exercised so that it can be more sensitive and responsive. Sometimes simultaneous vaginal and clitoral stimulation can be confusing, much like trying to concentrate on rubbing your stomach and patting your head simultaneously. And sometimes vaginal sensations are reduced because the G-spot is not getting stimulated.

If you would like to increase your vagina's sensitivity to stimulation, the following three exercises may prove helpful. If the difficulty resides in a lack of pelvic muscle tone, Kegel exercises can help. If simultaneous clitoral and vaginal sensations are distracting, the exercise of masturbating with something inside the vagina can bring about positive results. If you are unfamiliar with the G-spot, locating it and finding ways to stimulate it directly may increase the sensations you experience vaginally.

## The Kegel Exercises

In the mid-1900s Dr. Kegel developed a series of exercises to help women who suffered from urinary incontinence, i.e., they would inadvertently expel small amounts of urine if they coughed, sneezed, or had an orgasm. The exercises consisted of strengthening the pubococcygeal (PC) muscle, the muscle that, when squeezed, stops the flow of urine. The PC muscle turns out to be the same muscle that forms the orgasmic platform and, along with other pelvic muscles, contracts with orgasm. Consequently, when Kegel questioned women about their response to his exercises, they replied that not only was their ability to retain urine better after practicing the exercises, but they were experiencing more sexual sensations during intercourse as well. Kegel exercises are also recommended both before and after childbirth as a way of toning and strengthening the vagina. Postmenopausal women who use Kegel exercises find that they help to maintain lubrication (by increasing bloodflow to the vaginal area) and reduce the need for estrogen creams.

First, to locate the PC muscle, urinate with your legs apart; the muscle you squeeze to stop the flow of urine is the PC muscle. Practice stopping the flow of urine a few times in order to become familiar with the muscle. Then, lie down and put your finger in the opening of your vagina and contract the PC muscle. See if you can feel the contraction around your finger while taking care not to move your thighs, stomach, buttocks, or any other muscles in the pelvic region.

After practicing the following exercises for about six weeks, see if you notice any difference in the strength of your PC muscle when you put your finger in your vagina and squeeze.

### THE SQUEEZE-RELEASE EXERCISE

The first Kegel exercise consists of squeezing the PC muscle for three seconds, relaxing the muscle for three seconds, and squeezing it again. It may be difficult, at first, to contract the muscle for a full three seconds. If this is the case, contract for one or two seconds at first and build up the time as the muscle gets stronger. Carry out a series of ten squeezes and releases at three different times during the day.

### THE FLUTTER EXERCISE

The second exercise is much like the first except that instead of holding the squeeze for three seconds, the objective is to squeeze the muscle, relax it, squeeze again, and release as quickly as possible. Again, complete a series of ten squeezes and releases at three different times during the day.

When you first start doing this exercise, it may feel like a tongue twister; you may not be able to tell if you are contracting or releasing and for a while it may feel all muddled together. However, begin slowly and with practice you will gradually be able to do the Flutter more rapidly.

### THE ELEVATOR EXERCISE

The third exercise consists of exercising the entire length of the vagina. Imagine that your vagina is an elevator shaft and the elevator is at the opening to the vagina. Rather than squeezing, contract the muscles as you imagine yourself slowly pulling the elevator upward along the vaginal canal, beginning at the opening and ending at the uterus. After the three or four seconds it takes to go the entire length of the vagina, slowly relax the muscles as if you were lowering the elevator to the ground floor, and then begin again at the vaginal opening. Do three series of ten contractions daily. This exercise is good for strengthening the uterine muscles as well as the PC muscle.

The advantage of these first three Kegel exercises is that you can do them anywhere and at any time and no one can tell you're doing them. Practice when you stop the car for a red light or in the morning when you wake up. Or do them when you answer the telephone at home or at work, or when you are lying down to rest. The muscles surrounding your anus may move during these exercises, but if you find you are moving your thigh muscles, your stomach muscles, or your buttocks, you are probably squeezing the wrong muscles.

## THE BEARING-DOWN EXERCISE

This fourth exercise is more apparent to the observer, so you might want to practice it in privacy. It consists of bearing down as during a bowel movement, but with the emphasis more on the vagina than the anal area. Imagine there is a tampon deep inside your vagina and bear down as if you were pushing it out. The bearing down should be held for three or four seconds, as with the Elevator Exercise.

All four exercises should be practiced ten times each at three different times during the day in the beginning. As you progress with the Kegel exercises, slowly increase the number of repetitions in each series until you are able to do twenty of each exercise in succession. You can do them as frequently during the day as you can find time, but consider three times daily a minimum.

Some women hesitate to practice the Kegel exercises because they feel sexually aroused by contracting the PC muscle. While this can be disconcerting, it is a perfectly normal reaction. The muscle tension created by the exercises causes blood to flow to the pelvic region which is the same physiological process that occurs with sexual stimulation. So, if this happens to you, don't worry about it, just enjoy it. Other women discontinue practicing the Kegel exercises because they find the exercises fatiguing. If this is true for you, you are probably using muscles in your abdomen, buttocks, or thighs rather than exercising the PC muscle by itself. In this case, begin again by stopping the flow of urine without squeezing the muscles in the abdomen, buttocks, or thigh areas to isolate the correct muscle.

If you are carrying out the exercise correctly, but you initially notice some discomfort or tightness in the pelvic region, reduce the number of daily contractions, but do not abandon the exercises. Like any muscle that is being exercised for the first time, it may feel a little stiff initially. However, it is quite important to keep this muscle, like others in your body, in tone. The Kegel exercises should become as much of a habit as brushing your teeth, and like brushing your teeth, should be continued for the rest of your life.

## The Locating the G-Spot Exercise

In over 300 pelvic exams, Perry and Whipple never found a woman who did not report an area of vaginal sensitivity corresponding to the area first described by Grafenberg in 1950. The area known as the Grafenberg spot, the G-spot, or the urethral sponge is located in the front wall of the vagina and surrounds the urethra.† In the unaroused state, the G-spot ranges between the size of a dime and the size of a quarter but it is difficult to differentiate from the surrounding tissues. When aroused, this area doubles in size and is easier to find because it becomes more corrugated and puffier. The G-spot is only one area of vaginal sensitivity. Some women report sensitivity on the right side of the vagina, the left side, or the area closest to the anus.

Unless you have long fingers or a short vagina, it will probably be difficult for you to stimulate your own G-spot. However, give it a try. If you squat rather than lie on your back, it will make it easier to get your arm in position. Then, insert your middle finger and press your fingertip into the front wall of your vagina approximately midway between the top of your pubic bone and your cervix. The lump you are looking for is not on the surface of the vaginal wall, but deep within the wall, so press firmly. The slightly fleshy area will become more pronounced as you rub it. As the G-spot begins to swell, place your other hand on your abdominal wall just above the pubic bone to see if you can discern a lump between the fingers of your two hands. However, remember, if you are lying on your back and tensing your abdominal muscles while you reach inside the vagina, the tensed muscles may make it difficult to discern the lump between the two sets of fingers.

Many women report an urge to urinate when the G-spot is stimulated, so urinate before beginning the exercise. This response is

† See the diagram on page 58 for the precise location of the G-spot.

common because the G-spot is located around the urethra, close to the neck of the bladder. With continued stimulation, however, this initial sensation can be replaced by a feeling of pleasure.

If you think you have located your G-spot, you can stimulate it by rubbing and firmly pressing the area. It is likely that you will require more pressure than generally needed for clitoral stimulation. The awkwardness of this position can make it difficult to maintain firm pressure so you may prefer to carry out this exercise with your partner's assistance.‡

If you can comfortably stimulate your own G-spot, but do not find the sensations pleasurable after about five minutes, leave your fingers inside your vagina while masturbating in your usual manner. Notice if applying this additional pressure to the G-spot enhances your feeling of arousal. Experiment and explore. As with the other self-stimulation exercises, don't forget to create an erotic mood through the use of fantasy or erotica.

Some find that direct stimulation of the G-spot brings about an orgasm quite rapidly. Some women do not enjoy having the G-spot stimulated until they are at least somewhat aroused. And just as some women never find direct clitoral stimulation pleasurable, some women do not find direct internal pressure on the G-spot comfortable or pleasurable at any point in the sexual arousal process.

## The Increasing Vaginal Sensitivity Exercises

The following two exercises for increasing vaginal sensitivity require masturbating with a phallic-shaped object in the vagina. Many items can be used for this purpose: your fingers, small plastic battery-operated vibrators, vegetables such as zucchinis, carrots, or cucumbers. Glass objects or objects that might splinter or otherwise cause harm to the vagina should *never* be used. Plastic bottles should always be capped or inserted bottom end first. This prevents a vacuum from forming which could make the removal of the bottle difficult or dangerous. If vegetables are used, they should be washed thoroughly to remove any pesticides which could irritate the delicate membranes of the vagina. Some women prefer to take no

‡ See the G-Spot Stimulation Exercise on page 183.

chances and peel the vegetables. (I'll never forget the women in one of my groups who had the whole group in an uproar as she described picking through the pile of zucchinis in the grocery store, looking for the one that was the perfect size and shape.)

### THE SIMULTANEOUS STIMULATION EXERCISE

To learn to respond to simultaneous vaginal and clitoral stimulation, pick a suitable phallic-shaped object. Lubricate it with saliva, vaginal secretions, or products such as K-Y jelly or Albolene cream to facilitate its insertion. Avoid using Vaseline, as it is not water-soluble. Then masturbate in your usual manner. When you have reached a high level of arousal but are not yet close to orgasm, insert the phallic-shaped object in your vagina. Move the object in and out, in circular motions, or press it against the G-spot or other internal areas that are especially sensitive.

Stimulate yourself clitorally with one hand while you apply the vaginal stimulation with the other. You might find it increases your pleasure to move your pelvis in response to the inserted object. If you maintain your usual masturbation position and stimulation technique and only add the vaginal stimulation, you should cease to be distracted by the new vaginal sensations in a relatively short period of time. Within a few sessions of practice you will probably be able to reach orgasm this way. If you also change your masturbation position, for instance from lying on your stomach to lying on your back, or eliminate or significantly alter your clitoral stimulation method, orgasm may require considerably more trials. It is probably best to make one small change at a time. First add vaginal stimulation and wait until orgasm is achieved this way before experimenting further.

### THE VAGINAL EXPLORATION EXERCISE

Once you are able to have orgasms using this technique, you may want to vary your method somewhat in order to further increase your sensitivity to vaginal stimulation.*

---

* This exercise is also recommended by Carol Ellison for women who are more vaginally responsive and prefer to eliminate clitoral stimulation totally because they find it distracting.

Masturbate in your usual manner and once you begin to feel aroused, discontinue any clitoral stimulation and totally focus on the vaginal stimulation. Pay close attention to the sensations experienced *inside* your vagina. As with the last exercise, experiment with moving your fingers, a phallic-shaped object, or your body, in both thrusting and circular motions. Experience the different sensations as you apply pressure around the vaginal opening from different angles. Experiment with the sensations that occur when you simultaneously squeeze your PC muscle as if carrying out the Kegel exercises.

If you start out using clitoral stimulation, you will probably lose the sexual sensations fairly rapidly once you discontinue it, but don't let this worry you. Just continue to utilize fantasy or erotica while you explore your vagina. If you cannot regain the feelings of arousal after about ten minutes of moving the phallic-shaped object in different ways inside your vagina, reinstate the clitoral stimulation until you again feel aroused and then discontinue it once more.

The goal of this exercise is not to have an orgasm; it is to become more aware of and sensitive to the sensations that are experienced inside your vagina. You will probably need to spend a minimum of thirty minutes on at least three different occasions before you will begin to notice any *increase* in your vaginal sensitivity. If you want to have an orgasm, and the vaginal stimulation alone is insufficient, use simultaneous clitoral and vaginal stimulation or some other self-stimulation technique.

### The Fantasy Rehearsal Exercise Revisited

An adaptation of the Fantasy Rehearsal Exercise that was described in Chapter 5 is the last exercise to complete on your own before beginning the partner exercises. In this exercise, specific fantasies will be used to help bridge the gap between experiencing orgasms alone and climaxing with a partner. This exercise should also help make your first practice sessions with your partner more relaxed and comfortable.

When you try masturbating in new positions you might imagine, while you are stimulating yourself, that it is your partner's hand that is stimulating you. Or, you might pretend your partner is orally stimulating you. When you masturbate with something inside your vagina you might fantasize that while you are having intercourse, you are stimulating your clitoris or your partner is stimulating your clitoris.

To simulate intercourse more closely, you might first arouse yourself by masturbating in your usual manner. Then place the vaginal insert between your forefinger and middle finger at the point where the two fingers meet your palm. Introduce the phallic object into your vagina while you press the palm of your hand over your genital area. Use your other hand to move the insert in and out of your vagina and at the same time move your pelvis against the palm of your hand. Meanwhile, fantasize that you are actually having intercourse with your partner. Practice this exercise for thirty minutes to an hour each time you masturbate. It will require a number of trials before you are able to teach yourself to experience orgasm in this manner.

Now that you have practiced expanding your sexual response to include new types of stimulation and new sexual positions, it is time to take the experience out of the laboratory and bring it into your relationship. This does not mean that masturbation must be discontinued. Some women choose to make love to themselves sexually at various times during the week or year. Others, while finding masturbation useful as a learning tool, prefer to devote their sexual expression to the time spent with their partner.

The next step on our journey is to experiment during partner sex with the kinds of lovemaking positions and stimulation you use during masturbation. Some women separate masturbation and partner sex so completely that they would never consider trying out, in the presence of their partner, what works for them while alone. If they stimulate themselves clitorally while alone, they avoid having their partner touch their clitoris, and they would never consider touching it themselves when their partner is present. If they masturbate on their stomach, they may prefer having intercourse on their back. Basically, they have a tendency to throw all their sexual knowledge and expertise out the window, and then wonder why they are not orgasmic with their partner.

In order to carry out the necessary changes in making love with a partner, you may have to first confront your own inhibitions. Letting your body feel, in a partner's presence, what you experience alone means learning to relax. And even then, there may be additional concerns and fears in the way, such as, how to let your partner know what feels good without sounding critical of past lovemaking experiences or creating feelings of inadequacy, or how to express your needs when you are afraid of not reaching orgasm even when your partner follows your instructions. These and other problems commonly confronted during this process will be explored in the next chapter, along with physical lovemaking exercises designed to increase orgasmic response.

# Chapter 8

# ORGASM WITH A PARTNER

A variety of approaches have been successful in helping women to become orgasmic during partner sex. Different approaches and exercises work for different women. Some people prefer a step-by-step guide with clearly outlined activities, complete with time allocations and numbers of repetitions. Others hate rules; they spend their lives creating loopholes and making themselves special exceptions. For people who don't like to be told what to do, or who just enjoy being contrary, a very structured approach won't work. Such people do best with general ideas, using their own resources and creativity to determine the exact route to take. Still others fall in between—preferring some guidelines but no absolute structure.

Taking these different personalities into account, I have attempted to present the material in the rest of the book in a way that will enable you to create your own treatment plan. For those of you who want the theory and no structure, the information will be available. Examples of ways to approach the different exercises will be suggested for those of you who desire some structure. And specific guidelines will be presented for those of you who prefer a step-by-step treatment plan. Please remember that everyone is unique and an approach that works for one person may be inappropriate for another. Therefore, feel free to pick and choose the relevant exercises or to rearrange or modify the exercises to meet your own needs. Ultimately, what's important is that you learn to have orgasms with your partner. What appears to be the long way around to one person may be the most direct route for another. Trust your intuition. Before doing any exercises, read through the entire chapter to get a general overview, then use your best judgment in picking those exercises that seem appropriate for you.

If you choose to vary the sequence of the exercises or eliminate certain exercises altogether, be careful that you skip over only the ones for which you already possess the necessary expertise and knowledge. Do not skip exercises because they would be too anxiety-producing. Sometimes the areas we would prefer to ignore are exactly the ones we need to confront in order to overcome our blocks. For example, some women find the idea of receiving clitoral stimulation during sex absolutely horrifying. It may feel unnatural or raise concerns that a partner would feel emasculated. A woman who requires precise and direct clitoral stimulation will not reach orgasm during lovemaking if she refuses to carry out the exercises designed to incorporate clitoral stimulation into partner sex. Before she can relax and enjoy the stimulation that is most arousing to her, she will have to face negative feelings about clitoral stimulation. Therefore, skipping the anxiety-producing exercises would only be postponing the very step that could be most helpful.

## PROVIDING SEXUAL INFORMATION

If you are already very close to orgasm while making love with your partner, you may find that simply explaining your unique sexual preferences is all that is required. Through your journey so far, you have explored and discovered how you like to be stimulated. It is this information that your partner needs to know in order to stimulate you most effectively.

Most women expect their male partners to be the experts on sexuality and most men assume this role. However, few men have ever been given any explicit information about how to sexually please a female partner. Locker-room talk is generally limited to bravado with very little useful information. And since males don't even possess the same genital equipment as females, many men are at a loss as to what women enjoy sexually.

In Mangaia, an island in the South Pacific, boys are taught explicitly about sex. The Mangaian boy undergoes a superincision ritual, during which a slit is made on the top of the penis along its entire length, when he is about thirteen years old. The expert who performs the superincision instructs the boy in a variety of sexual activities. To remove the scab, the boy has intercourse with an experienced woman a few weeks after the operation. This woman teaches him various sexual acts and positions and trains him to hold back his orgasm until his partner is able to have one also. And interestingly, in this society, apparently all women learn to have orgasms.[1]

However, in our culture, men are not taught how to be good lovers. Yet, they are embarrassed to ask for information they feel they should already know. Consequently, men lament the fact that more women don't assert their sexual needs more fully. If they are taught in a caring and supportive manner, and not purposely insulted or made to feel inadequate, men are generally appreciative and ardent students. As previously mentioned, men who were initiated into sex by a communicative older woman not only remember her with special affection, but often credit her with their ability as a lover.

## Sharing

Before confronting any embarrassment you may have about describing your particular sexual preferences, imagine how your partner could best tell you how he would like you to make love to him. Consider how your feelings might be hurt—ways in which he might tell you that could cause you to feel clumsy, inept, or inadequate. Then imagine how you could be told so that you felt loved and important. What words or phrases would encourage you to follow your partner's instructions with enthusiasm? Then use this information to open the communication lines with your partner.

You could introduce the topic outside the bedroom by saying, "I just read this book on female sexuality and the author made some points I hadn't thought of before, and I thought it might be fun to share them with you." Or, "You know, I was reading this article and I was just amazed at how different women are sexually. I hadn't realized that what I like sexually might not be the same as what other women like. For instance, I realized . . ." and you could lead right into your sexual preferences. One woman said, "I think our lovemaking is great now, but with a little practice, it could be fantastic. Let me tell you some things about me that would make it even better."

Or, you could initiate the conversation by asking your partner what really pleases *him* sexually. Even if he responds with "Everything you do is terrific," you could inquire further. You could let him know that some things he does are more special for you and that he must have some preferences also. You might let him know that you would like to be the best lover he ever had and to do that you require more detailed and specific information about his sexual likes and dislikes. He's then bound to ask what you like, at which point you could describe what really turns you on. Remember to be specific. For example, you might say that your breasts are especially sensitive and that your arousal is heightened considerably when he sucks on your nipples or squeezes them between his thumb and forefinger. Or maybe it is a gentle touch of your breasts that you prefer. Possibly he doesn't realize how much you enjoy oral sex or how you like to be orally stimulated—like having your clitoris sucked or flicked by light, rapid movements of his tongue. You may not have made him aware that certain intercourse positions are more pleasurable than others and more likely to result in orgasm. You might want him to know that you appreciate kissing or stroking all over your body before any direct genital stimulation has begun. He may not realize that your mood for sex depends on the amount of intimate time you have had together earlier in the day and that when you both consciously set aside the time to be together, you start out feeling much more turned on. Your partner may already be well aware of some of this information, but some of it may be entirely new to him. For example, he may have realized that oral sex is a real turn-on for you but may not be cognizant of the specific hard or soft pressure that you prefer.

You might instead feel more comfortable presenting your sexual preferences as part of your lovemaking. Sex *is* a form of communication, and communication occurs in many ways—through body movements and sounds as well as words.

For some, talking while making love is a real sexual enhancement. It turns some people on to hear their partner say, "I love you," as they are approaching orgasm. Some like to give instructions in explicit sexual language, for example, "I want you inside me now," or, "Please go down on me. I want to feel your hot tongue on my clit." Others like to use graphic or "dirty" words as a way of arousing sexual feelings such as, "Fuck me harder," or, "Eat my cunt."

You could whisper in his ear that you love the way he is kissing your breasts. When you are in the middle of oral lovemaking, you could cry out in a pleasurable tone, "Oh, suck me harder" or "softer" or "Don't stop," as a way of letting him know what feels good. You could initiate the intercourse positions that you most enjoy either by just asserting yourself and maneuvering your body and his into the right positions or by saying something like, "Now I'd like to show you something very special; just relax and enjoy this." You could moan, "slower" or "faster," as a way to communicate the pace you would like. By pressing your hand down on top of his you could convey the message that you would like him to stimulate your genitals more firmly. In these ways, you could let your partner know what pleases you without sounding like an antiseptic instruction manual: "Rub two minutes on right side of clitoris, then squeeze nipples."

If you don't feel comfortable using words or if silence is important to your lovemaking, show your partner how you like to be made love to by making love to him in ways that you find pleasurable. The amount of information you can communicate using this technique is considerable.

The first time Deborah made love with Danny, he was very rough and forceful. Since he was not only a new lover, but one with whom she looked forward to having a long relationship, she felt the need to communicate her preference for softer, more leisurely lovemaking. However, she could tell that Danny was quite pleased with his performance and she didn't want him to feel unappreciated or incompetent. So she merely said, "That was terrific, now just lie back and relax while I show *you* something." And she proceeded to begin the lovemaking all over again, but this time according to her style.

Everyone likes to feel successful and appreciated. We don't like to be criticized or made to feel stupid, so give your partner *positive* feedback whenever possible. Clearly and frequently talk about what you appreciate about your lovemaking together. It's the old truism that you can catch more bees with honey than with vinegar. If positive feedback doesn't produce the results you want, and you need to offer more direct suggestions, remember to express your feelings of dissatisfaction with "I" statements.* These get better results than blaming.

Opening up the sexual communication can benefit your partner as well as yourself. Each man is sexually unique. You might not be aware that your partner has particularly sensitive nipples, or finds stimulation of his scrotum or light anal penetration especially pleasurable. With additional information from him, you will be better able to meet his sexual needs as well.

### The Anatomy Lesson Exercise

Men often lack not only information on the uniqueness of each woman, but basic anatomical information. Most men never saw a woman's genitals before they began having sex. During sex it is usually difficult to see because of inadequate light or just plain awkwardness about examining this private area. Describing your genitals to your partner, explaining the sensitivity of the different structures, and even showing him the illustration of a woman's genitals in Chapter 3† can provide a good starting point. For example, talking about the clitoris all day long won't help if your partner doesn't know exactly where yours is located. In this instance, verbal communication alone will not suffice. Most men must see and touch a woman's genitals before they can really understand them. And the best way to accomplish this is to sit before him nude, in the light, and, as unfeminine as it may at first seem, with your legs spread wide open.

While you could bring the subject of the Anatomy Lesson up when you are not being sexual together, this particular exercise is

* See pages 97–98.
† See page 53.

probably most easily initiated during lovemaking. You might quietly and warmly whisper that you think your partner might enjoy some more light so that he could really see how your genitals look when you are turned on. Or, as you are stroking and sucking his penis you might ask for more light so that you could see *him* better. After remarking about how beautiful his genitals are, you could question him about how he best likes having his penis touched, or you could play with him in different ways and ask which are most exciting. Then you might offer to trade information. You could tell him some things about your sexual preferences and let him see your genitals.

Once the light is on, you need only spread apart your legs and, in the way that feels most comfortable for you—seductively, sensuously, innocently, etc.—point out the different structures. Don't forget to indicate the areas that are unusually sensitive. You could show your partner how to bring lubrication down by inserting his fingers up into your vagina, and at the same time indicate where your G-spot or other areas of vaginal sensitivity are located. When you get to the clitoris, be sure to point out the clitoral shaft so that he can feel the ridge. Then you might place your hand over his hand. By guiding it, you can clearly indicate the exact strokes you like and the amount of pressure preferred. In this quiet and playful way you can teach your partner a tremendous amount about your particular sexual needs, probably more than even an hour lecture could provide.

Once you have shown him how and where you like to be touched you could reach back and turn out the light, if it is easily accessible, or close your eyes and make sounds of pleasure as he continues stroking your genitals. In this way the Anatomy Lesson can be just another part of your lovemaking.

## BAN ON INTERCOURSE

Women who are not getting pleasure or satisfaction out of sex often blame intercourse for their negative feelings. They may see intercourse as marking the termination of more pleasurable kinds of touching and complain about insufficient hugging, kissing, and fondling. If they believe that intercourse is all that interests their male partner, they may angrily focus all of their sexual dissatisfaction on the act of intercourse.

If you have built up very negative feelings about sex, you may want to put a ban on intercourse for a few weeks while you carry out the nonintercourse exercises. Although the ban on intercourse is mandatory in most Masters and Johnson-based sex therapy treatment programs, I have found that it is only essential when the woman holds very negative feelings about intercourse. If you do not feel this way, continue your lovemaking as usual, while setting aside extra time for the appropriate sexual exercises.

## Physical Touching

If you do place a ban on intercourse, it is important to maintain other forms of sexual activity during that period. Holding, kissing, and manual and oral stimulation can be substituted for intercourse. In addition, although intercourse may be off limits for a while, orgasm is not, particularly orgasm for your partner. Keeping your partner's support high by experimenting with other forms of sexual activity and release is highly recommended. There is no need to deprive your partner while you are expanding your own sexual repertoire.

Although men learn, while growing up, that touching, holding, hugging, and kissing are feminine needs and that "real men" only like intercourse, all humans have a need for physical touching. Research shows that institutionalized babies who are not held and cuddled become apathetic and, in extreme cases, waste away.[2] In an experiment by Harlow, monkeys were separated from their mothers and were provided with dolls of either wire or terry cloth to hold their feeding bottles. These monkeys clearly preferred the terry-cloth doll, which provided a warmer, more nurturing touch than the cold, stiff wire. Harlow concluded that, among other things, this demonstrated the inherent desire for bodily contact.[3]

Men and women who learn that any public display of physical affection is improper may experience problems in their intimate relationships, particularly if their partner finds physical contact important. Couples who don't touch outside of the bedroom can create an artificial separation between the expression of their emotional and physical needs. Being physically distant most of the time can create awkwardness when sexual touching is suddenly initiated.

Traditional masculine role scripting can lead men to caress their partner only when they want sex. When this happens, touching can begin to seem like a demand rather than an expression of love, and can elicit resentment. Also if all physical touching is interpreted as a sexual message, the man's partner may inhibit her physical expressions of affection for fear they will be taken as a sexual invitation when she just wants a little physical closeness and nothing more. This can further minimize physical touching outside the bedroom, and lead to more awkwardness inside the bedroom.

During the period of time that you have agreed not to have intercourse, you must be particularly careful to express your closeness and caring in other ways. The sexual exercises in this chapter, by themselves, are insufficient to meet all of your needs for intimacy as a couple. Saying "I love you," holding hands, making special phone calls during the day, and exchanging thoughtful gifts can help to convey caring as well. This way sex is not left bearing the total burden of expressing intimate feelings. Not surprisingly, as women begin to teach their male partners about the importance of hugging and cuddling, their partners often begin to experience more emotional fulfillment.

Touching is not only important in maintaining the intimacy of a relationship. It is also an important part of the sexual arousal process. The skin is the body's largest erogenous zone. Touching all over the body, before approaching the genitals, is the most certain route to arousal for most women. While men seem to respond more strongly than women to visual stimulation, women react more strongly to bodily touch. The following nonintercourse exercises are designed to reacquaint you with the pleasures of full body stimulation.

As touching and caring are increased, and as you gain greater satisfaction from these areas of your relationship, you may find yourself more willing to engage in a variety of sexual activities—including intercourse—even if it is done more to please your partner than yourself. Not every sexual activity need be equally enjoyed by both partners. Certain activities may be engaged in more for one partner's pleasure than for the other's. This mutual accommodation is generally no problem when both people's sexual needs are being satisfied.

## PREPARATION FOR THE PARTNER EXERCISES

The following exercises stress the receiving of pleasure, the communication of sexual preferences, and the practice of orgasm-enhancing stimulation techniques. Again, you don't have to do all of the exercises. Carefully read through the chapter to pick out those exercises suited to help your particular problem. If you are not sure whether an exercise is appropriate, err on the side of carrying it out. If it isn't helpful, nothing but a little time will have been lost.

You should expect to take a few months to reverse the orgasm problem. Of course, the more frequently you can practice the relevant exercises, the more quickly you can expect changes to occur.

### Setting the Scene

Create a pleasant environment on the days or nights you have set aside to do the exercises. Postpone discussions that are likely to generate stress, anxiety, or animosity. Take the time to be affectionate with your partner beforehand; make sure that your children's needs are attended to so they don't interfere; bring home flowers or chocolates or some other special treat that will help your partner feel particularly cared for. Sometimes the smallest gestures can have large emotional payoffs. Maintaining a good mood and expressing warm feelings toward one another sets the stage for good sexual experiences in general, and is particularly important when it comes to carrying out the sexual exercises.

Take care that the room is warm enough to comfortably remove your clothing. Change the lighting so that it is sensuous—dim lighting or candlelight usually works best. Sensual music can enhance your environment. Also, buy some oil with a consistency that is pleasant to the touch. Women I have worked with particularly recommend Albolene cream, massage lotion, baby oil, or coconut oil. You may want to pick out a scented oil together to ensure that it will appeal to both of you.

Take the necessary precautions to be sure that you will not be disturbed during this time together. You might want to take your telephone off the hook or place it where you are unable to hear it ring. If you have young children, it would be wise to set the time aside when they are sufficiently well occupied to ensure that they will not unexpectedly interrupt you, when they are staying at a friend's or relative's house, or after they are asleep. If they are old enough, you can let them know that you and your partner need to be alone together for a while for some loving and that they should not disturb you unless it is an emergency. Then tell them at what time you expect to be finished so they know when they can count on being with you.

## The Mental Setting

It is important to set the scene emotionally as well as physically. Many women find that their sexual response is directly related to how sexually interested they are when sex begins, and that preparing themselves mentally ahead of time increases their sexual enjoyment. If they allow their sexual feelings to simmer, like a stew or a soup, the feelings build and soon develop their own richness.

Women simmer sexual feelings in many different ways to purposefully build sexual interest. Some women do this by reading erotic stories silently to themselves or aloud with their partner immediately before lovemaking or even hours earlier. Others enjoy leafing through erotic pictures or magazines. Some build anticipation by fantasizing about the kinds of sexual activities that will take place. Some even tell their partners about their interest over dinner or by telephone during the day as a way to heighten the sense of anticipation.

Regardless of how the mental arousal process is set into motion, be sure that you feel turned on by the time you start the exercise. There is no question that your success with the exercises is likely to be greater if you take some time beforehand to focus your attention on simmering your sexual feelings.

## The Body Rub Exercise

There is a tendency for a woman who is not orgasmic to be overly concerned with her partner's pleasure and not concerned enough with her own. As a result, you may find that you stop your partner from pleasuring you before you are fully satisfied. Not believing that part of your partner's turn-on results from turning you on and seeing you fulfilled, you may worry that you are taking too long and that your partner is getting bored or tired or in some other way is not really enjoying the sexual interaction.

The Body Rub Exercise is an adaptation of Masters' and Johnson's sensate focus exercise[4] especially designed to help you accept the fact that your partner enjoys pleasuring you. It will also give you some beginning practice at communicating when a certain touch is uncomfortable—for example, when it tickles or hurts—so both of you can begin to freely communicate about sexual technique without worrying about hurting each other's feelings.

Even if you should feel aroused by this exercise, do not follow it with sexual intercourse or any other orgasm-oriented activity. Knowing that sexual intercourse is off limits and that nothing is expected frees many women from the fear of failure or disappointment and allows them to relax more fully and immerse themselves in the touching. This can result in feeling more sexual sensations than usual.

To ensure that the exercise will go as smoothly as possible, make certain that you set aside sufficient time for a relaxed, unpressured body rub. Plan at least thirty to forty-five minutes for the massage and discussion period afterward. If each of you wishes to both give and receive a body rub, reserve twice that amount of time.

People who are not accustomed to being stroked for an extended period of time may initially find the passive receiving role uncomfortable. This is often true for men who have been trained to feel that they are entirely responsible for the sexual event. In this case, it may be preferable to begin with a much shorter body rub—five to ten minutes—and then gradually extend the time with each practice session. It is far better to end a short massage feeling good than to spend a longer period of time and feel anxious or negative about the experience. Building on good feelings and good experiences is paramount when it comes to improving your sexual relationship.

Begin by deciding who will give and who will receive the first massage. Sometimes one of you may have a preference for a particular role. At other times the toss of a coin can offer a simple and fair way to make the decision.

The person receiving the first body rub should decide what area of his or her body will be massaged. If you are not comfortable beginning with a nude massage, you might prefer to have your face, hands, or feet massaged first. If nudity is comfortable for you, you might like to begin with a back, front, or leg massage or even a full body massage.

THE ROLE OF THE GIVER

The job of the person giving the massage is simply to stroke, caress, and in other ways attend to the area chosen by the receiver to be massaged. Since this first body rub is not designed to be sexual in nature, please do not overemphasize breasts or genitals. Include these eroticized areas within a front or full body massage but treat them with no more or less attention than you would more neutral areas such as the elbows or neck.

Don't worry about massage technique. Some people are intimidated by the word "massage," because they feel they lack experience or training in this area. If you haven't taken a massage workshop or read extensively in the field, you may feel less than adequate at touching your lover's body. However, the best massage instructors teach their students to feel comfortable doing what comes naturally. Technique is minimized and paying attention to what feels good is emphasized. So don't let concern about your proficiency as a masseuse hold you back from completing this exercise. On the other hand, if you would feel more comfortable reading something on the subject in advance, by all means do so. There are quite a few good books available.[5]

The body rub should be conducted from the vantage point of the giver's own interest and not just as an effort to please the receiver. This is a very important point. Most often, when we give a massage, we try to do it in the way that our partner will most appreciate and respond to. Our focus is more on our partner's reaction than on our own feelings about the experience of touching. However, this massage is to be carried out from a different perspective. The object is not to please your partner, although this is likely to occur, but to enjoy touching. You are not to rub your partner in an attempt to relieve his or her shoulder tension. However, for your own interest you may want to experiment with a firm pressure or pressing with your thumbs or fingertips while massaging certain areas. You may also want to experiment with a light touch, with circular motions. Try using your mouth, hair, or other parts of your body in the massage. You may want to scratch lightly with your nails or materials of different textures to add variety to the experience. Make the endeavor an interesting one. Learn new things about your lover's body, about its curves, muscles, skin, and bones.

Also, do not try to continue massaging once your interest has waned. If you are losing interest, see if you can figure out why. Are you getting bored because you are not used to stroking another person for a long period of time? Are you unable to think of any new ways of touching your partner that might make the experience more interesting to you? Have you used other parts of your body, fabrics, feathers, oil, fur mittens, or other things for variety? If you have tried to experiment and still have lost interest, it is best to let your partner know this and to terminate the exercise. Since one of the main objects of the massage is to convince the receiver that the giver is enjoying the experience, the giving must be genuine. If the giving is being done with resentment or disinterest, the receiver will only have more reason not to believe they are being given to joyously. However, if the massage is ended before interest has waned, the receiver will learn to trust the giver not to give beyond the point that is comfortable, thus the receiver will be able to relax and receive more fully.

To be comfortable and free of worry while giving the massage, you must be able to count on the receiver to let you know if you are in any way causing discomfort. To ensure this, you should agree ahead of time to elicit three negative responses from the receiver during the course of the exercise.

## THE ROLE OF THE RECEIVER

It is important that the giver be able to experiment with new touches without having to worry about making the receiver uncomfortable in any way. Therefore, when you are in the role of receiver, be sure to let the giver know when any touch is not enjoyable for you. Holding your breath and hoping that the way you are being touched will soon stop will only cut off your feelings of arousal. It's better not to grin and bear it—the object is pleasure, not discomfort. Some people have had very little practice at letting their lover know when they don't like something. They often feel they are protecting their partner from hurt by remaining silent, but in reality they are only building up negative feelings that can eat away at the relationship.

One man confided that he wished women would tell him more quickly when they are uncomfortable sexually. If a particular lovemaking position becomes unpleasurable or even painful to a partner, and she says nothing until she can bear it no longer, it can result in terminating or at least severely dampening the sexual experience. He would much prefer to be told early so that he can rectify matters while sexual interest is still high. Letting each other know what you don't like gives both partners practice at accepting a negative response without feeling devastated.

Consequently, the giver is to elicit three negative responses from the receiver. If the touching is positive or neutral, the receiver is not to say a word. Although sounds of pleasure should not be purposely inhibited, neither should they be exaggerated. However, if the touch is in any way negative, you, as the receiver, are to let the giver know in a positive way. In other words, rather than saying "Ouch!" "Stop," or "No, that hurts," let the giver know not only what to eliminate, but how the touch could be made more pleasurable. For example, you could say, "Could you please do that more firmly, that tickles." "The scratching of your nails on my skin is too rough, could you use your fingertips instead?" It is just as important for the receiver to be honest about any discomfort as it is for the giver to be honest about beginning to tire of the experience.

Except for correcting your partner's touch at least three times, the receiver's role in this massage exercise is to just relax and thoroughly enjoy being ministered to. As receiver, empty your mind of all worries and concerns. Forget business and children problems, the phone calls you didn't return, and the errands left undone. If you are having difficulty blocking out distracting thoughts, you may find it helpful to direct your attention to the exact place on your body your partner is massaging. Then focus on discovering exactly how your skin and muscles respond to the different ways your partner touches you. Think of words to describe the feelings —such as "tingling," "warm and creamy," "firm and strong." Concentrate on the moment. Attend completely to the touch your body is receiving.

INSTANT REPLAY

Once either the giver or the receiver is ready to terminate the body rub, or the time allotted has elapsed, the physical part of the exercise is over. However, it is very important to spend at least five minutes afterward discussing the experience. This instant replay provides an opportunity to review the event and become aware of aspects that may have been missed the first time around. This is the time to check out any of your worries or concerns. The giver can ask which types of touch the receiver liked best and which specific areas of the body the receiver most enjoyed having touched. The receiver can feel free to question whether the giver was truly interested in the experience or if the giver's interest began to wane at any particular point in the massage.

All concerns should be responded to honestly. In the long run it is far more important to build a sense of trust than it is to be polite. The expression of negative feelings gives greater credibility to the positive ones. It is hard to trust feedback when it is only positive and glowing. A balanced report is more believable.

Talking over the exercise is a first step in learning to discuss other and more intimate sexual preferences. Such discussions also enhance intimacy. Every conversation in which you share something about yourselves deepens your knowledge of each other, which then fosters caring.

After the discussion period has ended, you can either change roles immediately, with the receiver becoming the giver, or you can arrange to exchange roles in the next few hours or days. Some people feel that they cannot fully enjoy receiving a massage if they know that they have to return one immediately afterward. Other people feel uncomfortably indebted unless they are able to return the favor as soon as possible. So, set up the exercise in the way that works best for you. Repeat the exercise at least twice in each role, or as many times as necessary to feel comfortable receiving and giving for a minimum of thirty minutes each. Hopefully, after a few sessions of this exercise, you will not only be able to better communicate your desires and dislikes, you'll also be able to leave your tentativeness and concern about your partner not enjoying the sexual experience outside the bedroom.

**Reminder:** If the exercise is successful, the receiver may feel relaxed and turned on afterward. Acting on the feelings at this point can create problems, however. The object of the exercise is to create a foundation for future arousal. If this one attempt were to be the only success, there would be little point to the exercise. If you act on the sexual feelings prematurely, and the lovemaking ends with the usual disappointment or frustration, you will have taken a step backward. You will have only confirmed that you can't trust positive turned-on feelings to persist. Consequently, although it may be difficult to postpone sex when both of you feel sexually interested, it is better to build a reserve of positive touching experiences before moving ahead. Therefore, if you feel particularly close after the massage or postmassage discussion, limit your expression of physical caring to hugging and kissing. Anything beyond that, especially touching that might lead to orgasm, should be delayed for at least one hour after the massage.

Because this can be a problem area, it is advisable, before the exercise begins, to reaffirm your agreement not to have sex until at least one hour after the body rub. Acting in good faith and sticking to agreed-upon limits will help develop the kind of trust that is so important in an intimate relationship. If your partner pushes for sex despite your explicit agreement, and tries to make you feel guilty when you maintain your position, you may have to review together your expectations. Be sure your partner understands that the purpose of this exercise is to create the foundation for greater sexual interest and response on your part in the future, and not to produce an orgasm today.

## ACCEPTING PLEASURE

Accepting pleasure can be difficult outside as well as inside the bedroom. Many of us are more comfortable giving than receiving and consistently place the needs of others before our own. Feeling we deserve pleasure is another essential aspect of becoming orgasmic. If we remain riveted on our partner's needs, our partner may be fulfilled while we are not. We need to consider our own needs as much a priority as those of our partner. However, many of us have been taught that if we are concerned with our own pleasure, we are selfish. In our puritanical culture, selfish is tantamount to sinful. Somehow it indicates that we aren't good wives, good mothers, or good people.

The word "selfish" needs redefining. Being selfish about pleasing ourselves actually results in our being able to give more to others. The happier we are and the more satisfied we are with our own lives, the more energy we will have to devote to the needs of those around us, and the better we will perform in our roles as wife, mother, working woman. If we are sexually satisfied, our partner will also gain more from our sexual encounters.

Women who find it difficult to accept pleasure find it almost impossible to ask for it. Many of us carry around the notion that our partner should be sensitive enough to our needs to know automatically what we want. Sometimes we don't ask for anything directly because of a fear of rejection. We couch our requests in subtle language, hoping our wishes will be deciphered and fulfilled, but protecting ourselves in case they're not. Rather than asking for a glass of water we might say, "Boy, this heat sure can make you thirsty." Rather than asking for flowers, we might comment on how romantic it is when the leading man in a movie shows up at the leading lady's door with a bouquet. Unfortunately, the fear of not getting our wish can create a self-fulfilling prophecy. Not having been asked directly, our partner may not know what we want. And if we interpret not getting what we want as an indication that we were right not to ask because we wouldn't have gotten what we wanted anyway, then we won't make our needs known the next time either.

People who love one another basically want to please each other, although often they don't know how. Men report that they wish their partner would be clearer in specifying her needs so they wouldn't have to stumble around in the dark trying to decipher her wishes. By not being specific with your partner about your sexual preferences, you are depriving him of the pleasure of pleasing you, as well as depriving yourself of sexual pleasure.

Some people feel that they are not being independent or self-sufficient if they ever have to rely on someone else. Somewhere in their lives they learned to only count on themselves. Perhaps when they relied on others they were disappointed, so now they protect themselves by withholding their vulnerability—and with it, their orgasms. Practicing being vulnerable by putting your needs out in the open—to be accepted or rejected—is one way to build trust in your partner. A willingness to trust your partner and be vulnerable is sometimes a prerequisite for orgasm.

## The Yes Exercise

The Yes Exercise is designed to enable you to raise your level of contentment with your life. It has been created for people who have difficulty asking for what they want and who tend to put their own needs last.

Basically, the Yes Exercise consists of asking for or letting yourself have three things each day that you would like to have, but usually wouldn't ask for or allow yourself to enjoy. If you are accustomed to asking your partner for something—to make dinner, for example—this request would not count. Begin with simple things that are not of earthshaking importance—things which would not devastate you were they not granted. For example, you might ask a friend or relative to take care of your children so you can go away for a weekend, or have your child run an errand that would free some time and energy for yourself, or ask a friend to help you with a task that could be completed far more easily if two people combined efforts. You might allow yourself to go out to a nicer restaurant than usual with your partner or friend or to buy a piece of clothing you admire but would generally consider too much of a luxury, or to spend an afternoon lounging in the sun and let the chores wait.

The object of this exercise is not to get what you ask for—but just to ask. Whether or not your wishes are fulfilled, you will have learned something. It is also important to distinguish between a refusal to fulfill a particular request and a personal rejection. Think for a minute about your own experience of being asked to do something, and your motivation for denying the request. For example, if you did not want to or were not physically able to pick up your child from school at a certain time, would you consider it an indication that you did not love him? It is important to remember that circumstances, preoccupations, and priorities can limit someone's availability.

If you don't feel comfortable turning down someone's request, you may worry that asking for something would place the other person in the same uncomfortable position. Because of your own discomfort with turning down requests you may fear that someone else might say yes out of a sense of obligation, as you sometimes do. Then you may worry that they will harbor negative feelings toward you afterward. Although this is a reasonable concern, it is possible to recognize when a person is responding out of politeness rather than out of a genuine sense of giving. If the former is the case, you can make it easier for the person to turn down your request through assurances that you will certainly be able to find someone else to help you out.

Learning to ask for what you need as soon as you become aware of it can eliminate the experience of waiting so long that you feel desperate and vulnerable when you finally do ask. Also, asking early gives you lots of time to find an alternative source of assistance if the initial one is not available.

The reason you should ask for *three* things each day, as opposed to one, is that asking more frequently for smaller things dissipates the pressure that could build up around one large request. Also, if you only had to make one request per day, you might forget about the exercise altogether. Making three requests requires you to pay attention to the exercise throughout the day and keeps you aware of opportunities to ask, including those you inadvertently let pass by.

Don't become concerned, however, when you miss an opportunity. There will be others. Since you may not readily think about how others can assist you or how you can better give to yourself, it is only natural that initially some opportunities will slip by unrecognized. Noticing the ones you miss will help develop awareness, which is the first step toward action. With attention and practice, you can expect to get better at picking up on opportunities that present themselves.

In the beginning, you may want to use the Fantasy Rehearsal Exercise‡ to practice making requests before approaching the real person. Going over the exact words you might use and imagining possible responses, both negative and positive, can build self-confidence.

It may also be helpful to view the situation from the other person's perspective. You might consider how you would like to have the identical request made of you. What words would make you feel like fulfilling the request? How could the request be made so that you would not feel guilty if you wanted to turn it down? This kind of fantasy rehearsal can be very beneficial.

The attainment of orgasm is nothing more than the release of built-up sexual pleasure. A deep feeling that the experience of sexual pleasure is really not acceptable is sufficient to block orgasm. Learning to ask for and allowing yourself to experience receiving pleasure outside the bedroom can develop a sense of confidence that can be transferred to the bedroom, enabling you to ask for what you need sexually and to enjoy the process of receiving.

No matter how your initial attempts at asking for what you want turn out, ultimately, the more capable you are of making requests, the better you will be able to fulfill your own needs. The more you practice asking, the easier each request will become. One woman is fond of saying that if she isn't turned down three times a day, she hasn't asked for enough. She expects some portion of her requests to be turned down, and so she isn't bothered when this occurs. The more we ask for, the more we are likely to receive in the end. After all, if we only ask for one thing and get refused, we have nothing. But if we ask for six things and get refused on three, we have had three more requests met than we would have if we had never asked at all.

Finally, the more willing you are to rely on others, the easier it will be for others to make requests of you. Most of us are more than

‡ See pages 99–100.

willing to assist a friend. Helping another gives us a chance to feel needed, to feel useful, to share our love. By asking others for help, we provide the opportunity for them to experience these same positive feelings. When we don't ask, we deprive others of giving and may also inhibit them from asking for help from us. When we impose on them, we free them to impose on us—all in a loving way.

## The Sexual Request Exercise

Once you are able to ask for or allow yourself pleasure outside of the bedroom, the next step is to ask for what pleases you during sex. Many women had no experience talking about sex while growing up. Consequently, they have difficulty saying sexual words. Some have never even developed an adult sexual vocabulary and have only their childhood names for anatomical parts and no names for many sexual activities. Some words are perceived as dirty and not to be spoken by a respectable woman. Some women have concluded that only silence belongs in the bedroom. Others consider offensive or unfeminine the assertiveness required to communicate their sexual desires.

Finally, some women believe that something given without their asking is superior to something they have to ask for. The problem with this myth is that it invites disappointment because most partners are not mind readers and do not automatically know how to please the one they love. In fact, given the uniqueness of each individual woman, without specific information most partners are lost. As one man said, "Each woman should come with her own individual guidebook so a man will know how best to make love to her."[6]

If you experience discomfort talking about sex or have trouble asking for what pleases you, the Sexual Request Exercise can help. This exercise is a combination of the Body Rub Exercise and the Yes Exercise. Massages of thirty to forty minutes are to be traded. Less time can be allocated if this is too long. Again, it is better not to risk a negative experience by setting expectations too high or by setting a goal that would make the experience feel more like work than relaxation and enjoyment.

As in the Body Rub Exercise, appropriate preparations should be made to ensure undisturbed time together in a comfortable atmosphere.* Determine who is to be the first massage giver and who is to be the recipient. Some people who find it particularly difficult to take pleasure often appreciate being the giver first. Once they have fulfilled their partner's needs, they are more able to relax and receive pleasure themselves.

## THE ROLE OF THE RECEIVER

As receiver, gather any powders or other accessories that you would like to be able to choose from. Begin by telling the giver where to start on your body and how you would like to be touched. For example, "I would like you to begin at my shoulders with a very light stroking motion—pretend you are a feather . . . now use your fingertips to caress my whole body . . . oh, that feels good, yes, just like that . . . now could you begin massaging my stomach using a stronger touch, maybe in a circular motion . . . I'm going to be quiet for a few minutes while you do that just so I can enjoy it," etc. As the receiver, it is important that you give a fairly constant flow of suggestions. Such constant instruction-giving may feel like over-kill at first. But this exercise is designed to exaggerate the process of explicit communication, both to help you make your sexual needs known and to provide the giver with information to meet your needs in the future.

## THE ROLE OF THE GIVER

It is the giver's responsibility to see to it that the receiver gets everything he or she asks for. This will help establish trust and re-inforce the attempts to communicate sexual preferences. As giver, explicitly follow the directions of your lover. You can add those things that you feel would further enhance the receiver's experience, but for this exercise you should stick primarily to following the receiver's instructions.

Once again, whether the massages are exchanged during one time period or given on different occasions, sex should be prohibited for at least one hour following the exercise to prevent the possibility of

---

* You may want to reread pages 159–60 on hints for setting the scene.

performance pressure and to facilitate relaxation. Again, this should be clearly understood and acknowledged beforehand so that neither of you will be disappointed.

INSTANT REPLAY

A five-minute replay or debriefing session should follow the exercise, not only to share how it felt to give and receive explicit instructions, but also to cover what both found particularly enjoyable about the touching experience. If any misunderstanding occurred during the massage, this period can be used to clarify the miscommunication. This is also a good time to discuss how you might want to modify the exercise during future practice sessions. Remember that the objective of the exercise is to open up explicit sexual communication. It may be necessary to carry out the exercise two or three times before you become comfortable expressing your sexual likes and dislikes and your partner develops some new awareness of your sexual preferences.

## The His and Her Exercise

The His and Her Exercise is designed to change the routine of your lovemaking and to better enable both of you to enjoy the experience of being totally passive and receiving as well as totally active and giving. It has been created to provide you with an opportunity to receive without feeling self-conscious, selfish, or worried about your partner's pleasure, and to initiate sexually so that the sexual activities that transpire are ones that are most pleasurable for you.

The idea for this exercise originated from a couple who used this method as a way of sexually pleasing one of them when the other wasn't really in the mood to be sexually aroused. The disinterested partner was more than willing to please the turned-on partner. They enjoyed this process so much that they began reserving nights ahead of time to trade off roles.

Now that you have had some practice receiving sexually, and have communicated some of your sexual preferences, it is time to incorporate these components into a total sexual experience. Set aside an evening during which you will exclusively give to your partner. The next time your partner can totally give to you. Breasts and genitals are *on* limits for this exercise and should, at times, be concentrated on. Intercourse should not occur when the woman is the receiver so that there is no pressure to reach orgasm. However, on "his" night the woman can feel free to incorporate intercourse into the pleasuring session.

The object is for the receiver to experience as much sexual arousal as he or she is capable of, and for the giver to be as creative a lover as he or she can be. Set aside a minimum of thirty minutes for the assignment. Decide who will be the giver and who will receive.

Although it is best to discuss this exercise before carrying it out, this is not essential, and initiating it, even with a relatively new partner, is fairly simple. At the beginning of a sexual encounter with a new partner, merely suggest that he lie back and relax. Explain that you don't want him to do anything, that you would appreciate being able to just give to him sexually. He need do nothing active, just receive. If he so desires he can return the favor next time.

### THE ROLE OF THE GIVER

Act as if you have all the time in the world and thoroughly allow yourself to enjoy giving to your partner. This situation gives you the opportunity to explore and experiment, expanding on methods used for body pleasuring in the previous exercises. After a period of time, focus more attention on your partner's genitals and other sexually sensitive areas.

### THE ROLE OF THE RECEIVER

When your partner is the giver, you can completely relax and just respond to the pleasure provided. Try to focus totally on the pleasurable sensations. You can give directions if you feel the need, or not say a word.

As with the Body Rub Exercise, if the touching is unpleasurable, it is important to communicate this to your partner. Try to describe in a positive and helpful way how the touching can be changed to make the experience more pleasing.

Ellen had problems allowing herself to relax and receive sufficient pleasure to reach orgasm. When it was her night and her partner would not allow her to reciprocate in any way, she found her sexual feelings building. She noted when she felt the urge to change positions, to concentrate on him, or to do something different, but she restrained herself from doing any of these and instead continued to focus on the pleasurable sensations. To her surprise, she felt an orgasm coming on. Again, she nearly stopped herself, but the feelings felt so good, and her partner seemed to be enjoying pleasuring her so much, that she relaxed and experienced her first orgasm with him. From this experience she realized that all she needed to do was allow her partner to completely pleasure her without feeling guilty about taking or feeling awkward about visibly expressing her arousal.

The His and Her Exercise is really a transition exercise. The exercises in this chapter have been carefully circumscribed activities designed to provide you with practice at giving, receiving, and communicating in new ways. The exercises in the next chapter, however, are much less self-contained. Instead, they consist of small changes that can be incorporated into your normal lovemaking experiences to make them more pleasurable and more likely to result in orgasm.

*Chapter 9*

# MODIFYING LOVEMAKING

The exercises in this chapter provide opportunities for transforming your sexual experiences through experimentation, communication, and different kinds of sexual interaction. These exercises can be integrated into any sexual encounter and do not necessarily have to be discussed with a partner ahead of time to be carried out effectively. Also, it is no longer necessary to maintain any ban on intercourse. Sex as usual, with some additions, will be the focus.

## The Sexual Assertiveness Exercise

While many of us are able to decline sexual activities which we don't find appealing, few of us are able to comfortably initiate the sexual activities we would most enjoy. Initiating different sexual positions and activities is one way to see that our sexual needs get met.

Before your next sexual interaction with a partner, sit quietly for a few moments and think about the kind of sexual activities that are particularly arousing for you. Do you enjoy oral sex? Anal stimulation? Certain intercourse positions? Pick out something specific that you would like to experience the next time you make love. Pick an activity that may have occurred occasionally in the past but which does not ordinarily take place; or select a new activity that you have never tried together.

Next, in fantasy, imagine initiating the activity that you have decided upon. Specifically, imagine at what point in the lovemaking you would initiate it and exactly how you would go about it. How could you maneuver your body so that you are in a position for oral sex or move your partner's hand to the part of your body that you would enjoy having stimulated? Repeat the fantasy a few times, each time initiating the activity differently. If you go through these motions mentally, it should be easier to initiate the activity when the opportunity arises.

The final step of this exercise is to carry out the activity the next time you have sex with your partner. It doesn't matter if you continue with the activity for five seconds or twenty-five minutes. The object is to physically assert yourself in order to receive the kind of stimulation that you desire during your lovemaking.

Once you have been successful at initiating the first activity, initiate some new sexual activity each time you make love. You might want to repeat activities you particularly enjoy; it is not necessary to initiate something different each time. However, it is important to keep asserting yourself in an active way. For example, the first time you carry out this exercise, you might initiate stimulating your partner orally. The next time you might arrange it so that you can have intercourse while you are sitting astride. The third time you might let your partner know that you would like to be orally stimulated. If you require direct clitoral stimulation to reach orgasm, you could initiate prolonged clitoral stimulation as one of the new activities. The following time you might try the astride intercourse position again. Subsequently, you might initiate the entire sexual encounter by letting your partner know in a more overt manner than usual that you are in the mood for sex. You could ask early in the day to reserve time later that evening for making love, or you could leave a note to that effect on his dinner plate.

## CLITORAL STIMULATION

The next two assignments specifically deal with the integration of direct clitoral stimulation into partner sex. The first exercise focuses on you applying the stimulation yourself and the second on teaching your partner to stimulate you.

Many women are shocked by the idea of stimulating their own clitoris while having sex with their partner. After all, this form of stimulation has been ingrained as being not only private, but shameful. For someone to know that we do it is bad enough, but to actually let them see us do it may seem inconceivable.

There is a myth that it is somehow wrong to touch yourself while making love with someone else. An unspoken rule dictates that you only touch me and I only touch you, but neither of us should ever touch ourselves.

Concern over a partner's reaction to our touching ourselves during lovemaking can make initiating this exercise difficult. Talking about it ahead of time, especially if you have been working on the exercise progression together, will help matters. If you don't wish to discuss it beforehand, you can still initiate the activity.

If your partner has never been with a woman who has touched herself during sex, this may be uncomfortable at first. It is important to remember that men and women have both grown up with and incorporated cultural ideas that stand in the way of sexual growth. As difficult as it is for us to assert ourselves and feel comfortable stimulating ourselves during sexual play with a partner, it may be equally difficult for our partner to accept this activity.

Many men feel that the only proper way for a woman to be stimulated is by their penis. They may consider a woman touching herself to be emasculating, as if she were trying to take over their role. One man even asked a preorgasmic group member to stop touching herself the first time they made love together. He said *he* would take care of her.

By explaining to your partner that it is impossible for him to know at each moment what you need clitorally, you can help reduce some of the societal pressure he may feel to perform. By assuming some of the responsibility for stimulating yourself you can liberate him from continually worrying about your sexual enjoyment, thereby allowing him to concentrate more fully on his own sexual pleasure.

Not all men respond negatively. Some find watching their partner stimulate herself a real turn-on. One man mentioned that he was not feeling particularly turned on one night when his wife of ten years surprised him by beginning to masturbate. They were in bed watching television together when he became aware of subtle movements on her side of the bed. When he looked over, the cover was no longer on top of her, and she was in the process of stimulating herself. After watching for a while, he became very much aroused and joined in. This experience remained memorable as one of their best times in bed together.

## The Self Clitoral Stimulation Exercise

If you have any negative feelings about the need for clitoral stimulation you may find this exercise difficult to carry out, but because it has been instrumental in so many women becoming orgasmic, it is highly advisable.

Once you can masturbate to orgasm while thrusting something in and out of your vagina,* there is no reason why you should not be able to experience orgasm during intercourse while simultaneously stimulating your clitoris. And this is precisely the purpose of the Self Clitoral Stimulation Exercise: to stimulate your clitoris manually or with a vibrator before and during intercourse.

Your partner's participation in this exercise (whether or not he is aware of it) is just to make love to you in his usual manner. He need do nothing different. You are the one who will be trying something new.

If you find it difficult to begin immediately stimulating your clitoris, you might first want to begin by just stroking your breasts. On another occasion, you could move your hand down to your stomach and begin erotically massaging that soft, sensual area. On the next sexual encounter you could continue moving your hand downward until you reach your clitoris.

If you would like to use a vibrator instead of your hand, make sure that your vibrator is plugged in next to the bed before you make love so that it is easily accessible. If your partner has never seen your vibrator, introduce it as a toy that enhances lovemaking for you. You might want to show him how it works by using it on his shoulders and back before stimulating yourself. I would not recommend that you try it on his genitals initially. Both men and women have highly individual responses to vibrators—some love it and some hate it. Let him ask to try it out on his penis or invite

* See the Increasing Vaginal Sensitivity Exercises, pages 145–47.

him to experiment with it after you have used it clitorally on yourself.

You can stimulate yourself clitorally in almost any intercourse position. The positions that are the most comfortable for you will be dictated by how your two bodies most comfortably fit together. Some positions are better for some couples than others. The woman-astride is generally a good one. The rear-entry positions can be easily adapted to provide access for direct clitoral stimulation. Whether you are flat on your stomach with your partner lying on your back, on your sides curled together like spoons, or on your hands and knees, it is possible for your partner to enter you vaginally from behind leaving you considerable space and freedom to stimulate your own clitoris. Also, if you are on your back and your partner is on his side, almost perpendicular to your body, with his legs between yours or alternating with yours, he can enter you from the front, leaving ample access to your genital area. You can stimulate your clitoris in the man-on-top position as well. If your partner lifts himself up by extending his arms, it will create sufficient space for you to slip your fingers or a small vibrator between his pubic bone and your genitals.

Choose the position that most closely resembles the one you use when you masturbate alone. Make use of the pattern your body has become accustomed to over the period of time you have been masturbating. Adapting what already works well is most likely to lead to success.

You will probably have to experiment with stimulating your own clitoris during intercourse a number of times before you will be able to have an orgasm. The first time you stimulate your clitoris while making love with your partner, do so for only a short while with no intention of reaching orgasm. As you become more comfortable with touching yourself in your partner's presence, you can prolong the stimulation. It will take substantially longer to reach orgasm while interacting with a partner than it ever takes when you masturbate alone. So don't get discouraged, just relax and pleasure yourself in the ways you enjoy.

In many cases, it may be necessary to maintain the clitoral stimulation beyond the point when your partner ejaculates. One woman realized that she could not fully relax until her partner had climaxed. No matter how hard she tried, she was too concerned about his pleasure. However, after he had his orgasm, she was no longer preoccupied with his needs. At that point she could more fully relax and respond to the clitoral stimulation while her partner's penis remained inside her.

Once you are able to experience orgasm while stimulating yourself manually or with a vibrator, during or outside of intercourse, you have a technique that you can always rely on. Although you may still want to teach your partner to stimulate you more effectively, you do not have to remain sexually frustrated while he is learning. You can always stimulate yourself to orgasm during lovemaking.

## The Partner Clitoral Stimulation Exercise

Teaching your partner to stimulate you clitorally is more difficult than applying the stimulation yourself. A verbal explanation may not suffice. Your partner may not grasp the nuances of the stimulation you need. After all, your partner does not have the immediate feedback that you have when you are stimulating yourself. If the motion is too hard, you instinctively lighten the touch; if the stimulation becomes irritating or too repetitive, you automatically vary the stroke. Your partner's stimulation is bound to be less precise and will require constant monitoring in the beginning until he learns *what* you like, and *when* you like it.

With the idea that a picture is worth a thousand words, you might use the Self Clitoral Stimulation Exercise to show your partner how you like to be stimulated. Pick a position that enables your partner to clearly observe you. Your partner might want to caress your body while you are stimulating yourself. Then, after about four or five minutes of close observation, allow your partner to assume the clitoral stimulation. As you carry out the assignment, don't worry about having an orgasm. The object is just to teach your partner to stimulate you clitorally in the way you enjoy. It may take a number of sessions before you respond to your partner's touch with orgasm. In the meantime, you can always provide the clitoral stimulation yourself when you desire release.

Pauline was brought up in a strict religious environment that declared masturbation a sin. When we mentioned the idea of masturbating in front of her partner, she was shocked. But as other women in the group carried out the assignment successfully and without negative repercussions, she decided to try it herself. When she mentioned to her partner that she would like to demonstrate for him how she liked to be touched, he seemed more than a little interested. It turned out that he found the idea really exciting. One of his fantasies had always been to watch a woman masturbating. When she began the demonstration, Pauline felt awkward and uncomfortable. She found herself wishing she were somewhere else. When she remembered that she didn't have to have an orgasm, only touch herself, she began to relax a bit. Her partner seemed very interested in watching her, when he suddenly left the room. Momentarily he returned with a few tissues and lay down next to her and began stimulating himself. To her surprise, Pauline was fascinated. She had never seen a man masturbate before. Although she did not reach orgasm the first time she stimulated herself in front of him, she reported that his technique had improved a thousand percent when they made love afterward. She also felt that her ability to manually stimulate him improved. With time she found herself more aroused by his touch. Then one evening after an unusually long period of lovemaking, she had an orgasm while he was manually stimulating her.

When your partner begins to practice what you have demonstrated, be careful not to take over the stimulation yourself and thereby preclude responding to your partner's touch. Women who are concerned that they will lose the orgasm tend to do this when they experience feelings of high arousal. Some women do it because they are concerned about becoming overly dependent on a partner who can stimulate them to orgasm. Some women who are only able to respond to vibrator stimulation may be using the machine to avoid being vulnerable to their partner. Sometimes the ability to respond to your own hand or vibrator stimulation but not to stimulation by your partner is an indirect expression of anger—almost like saying, "I can have an orgasm, but you aren't able to do it for me." If you think that fear of intimacy, fear of vulnerability, or a need to indirectly punish your partner is stopping you from responding to your partner's touch, you might resist taking over the manual or vibrator stimulation yourself to see what happens if you allow your partner to continue at it a little longer.

## VAGINAL STIMULATION

### The G-Spot Stimulation Exercise

You can add stimulation of the G-spot with very little difficulty while your partner is clitorally stimulating you. After you have become sexually aroused by whatever foreplay techniques you enjoy most, have your partner stimulate your clitoris either manually or orally. When you feel ready, have him insert both his index and middle fingers to about the depth of the middle knuckle. If you are on your back, his fingers should be inserted palm up. If you are on your stomach, they should be inserted palm down. If after he inserts his fingers, he firmly puts pressure on the front wall of the vagina just above the point when the pubic bone ends, he will be stimulating the G-spot. Some women find that this simultaneous clitoral and G-spot stimulation heightens their arousal considerably.

### The Intercourse Exercise

Some women find it particularly arousing to have intercourse in positions which provide more direct stimulation of their G-spot. To carry out the Intercourse Exercise, let your partner know before lovemaking that you would like to determine when intercourse begins and which position to use. Be sure to spend the necessary time building up your arousal. Some women who are vaginally responsive believe that their responsivity is largely determined by how aroused they are before intercourse begins. For many of these women, this arousal level is determined as much by their mental set and the fantasies and thoughts they have, as it is by the physical stimulation.[1] Therefore, make sure that you begin intercourse only when you feel ready. Take all the time you need to warm up. When you are ready, lead your partner, through verbal or nonverbal guidance, into an intercourse position that stimulates the front and top part of the vagina. This will be different from most positions that provide clitoral stimulation. The specific intercourse position that will work best for you depends on the unique way you and your partner fit together physically. Many women find rear-entry positions, whether they are on their hands and knees, stomach, or side, best for G-spot stimulation. For some women, arching their back in this position is necessary to create the precise angle that allows for stimulation of the G-spot. For others, stimulation is best when their partner is on top but with his arms outstretched and his back arched. For some, the position of greatest stimulation is sitting on their partner's lap while he is also sitting. Some find that positions in which the man is kneeling are most conducive to G-spot stimulation. He can either be kneeling at the foot or side of the bed while she lies on her back on the bed, or he can be kneeling over her while she is on her back with her knees raised over his shoulders. Other intercourse positions may be more pleasurable depending on your particular areas of vaginal or clitoral sensitivity and your anatomical fit with your partner. Experiment with a different position each time you have intercourse until you can determine which positions provide you with the most pleasure. Also, some women's diaphragms fit in such a way that they interfere with stimulation of the G-spot. You may want to have your gynecologist check yours if you think this may be a problem.

### The Expanding Pleasure Exercise

The amount of time spent on lovemaking is important. Gebhard's analysis of Kinsey's research of the 1940s showed that only 7.7 percent of the women who regularly spent twenty-one minutes or longer on foreplay *failed* to experience orgasm.[2] Hunt's data, accumulated in the 1970s, showed that most couples spend less time than that. "The median duration of foreplay for our single people under twenty-five is fifteen minutes and of those ages twenty-five to thirty-four, is about twenty minutes, while for married persons in both age groups it is about fifteen minutes."[3] He goes on to add that older couples spend even less time. No wonder so many women are not orgasmic. They are getting roughly two thirds of the time they need to build arousal.

Sometimes a woman is not orgasmic during intercourse because her partner ejaculates almost immediately after he enters her. And with his ejaculation comes the end of the lovemaking. Many men ejaculate rapidly because they learned to masturbate surreptitiously and quickly so they would not be discovered, or because their first sexual experiences in basements or the backs of automobiles were filled with anxiety and had to be carried out rapidly so they wouldn't be caught. As a result, these men taught themselves to come to orgasm after only a brief period of stimulation and they never learned to control the arousal process. Luckily, while rapid ejaculation is a very common sexual problem, it is one of the easiest to reverse. Sex therapy is effective in nine out of ten cases, and many men can be helped by carrying out the exercises described in self-help books without any professional assistance.[4]

While women seem to require more time than men to get warmed up, most women attempt to fit themselves into their male partner's sexual pattern by trying to achieve orgasm as quickly as possible. It has always been the woman's role to adapt. But in this situation, to experience orgasm quickly is to curtail the pleasure for both people.

To see how much time you generally spend making love, just glance at the clock when you begin having sex and then again when you stop. Often, what seems like an hour of lovemaking is only fifteen minutes. If your clock watching indicates that you generally spend less than twenty-five minutes in foreplay, that is, all those activities prior to intercourse, you should carry out the Expanding Pleasure Exercise.

Set aside forty-five to sixty minutes for making love with your partner. Since this is longer than you usually spend, either start earlier in the evening or choose a morning or afternoon when you have no pressing plans. Spend a minimum of thirty minutes on foreplay. After this period, you can include intercourse if you desire.

If you are not discussing the assignments openly with your partner, you could just mention as you begin making love that you would really enjoy spending an especially long time kissing and caressing each other before having intercourse. You might even tantalize him by saying that you want to wait until you are so turned on that you are consumed with the desire to have him inside you. Let him know that you want this to be the longest and best experience you have ever had. Then, you will have the security of knowing that you don't have to rush, that you will have ample time to relax and enjoy the slow buildup of sexual sensations.

Enjoy covering every inch of your partner's body with kisses. Spend ten or fifteen minutes rubbing each other all over before attending to the genitals. Extend oral sex if you both enjoy it. Don't forget to use sufficient oil or lubricant on the genitals to enhance manual stimulation. Creatively explore different touches and different rhythms. If you should feel his orgasm drawing near, back off and tease him more gently, or discontinue stimulating his penis altogether while attending to other parts of his body. You might want to share some of your sexual fantasies or erotic thoughts during this time or just silently experience them on your own. There is no need to think ahead about how you "should" already be feeling, or worry whether orgasm will occur. Just relax and enjoy the time together. It will probably take a few repetitions of this assignment before you can fully drop some of the concerns which block orgasm. Meanwhile, pay attention to the sensations you do feel.


## PRACTICE AND ORGASM

If you've made some gains, but aren't experiencing everything you had hoped for before beginning the exercises, don't be at all discouraged. As with anything else, continued practice should bring forth ever-increasing results. The small improvements experienced now are the seeds of better things to come. High oak trees grow out of small acorns, and without the acorn nothing more could develop. Women who attend preorgasmic groups slowly continue to build upon the progress made in their therapy group throughout the year after it ends.

You are now in a position to develop and expand sexually. It may take a while before you feel your journey is complete, so enjoy the process as it unfolds. You can only be where you are at this particular moment anyway. You might as well not try to rush things.

Some women discount their orgasms if they still require clitoral stimulation. If this represents your feelings and your situation, I can only reiterate that vaginal stimulation does not produce a vaginal orgasm and clitoral stimulation does not produce a clitoral orgasm. An orgasm is a full body response.† Every woman responds

† Reread pages 27–29 and pages 54–69.

differently. Differences in response reflect differences in learning and physiological predisposition. While some women reach orgasm through vaginal stimulation, there is no indication that they get more enjoyment out of sex than women who are most responsive to clitoral stimulation and vice versa.

## BLOCKING

If you have made no gain after completing all of the previous exercises a number of times, or if, despite your gains, you feel you are somehow blocked in your experience of orgasm with a partner, there are a number of possible explanations. You may require more erotic mental buildup than you are getting; there may be psychological issues tied to your expectation of orgasm; or you may have serious unresolved relationship problems that are standing in the way.

### The Fantasy Enhancement Exercise

Some women need to fantasize in order to experience orgasm.‡ This can be a problem if you believe that orgasm without fantasy is a purer emotional response and that a partner should provide all of the cues necessary for arousal. Women who believe that fantasy is wrong or abnormal cut off the mental component of their arousal and in so doing, limit their physical arousal as well. If you have, over the years, incorporated fantasy into your masturbation, you may require fantasy as much as clitoral stimulation or vaginal penetration to bring about orgasm.

By stifling your fantasies you can also stifle sexual feelings. Consequently, if you are not yet orgasmic during sex with your partner, check to see if fantasy is an important component of your masturbation experience. If it is, consciously add elements of your favorite fantasies while you are making love with your partner. You may want to enjoy your fantasy privately, or share it with your partner aloud. Talking about fantasies together can be a way to add excitement and variety to a sexual relationship. You may also want to enact some of your fantasies with your partner.

‡ See pages 113–14 for more information about fantasy.

One woman was turned on by fantasies of high passion and uncontrollable lust. She and her husband would occasionally act out these feelings by wearing old T-shirts and tearing them off one another as part of the seduction. In this way they could freely give reign to the intense and passionate feelings in total safety.[5]

## Psychological Blocks

If fantasizing during sex with your partner does not help you begin having orgasms together, you may have other issues connected to orgasm which are blocking your progress.

Although most women who don't have orgasms readily believe that they have some deep underlying psychological problem, this is rarely the case. Most women don't experience orgasm because of learned sexual inhibitions, insufficient sexual information, and an inability to relax and receive sexual pleasure—not because they are neurotic. In fact, very neurotic women and quite psychotic women can be highly orgasmic. Mental problems do not necessarily interfere with sexual responsiveness. When they do, the psychological issue may have to be disconnected from the issue of orgasm in order for the orgasm to occur.

For example, some women believe their whole life will be different once they become orgasmic. Such a woman may expect to feel perfectly secure and content once this particularly dissatisfying aspect of her life is resolved. And while one might think that this expectation of nirvana would propel a woman forward toward making changes, we have found the opposite to be true. Imagining that having orgasms will change one's life can bring up perhaps unrecognized fears that can actually inhibit a woman from becoming orgasmic. For one thing, while a changed life might be enhanced by excitement, it may also be fraught with new problems and fears. Some things might change for the worse. Even though the status quo may not be totally fulfilling, there is some sense of safety in knowing how a situation will turn out, even if that means not having orgasms.

As mentioned earlier, some women fear that if they were to become orgasmic with a partner, they might then be devastated if they were to lose him. Fear of excessive dependency causes them to unconsciously withhold the orgasmic release. However, it is unlikely that having orgasms will make you any more dependent on your partner than you already are. Depriving yourself of sexual pleasure throughout your life to avoid being vulnerable in the end is not a positive and fulfilling way to live. Also, if you learned to be orgasmic with your partner, and something did happen to your relationship, you could carry this ability into a future relationship.

Some women fear that if they become orgasmic, their partner will have some hold or some control over them. But, in fact, your orgasm is your own; your partner has no real control over you. You can always keep yourself from having an orgasm if you want to. You have been doing so for years and are unlikely to lose this long-standing ability. Your orgasm results from your willingness to let your partner pleasure you. You actively participate in creating any orgasm or satisfaction that occurs during a sexual experience.

Some women fear that if they become orgasmic with their partner they will become promiscuous. One woman was convinced that she would become sexually insatiable and would be uncontrollably driven to have sex with every man she encountered. In her case, the fear of being promiscuous came from the frustration of having repressed her sexuality for so many years. She feared that once she let herself go, she would lose control and make up for the years lost all at once. However, I have never yet seen any woman change her basic moral attitude because she became orgasmic.

Women who have been molested or who have had an incestuous relationship may fail to experience orgasm later in life as a way to justify their anger for the injustice done to them. Unfortunately, some of these women continue to cut off their own pleasure in order to preserve their scars. A child who is beaten and suffers a broken leg has the right to remain angry over the beating and the painful experience, even after the leg has completely healed. She doesn't have to wear a cast the rest of her life to justify her anger. A woman who has been sexually molested has a right to maintain her anger toward the one who hurt her without having to make herself a sexual cripple.

Concerns over intimacy may also inhibit orgasm. Some women feel emotionally overwhelmed by the intimacy of a loving relationship. They may have difficulty separating their thoughts and feelings from those of their partner. This confusion seems to get exacerbated at the point of orgasm when the heightened state of arousal blurs the senses anyway. To avoid this feeling of merging with her partner, a woman may cut off her arousal at this point.

Finally, some women do not become orgasmic because not having an orgasm protects them from something worse: extreme marital unhappiness, depression, or a deep sense of inadequacy. Some women prefer to take the blame for a sexual problem rather than expand their own sexuality and expose their partner as inadequate. One woman who was living with her partner said that if she were orgasmic, there would be no reason *not* to get married. To maintain a safe level of intimacy and independence, she cut off her orgasms. A woman may prevent herself from becoming orgasmic so she can blame her problems on this sexual symptom. In this way, she doesn't have to experience the anxiety that would arise if she faced the *real* problem. It would be like insisting that you were overweight when you were really pregnant, and concentrating on dieting rather than facing the fears and concerns about having a child.

If you are willing to truthfully confront your progress thus far, you can probably assess whether or not a deeper underlying factor is responsible for keeping you from becoming orgasmic. Did you complete all of the relevant exercises? When you did them, did you feel that you were carrying them out fully or did you feel that you were holding yourself back? Did you do some exercises only once or not at all when they should have been repeated a number of times? Did other tasks or outside activities or appointments keep you from attending fully to the exercises? Did you squelch the feelings or maybe even temporarily take a break from the homework when you started to feel more sexually excited? If you can see a pattern of making excuses not to complete the assignments or not completing them wholeheartedly, you might think about what in your life might be worse were you to become orgasmic.

Sit quietly and contemplate the question. Consider whether your relationship might get worse. What do you feel you would have to do if you were orgasmic that you don't have to do now? For example, one woman did not want to have sex as often as her husband did. She felt that if she were orgasmic, she would have no acceptable excuse for turning him down when he was interested in sex and she wasn't. By not being orgasmic she had a legitimate reason for not wanting sex as often.

## Relationship Problems

Anger and resentment resulting from the buildup of unresolved relationship problems may make you unwilling to become orgasmic. You might feel that by becoming orgasmic you would be giving up the only control you have in your relationship. If you don't feel safe enough to express your feelings directly, withholding orgasm may be the only way you have of expressing anger toward your partner. You may unconsciously fear that losing this power would render you helpless.

If psychological or relationship problems are creating your orgasm problem, you may require the assistance of a psychotherapist or marriage counselor.* If you are orgasmic with masturbation, you should be able to surmount the block that keeps you from experiencing the same release while interacting with your partner, though it may not happen quite as quickly or as easily as you first anticipated.

Once you are able to have an orgasm in your partner's presence, whether you have achieved it with the help of these exercises or the assistance of a sex therapist, the most difficult part of the process is over. Each time you have an orgasm, you will become more confident of having one in the future. This makes it easier to relax, which in turn increases positive results. After a number of successful orgasmic experiences, even if they are all in response to the same stimulation, you are in a position to experiment further to broaden your repertoire. You may want to add new ways of stimulating yourself so that you create greater variety in your responsivity, though you never want to stop using any techniques that work.†

Now that we have confronted problems concerned with orgasm, it is time to enter another area that can affect sexual relationships— physical discomfort during sex.

* See Chapter 15 for information on choosing a therapist.
† See Chapter 14 for exercises designed to help you expand your sexual repertoire.

*Section IV*

# SEXUAL DISCOMFORT

# Chapter 10

# PAINFUL SEX

Physical discomfort with intercourse is a far less common complaint than lack of orgasm and lack of sexual interest. Yet for women who have this problem, the results are just as devastating. While a minimal amount of pain can enhance the arousal of some women—creating a sort of bittersweet feeling—a greater level of pain can totally interfere with the experience of sexual pleasure. Whether the pain is experienced at the opening to the vagina, deep inside the vagina, or as a result of an illness or injury in some other part of the body, the presence of pain almost universally signals the end to pleasure. The sexual arousal process is a fragile system. Although procreation is important to a species, it is not necessary for the survival of an individual. Therefore, anything that signals bodily distress can interfere with the sexual-arousal process.

Pain frequently indicates a physical problem. Since a self-help book is thoroughly inadequate for solving a physical problem that requires medical attention, this section will be limited to helping alleviate discomfort that results from fear and anxiety. However, even emotionally caused symptoms, such as ulcers, can have real physical manifestations. If there is a real physiological problem, we hope that the information in this chapter will help you to isolate and better describe your symptoms to your physician.

Many women are uncomfortable having a gynecological exam. A

medical examination of areas of the body which are considered private may feel like a personal invasion. However, you have only one body and it is in your best interest to keep it healthy. Attending to a physical problem in its initial stages, before it has had time to develop into a more serious condition, can be crucial.

Whenever you experience pain or discomfort during sex, you should receive a thorough gynecological exam to rule out the possibility that medical factors are causing the distress. To help your physician assess your situation most effectively, try to isolate the exact point during lovemaking when physical discomfort begins and the exact place in your body that is painful.

The three areas where pain is most frequently felt are: at the vaginal opening during the initial stages of penetration, deeper in the vagina during thrusting, and at the clitoris during any point in the lovemaking.

## CLITORAL PAIN

Clitoral stimulation can be painful as a result of a number of conditions. Is your clitoris always tender when touched or only when touched in particular ways? Is the discomfort a long-term problem or a recent occurrence? If the pain has only occurred recently, you might want to visually check your sensitive clitoral glans by moving the clitoral hood back until the glans appears. If the clitoris is red or swollen it is possible that you or your partner inadvertently scratched it. Five days of sexual abstention should provide sufficient time for any minor scratch to heal. If you notice a canker or open sore, you may have one of the signs of a vaginal infection, or a venereal disease, and should have an immediate physical evaluation.

If your clitoris has been tender for an extended period of time, you may be suffering from grainlike deposits of smegma which can form under the clitoral hood, causing irritation and pain when the hood of the clitoris moves over the glans. You may be able to remove the deposits yourself by carefully washing the area with warm water. If this does not remedy the problem, a visit to your gynecologist is advisable.

Sometimes clitoral adhesions, which are small membranes that attach the clitoris to the underside of the hood, keep the clitoral hood from moving freely over the clitoris. While clitoral adhesions are not generally painful and do not normally interfere with enjoyable sex, they can become stretched, torn, or inflamed.

A yeast or other vaginal infection may have irritated the sensitive tissue at the vaginal opening and around the clitoral area. Or you may have developed an allergic response to the oil, bath soap, or laundry detergent you are using. In any of these cases, a visit to your gynecologist should clarify the problem as well as provide a medical approach to relieving it. Obviously, if you think you may be experiencing an allergic response, immediately discontinue use of the offending product.

If your clitoris does not become painful until after it has been stimulated for a period of time, it is probable that the direct stimulation is the cause of the problem. The most common reason for pain arising from clitoral stimulation is lack of lubrication. The second most common cause is a partner's rough and callused hands. Both can produce excessive friction on the genital tissue. Additional lubrication in the form of saliva, coconut oil, or water-soluble products such as Albolene cream can reduce the friction. Having your partner use hand cream on a daily basis may help. Also, stimulation where the hand is not merely rubbing back and forth *over* the skin but providing a deeper massaging of the structures beneath the surface may be found to be more comfortable.

To see if irritation caused by too much roughness or friction is the problem, compare direct manual clitoral stimulation with oral clitoral stimulation. If you have pain with manual stimulation, but not oral stimulation, callused hands or excessive rubbing and insufficient lubrication are the likely causes.

If both oral stimulation and manual stimulation are not initially painful but become uncomfortable after a period of time, there is a good possibility that what you label as pain is really *intensity*, especially if this feeling occurs prior to orgasm or interferes with your ability to experience orgasm. Once you experience orgasm, this sensation should go away. However, a different kind of clitoral sensitivity is often experienced immediately *following* orgasm. After orgasm, the clitoris of some women becomes excruciatingly sensitive, making any direct clitoral stimulation intolerable for anywhere from a few seconds to a number of minutes. If this is the case, don't worry about it. Enjoy nongenital touching until sufficient time has elapsed to reinstate comfortable clitoral stimulation.

## VAGINAL PAIN

There are two kinds of pain generally experienced with intercourse. The first occurs at the point of penetration. Sometimes this pain or an actual spasm of the muscle surrounding the vaginal opening—called vaginismus—makes penetration impossible. The second type of vaginal pain occurs with deep thrusting.

### Pain at the Vaginal Opening

Pain or discomfort that occurs at the onset of intercourse can have a variety of causes: infection, unhealed scar tissue, allergic response, insufficient arousal, and lack of lubrication. If your vaginal opening is sensitive and tender at all times, you may have a yeast infection or some other chronic vaginal infection. This is particularly likely to be the case if a strange odor or excessive discharge accompanies the tenderness.

Tears or episiotomy scars following childbirth are often slow to heal, and some women's vaginas remain very tender for many months or even a year after delivery. Occasionally, within the first six months of delivery, breast-feeding women find intercourse painful or very uncomfortable. This is because prolactin, the hormone released during breast feeding, has an antiestrogenic effect. The lack of estrogen can cause a temporary thinning of the vaginal lining, similar to the process that takes place after menopause, and irritation during intercourse may result. In this case, K-Y jelly and gentle persistence can ease the discomfort. In extreme cases, a physician should be consulted to discuss the benefits of briefly using an estrogen cream.

It is also possible that you may be allergic to the chemicals in your contraceptive cream, foam, or jelly, or to a commercial vaginal douche if you use one. There is also a possibility an oil you use to augment your lubrication may contain alcohol, which can irritate the genitals. Or you may have developed an allergy to the particular product. Even if you have been using the same oil over a period of time, it is still possible to develop an allergic response. One woman used an oil for masturbation almost daily for a month before she had any adverse reaction. To test for an allergic response, substitute saliva for the preparation you have been using and see if the tenderness, pain, or burning sensations subside.

The most common cause of discomfort at the point of penetration is insufficient lubrication. This is frequently caused by intercourse commencing before the woman is quite ready. Since lubrication is the result of sexual excitement or arousal, if there has not been enough foreplay to make you sufficiently turned on and ready for intercourse, the vaginal opening may remain dry. This could cause your partner's penis to meet resistance as he attempts to enter you. This dryness may be your body's way of informing you that you require more sexual stimulation before intercourse. The next time you feel pain upon penetration, check with yourself to see if you feel ready to move on to intercourse, or if you would prefer to prolong the foreplay a bit longer.

If you feel that you are sufficiently aroused when your partner attempts penetration and yet you experience discomfort, your problem might still stem from inadequate lubrication. Sometimes there is sufficient lubrication internally, but not enough at the vaginal opening. To see if this is the case, check your vulva to see if it is moist enough before your partner tries to insert his penis. If it is not, you might insert your finger deeper into your vagina to see if there is more lubrication there. If there is, use your finger and bring the lubrication down to the opening. Or, you might prefer to ask your partner to do this before attempting intercourse.

No matter how aroused some women get, they just seem to have less than adequate lubrication or lubrication that is not viscous enough to protect the vaginal tissues from the friction created by the thrusting of the penis. Sometimes this is simply a normal individual variation. At other times it indicates a hormonal imbalance or a response to a particular medication or drug. Antihistamines, for example, are a common offender. Drugs that dry out the nasal passages dry out the vagina as well. Some women report that marijuana affects them in a similar way. Birth-control pills have been another common cause of lubrication problems. They can either reduce lubrication or change its consistency, rendering what appears to be more than sufficient lubrication virtually useless.

Some women find that their lubrication decreases with age. Women in their sixties and seventies have reported decreased vaginal secretions that can create discomfort with intercourse if no additional lubricant is applied. Sometimes estrogen creams are useful for replenishing the vaginal lining that becomes thinned with age. If estrogen creams are not desired, a lubricant such as K-Y jelly, Albolene cream, or saliva can be helpful. In any case, it appears that the most important factor in retarding the negative effects of the aging process is an active sex life. As with other parts of our body, the more we exercise, the better our physical condition.

Finally, we are all physically different, and some perfectly normal women have inadequate lubrication or lubrication of a thinner consistency than required to make intercourse comfortable. This is one of the reasons why K-Y jelly was manufactured. Generally, a small dab will suffice, and you'll have no reason for further concern.

If you are very turned on and well lubricated before intercourse, but find that your vaginal opening is extremely tight and makes penetration difficult, there is a good chance that you are exhibiting the normal physiological signs of high sexual arousal. Blood flows to the vaginal area during sexual excitement. As arousal mounts, the walls at the entrance of the vaginal opening swell to form the orgasmic platform. This swelling of the walls actually narrows the size of the vaginal opening which makes the opening tighter.

One way to ameliorate discomfort which is caused by being overly aroused is to bear down as your partner attempts penetration, as if you were trying to push a tampon out of your vagina. Although pushing out may seem to be just the opposite of what you need to do, it actually facilitates entry. While you are pushing out you cannot contract the muscles, which is what often happens when pain is anticipated.

The anticipation of pain can actually cause pain. If you expect penetration to hurt, the normal response is to tighten up as a way of trying to protect yourself from the pain. This tensing up causes the muscles at the vaginal opening to contract even tighter, makes penetration more difficult and causes more pain. Thus, pain during one experience can cause you to tighten up in anticipation of pain the next time you are penetrated, creating a vicious cycle. Martha began experiencing pain with intercourse right around the time her husband's business began to fail. In effect, she was expressing physiologically the emotional stress and anxiety she was feeling. Her tenseness and fear cut down on her production of lubrication, and with less lubrication, Martha found penetration painful. After a few experiences of pain with intercourse, Martha began to anticipate the pain and tensed up as a way of guarding against it when intercourse was initiated. As a result, even when her husband got back on his feet financially and the original cause of the pain was gone, she still experienced the pain that resulted from tensing up.

If you think you are caught in this vicious cycle, first make certain that you are sufficiently aroused before having intercourse. Then check to make sure you have enough lubrication. If not, use a lubricant, and bear down as you receive your partner's penis. If the pain has existed for a protracted period of time, you may want to follow the exercises in the next section for overcoming vaginismus.

## The Vaginismus Exercise

Vaginismus is the spasmodic tightening of the vaginal opening which prevents penetration. Many women who have vaginismus have never been able to have intercourse. Some cannot even insert a tampon. Sometimes fear causes the tightening of the muscle surrounding the vagina. Sometimes vaginismus results because the woman's hymen is so thick and tough it makes penetration very painful or even impossible. If an overly thick hymen is responsible for the problem, a hymenectomy, or surgical removal of the hymen, can be performed. However, if tightness and pain at the vaginal opening prevents intercourse, and you have seen a gynecologist and there is no physical basis for the problem, here are a number of steps that can be taken to ameliorate the difficulty.

The first step is to relax. Most women with vaginismus worry that they won't be able to achieve intercourse and that the attempt will cause pain. Hence beginning the sexual act with anxiety is the norm. To break the pattern of tightening up in anticipation of pain, it is necessary that you learn to relax. To do so, try the following process on your own.

Find a comfortable, private, and warm place in your house where you are assured of not being interrupted. Remove your lower garments including your underpants. You may want to leave a blouse or sweater on for warmth or you may prefer to have the covers over you. A bed or couch where you can lean back, propped up by some pillows, is an ideal place to practice these exercises.

Now, close your eyes and take three deep breaths. Each time you exhale, imagine all of your physical and emotional tensions leaving your body through your breath. You might visualize a symbol for your tension and imagine it leaving your body through your nose or mouth. Or you might concentrate on the physical sensation of your tension evaporating as you exhale.

Next, spend two or three minutes thinking about being in one of your favorite places. Pick a place that has fond memories for you—where you felt peaceful and secure. For example, you might think about a recent excursion to the beach and recall how the sun felt on your back as you were lying on the sand; or you might choose to remember a lazy Sunday, reading the newspaper in bed; or a cozy evening spent in front of a fire, sipping some cognac while the snow fell gently outside. Just imagine yourself back in that relaxing scene.

Take three more deep breaths and, while semi-reclining, bear down as if you were pushing something out of your vagina. Then, lubricate your little finger or a Q-Tip with K-Y jelly. While you are bearing down, place your little finger or the Q-Tip just barely into your vaginal opening. If you have never had anything inside your vagina before, you may find the sensation not only unfamiliar but possibly a little uncomfortable or scary. If it doesn't feel comfortable, don't push your finger or the Q-Tip in farther, but don't pull it out either. Just take a few deep breaths as you become accustomed to the new sensations. You should leave your finger or the Q-Tip inside your vagina for about five minutes in order to get used to the new feelings before continuing with the next step.

After five minutes, bear down again and slowly push the Q-Tip or finger in until it has been inserted one inch. Rest and relax by taking a few deep breaths if you need to, then continue to insert it until it has reached a depth of two inches. If you choose to stop here and continue the deeper insertion on a subsequent day, make certain that you begin again with the relaxation and deep breathing. Every time you explore your vagina you should relax first.

If you began with a Q-Tip, you should proceed to inserting your little finger before trying something larger. Once you can leave your little finger inserted two inches in your vagina for five minutes, you can continue by inserting objects of gradually increasing girth. For example, next time you might try your index finger. When you can put that in to its full length and leave it in for five minutes, advance to your middle finger. After that, you could insert an unscented tapered candle, which allows you to extend the thickness gradually; or you could peel a zucchini or carrot so that it is just a bit thicker than your finger.

Vegetables are good to use because you don't have to worry about breaking them or having them splinter inside you. Just make certain you thoroughly wash or peel them to prevent any allergic reaction to insecticides. Also, many women recommend leaving the vegetables out of the refrigerator so they will be at room temperature when they are used.

Each time you practice the exercise, use a phallic-shaped object of increased size. Remember to relax before insertion, lubricate the object, bear down while you insert it, and leave it in for five minutes to get familiar with the feelings it produces. Next, slowly move the object back and forth in your vagina until you grow accustomed to the sensations that are produced. When you have advanced to the point where you can insert an object the size of your partner's erect penis (a zucchini or small cucumber might do) and you can move it in and out comfortably, you are ready for the next step.

Be sure to take a few weeks to gradually increase the circumference of the object used. Don't try to jump too quickly ahead and use a much larger object than the preceding one. It is preferable to move ahead slowly rather than to try to do too much too soon and encounter some discomfort. A painful experience can cause a setback by reinstating the old vicious cycle of tensing up in anticipation of the pain.

If you experience pain at any point, merely discontinue the exercise for that day and begin the next day by using an object the size of the one that you used the time before you experienced the pain. Since that size object was comfortably inserted before, you should have no problem inserting it easily again. If you cannot do this, you are probably not sufficiently relaxed. In this case, you should spend more time relaxing before inserting the object into your vagina.

Once an object the size of your partner's penis can be inserted comfortably, assume a kneeling position and imagine your partner lying on his back between your legs. In this position, bear down and insert the object into your vagina. Remain on your knees for five minutes and simulate intercourse by moving the object in and out of your vagina. While you are doing this imagine that your partner is beneath you with his penis moving in and out of you.

The final step is to repeat the last exercise, but this time with your partner. Enjoy foreplay until you feel ready to begin intercourse. At this point, kneel over your partner as you imagined doing in the previous exercise and remember to take a few relaxing breaths. Take the time to remember one of your favorite relaxing scenes. Your partner should remain fairly passive during this time. You might want to stimulate his penis orally or manually if he does not have an erection. Once he has attained an erection, lubricate his penis, relax, bear down, and *you* insert his penis slowly. Your partner should not move. However, when you feel ready to do so, you can move slowly up and down on his penis. If you should feel at all uncomfortable, stop the motion and rest, but leave his penis inserted.

Before you practice with your partner the first time, it should be made clear that neither of you will try to have an orgasm with intercourse. At this time you only want to move very slowly to build up your confidence that intercourse can occur painlessly. This is why your partner should remain passive while you control the thrusting movements. By being in control, you can ensure that the thrusting movements will not be too forceful or in any way uncomfortable.

Once you can have intercourse without pain, you are ready to have your partner begin moving very gently while he remains on his back. Talk throughout the process so that your partner knows how slowly and carefully he should move—or if he should even move at all. In the beginning it will be up to you to control the pace of your progress. Your partner should be prepared to discontinue movement if you tell him you are uncomfortable. It is far better to have a few painless experiences of less than satisfying sex than to try to move ahead too quickly and experience pain again. Therefore, move very cautiously. Once you have repeated this step three or four times without pain, you can increase the vigor of the thrusting.

To prepare for having intercourse in a different position, insert a vegetable about the same size as your partner's penis while you assume the new position. After you can do this alone comfortably, use this new position with your partner. Each time you try a new position, be sure to remember to relax, lubricate your partner's penis well, and bear down while *you* insert his penis. He should not push. Go as slowly as you like and take as much time as you need.

## Pain with Deep Thrusting

A physician should always be consulted when pain is experienced with deep thrusting. To better enable your physician to diagnose your problem, note exactly where and when you feel the pain. Does it always occur in the same intercourse position? Does pain coincide with those times when you feel less aroused? Does it occur when your partner moves in a particular way? Is the pain experienced during a particular phase of your menstrual cycle?

There are some common causes for pain during deep thrusting when no medical problem exists. In certain intercourse positions, you may find that your partner's penis rams into your cervix or uterus. Or, if you attempt intercourse before you are sufficiently aroused, your uterus may not have lifted far enough up in the vaginal barrel to be completely out of the way.

When the penis rams the cervix (which is connected to the uterus), it causes a jarring of the broad ligaments that connect the uterus to the abdominal wall. Although the cervix itself has no nerve endings that would sense this kind of pain (it does have nerve endings that respond to pressure and stretching), the sudden stress placed on these ligaments can cause pain.

While the cervix does not respond to pain, the uterus does. And although the cervix generally buffers the uterus from the penis, some women find that in certain intercourse positions the underside of the uterus can be hit by the penis during deep thrusting. The painful position or positions involved depend upon the anatomical structure of the woman and her partner. Women who have a retroverted or a tipped uterus are somewhat more susceptible to this problem because of the way their uterus is tilted. In some cases, the pain stems from an ovary getting trapped between the back wall of the vagina and the uterus. The ovary is then compressed by the thrusting of the penis. The obvious solution for these problems is to abandon those intercourse positions that result in the experience of pain and to utilize those which do not cause discomfort. If you don't want to give up the uncomfortable positions entirely, limit their use to those times when you feel very highly aroused. If you still experience pain even in a very aroused state, you should entirely avoid the intercourse positions that cause it.

Finally, during certain times in the menstrual cycle, particularly during ovulation, many women seem to be more sensitive to deep thrusting. In some cases, an ovarian follicle cyst can form which results in pain sometimes on one side and sometimes on the other. The pain occurs from midcycle to the period and ceases with the menses when the cyst spontaneously disappears.

If you find that pain occurs periodically, keep a journal. Include in your journal not only those days during which you experience the pain, but those during which you do not. Detail the painful positions involved and any other factors you intuitively feel are important—the size of the meal you ate beforehand, whether you were angry at your partner, whether you really wanted to have sex, whether you were feeling highly aroused or not very much aroused when you became aware of the pain, etc. By ascertaining what causes the pain, you should be better able to avoid it.

There are some conditions where chronic pelvic pain becomes worse during intercourse and indicates a problem for which a physician should be consulted. Pain persisting on only one side and persisting after the period might be an indication of another type of ovarian cyst that requires medical attention. Occasionally, fibroid tumors in the uterus cause pain with intercourse. Persisting abdominal pain on one side accompanied by a late period and spotting may be symptoms of a tubal pregnancy. Painful intercourse in addition to painful periods are common signs of endometriosis, a condition in which cells from the uterine lining begin to grow in the pelvis, forming scar tissue between the uterus and the back wall of the vagina. And pain during intercourse results in approximately 25 percent of the cases where a tubal ligation was performed through the vagina as opposed to through the abdominal wall.[1]

Some women experience a severe cramping pain after their partner has ejaculated inside them. In these rare cases, the cramping can be a reaction to the seminal fluid deposited directly into the cervix. Seminal fluid is rich in a substance called prostaglandin which may cause violent muscle contractions of the smooth muscles of the uterus. This is the same substance that is produced when the uterine lining breaks down which causes menstrual cramping. Prostaglandin is also used to induce labor and abortion. Condoms and diaphragms will prevent this problem. Women who wish to conceive may find the woman-astride position helpful, or a physician can be consulted for one of the antiprostaglandin drugs which can be taken thirty to sixty minutes before intercourse to relieve the cramping.

## SEXUAL DYSFUNCTION

Women who experience painful sex that appears to have no physiological basis should obtain more than one medical opinion. However, if two or three examinations by different physicians fail to indicate any medical problem, it may be that sexual dissatisfaction is at the foundation of the difficulty. If the suggestions in this book are not helpful, it would probably be wise to consult a psychotherapist. For some women, experiencing pain may be the only way they feel they can say no to their partner's sexual advances. Unfortunately, this can create problems of its own. A considerate man who doesn't want to inflict pain upon his partner may completely stop pursuing sex. One man confided to me that he and his wife had not had any sexual interaction in ten years because he could not bear to cause her pain. Since then he had simply sublimated his sexual desires for her or had periodic extramarital affairs. He is quite sure she has no idea why they stopped having sex.

When pain is caused by emotional problems in a relationship, the problem really isn't a sexual one—even though the symptom may take on a sexual form. Lack of desire can also be caused by relationship issues. This will be discussed in the next section.

*Section V*

# SEXUAL INTEREST

## Chapter 11

# WHAT IS NORMAL SEXUAL DESIRE?

Since the advent of sex therapy by Masters and Johnson, a new sexual problem has become evident. An increasing number of couples are seeking sex therapy as a result of what they consider a lack of sexual desire or interest. Lack of sexual interest is generally considered by sex therapists to be the most difficult sexual problem to treat because its causes are numerous and complex.

Sexual drive or sexual appetite refers to a person's innate physiological desire for sex. The basic physiological need for sex will vary from person to person. In addition, environmental, emotional, and physical factors will affect an individual's desire for sex at any particular time. Learned sexual inhibition, severe trauma, and unresolved relationship issues can have a negative impact on sexual interest. Physical illness, various medications, stress, and fatigue can also decrease one's level of sexual desire. On the other hand, factors such as being in love, feeling relaxed, or being on vacation can increase one's desire for sex.

Since we do not need to have sex to survive, most physical and emotional dangers will diminish sexual desire. We usually allow sexual desire to emerge under safe circumstances and inhibit it in situations we believe to be unsafe. While this response is adaptive under dangerous circumstances, for example, during a rape or sexually sadistic interaction, it becomes maladaptive in situations we may imagine to be dangerous but which are actually quite safe. For instance, sometimes we respond to our past experiences of destructive relationships or strong parental admonitions against sex as if they were applicable to a current sexual relationship.

To further confuse matters, it is very difficult to define a normal level of sexual interest. There are tremendous differences between individuals. A sexual behavior study carried out in 1972 found that the average person has sex approximately two times per week, and the frequency generally decreases with age.[1]

However, it is important to remember that a national average is precisely that—an average. Millions have sex more frequently and millions have sex less frequently. What one person considers a lack of interest is quite normal interest for another person. Many factors account for differences in sexual desire, including partner availability and the relative importance of sexual activity in comparison to other activities. Furthermore, some people who consider themselves lacking in sexual interest are not disinterested at all. Their real problem may be unrealistically high expectations created by the media or a discrepancy between their interest and that of their partner.

## EXPECTATIONS AND THE MEDIA

Sex is so prevalent in the media that it makes some of us feel that if we are not making love more frequently than the national average, we are not only lacking in libido but missing out on one of the world's greatest thrills. Since few of us have ever talked openly or honestly with friends or co-workers about how often we want sex, we may be left believing that our sexual desire must be less than or greater than everyone else's—especially if our partner's sexual needs differ considerably from our own.

In reaction to the sexual repression of the past, the pendulum has swung in the opposite direction. Now the emphasis seems to be on spectacular sexual activity and responsiveness. Since it is possible to remain sexual throughout our lives, the media presents the coercive message that we "should" remain sexual until death. If our interest wanes in our later years we may take this as a negative statement about our vitality and our worth.

## DESIRE DISCREPANCIES[2]

Some women and men consider themselves lacking in sexual interest if they desire sex less often than their partner does or oversexed if they want sex more frequently than their partner. However, these differences usually represent a disparity in the partner's sexual interest rather than a problem on one partner's part. After all, it is unreasonable to expect two very different people to have exactly the same sex drives.

Sexual discrepancies are similar to other discrepancies in a relationship. Often one partner is an indoor person, while the other partner enjoys out-of-door activities. Or one partner likes opera while the other prefers jazz. Discrepancies in sexual interest can be a problem if the couple is unable to compromise on sexual activity in the same way they would compromise on other issues such as choosing a restaurant when one partner is in the mood for Chinese food and the other has a craving for pasta. In sex, as in other areas, each partner must learn to be sensitive to the other's needs and take them into consideration when making plans.

However, special problems arise when it comes to discrepancies in sexual interest. Whereas in other areas of interest one partner can go off with a friend for a few hours or even a weekend and enjoy a particular activity separately, this is more difficult to do with sex. Since most relationships are monogamous, having one's sexual needs met by a third party often poses a threat to the security of the primary relationship. Because of this, when one partner desires sex, there is more pressure on the less interested partner to increase the frequency of sexual activity than there would be if the issue were the number of ski weekends or evenings at the symphony.

Furthermore, in our society, the media and even sex therapists seem to hold a "more is better" attitude. As a result, the partner who desires sex less is frequently labeled abnormal. We rarely consider that the more sexually interested partner may be the one with the problem. However, for some people, sex serves a multitude of purposes beyond sharing intimate communication and expressing lusty feelings. It may act as a pick-me-up when they are depressed or a tranquilizer when they are anxious. For people who are unable to express their needs to be touched in nonsexual ways, who cannot ask for a hug or a shoulder to cry on, sex is sometimes the only outlet for a variety of emotions. Such people put high expectations on sex, asking it to fulfill diverse emotional needs. Since it is not possible for sex to meet all of one's needs, dissatisfaction can result.

Although every couple is bound to have slight discrepancies in sexual interest, serious problems arise when minor discrepancies grow into polarized positions. When other areas of the relationship are not going well, control over the frequency of sexual activity can become the battleground and obscure the real issues.

## The Persist/Resist Battle

Sometimes a small difference in sexual interest gets blown out of proportion. Before long, the partner with the greater interest in sex begins making sexual overtures at every available opportunity, thinking, "If I don't have sex now, who knows when I'll have another opportunity." The partner with the lesser interest reacts against the advance, thinking, "If we have sex now, it will just be one more time, so I'll try to avoid it." The more the one initiates, the more the other withdraws, and the more the second withdraws, the more the first initiates. Often neither person is considering whether he or she really feels like having sex at that moment. Both are reacting more to their partner's anticipated response than to their own needs.

After seven years of marriage and two children, this persist/resist sexual battle totally colored Rob and Natalie's relationship. Natalie was becoming less and less interested in sex as Rob made almost constant sexual overtures. It had reached the point where Rob had even begun making remarks about his wife's "frigidity" when they were out with friends, and Natalie had begun to avoid all social engagements. This in turn led to Rob's spending frequent evenings away from home socializing, which only increased Natalie's animosity. Initially, Natalie had enjoyed sex, though to a lesser degree than Rob. However, as Rob pressed for more frequent sex, Natalie grew to hate it. For Natalie and Rob, there was a lot more involved in the sexual problem than sex. Each was trying to prove strength and control over the other—Rob by pushing for sex, and Natalie by withholding it.

The persist/resist battle is a common manifestation of a power struggle in a couple's relationship.* Lack of interest in sex can be a powerful position. It can make the more interested partner feel not only deprived and powerless but unattractive and undesirable. At the same time, the more interested partner has an equally powerful position. He or she can make the less interested partner feel sexually inadequate and guilty for being so unresponsive. If the woman is the one more interested in sex, she may feel indecent or not worthy of respect, since, according to her role scripting, she is supposed to have better control of her baser emotions.

## Lack of Touching

Regardless of whether the man or the woman is more interested in sex, when the sexual advances of one partner are refused over a period of time, hurt feelings and withdrawal are the likely consequences. This withdrawal leads to a further reduction in the amount of both sexual and nonsexual touching. Physical avoidance becomes a means of protection. The more interested sexual partner thinks, "If I don't reach out, then I won't be rejected." The less interested partner also curtails any physical demonstration of affection for fear it might be interpreted as a sexual invitation or tease. The discrepancy in sexual interest can thus create a deficiency in physical contact which then reduces the intimacy and closeness experienced by the couple.

Touching is an important expression of intimacy. Walking arm-in-arm or holding hands maintains an affectionate bond. Stopping for a hug or a brief kiss on numerous occasions during the day or evening can keep positive and affectionate feelings high. Intimate nonsexual touching enhances a relationship as much as passionate sex. Without it, feelings of isolation and a breakdown of intimacy can result.

## Lack of Sexual Initiation

Sometimes when a discrepancy in sexual desire exists, the more interested partner complains that the less interested one never initi-

* See Chapter 2.

ates sex. The less interested partner, in turn, claims never to have a chance. In this case, the more interested partner might say, "If I didn't initiate, you'd never get around to it and I'd be sexually starved." The less interested one might reply, "You're already after me before I've even had time to realize that I want sex. And we have sex so often that I have barely enough time between sexual encounters to begin to build up some horniness."

Sometimes a woman who does not initiate sex is just reflecting her female training which dictates that a nice girl doesn't have a sex drive of her own—she just responds to the sexual needs of her partner. Such a woman may enjoy sex when she has it, but may have suppressed her sexual awareness to such a degree that the thought of being sexual simply never enters her mind without the prompting of her partner.

Marla and Fred had been married for six months and were still in the honeymoon stage of their relationship when they made an appointment to see me. The problem was that Marla never seemed interested in sex. After I talked with them for a while, it became clear that they had an excellent and loving relationship and could openly discuss just about anything. They had even talked about their sexual concerns at great length before deciding to see a sex therapist. They wanted to ensure that what was now a fairly minor problem did not grow into a nasty thorn in their relationship.

Marla, very quiet and demure, enjoyed sex considerably once she was involved in it, but felt no sexual drive of her own. She had never masturbated, and before she married she would regularly spend periods extending over many months without sex, unless she was involved in a very serious relationship. Fred, on the other hand, had a strong sexual drive. Even with regular marital sex he found that he enjoyed masturbating a few times a week. In fact, out of consideration for his new wife, Fred masturbated a bit more than he would have liked and had sex with Marla a bit less.

After we had spent a few sessions discussing the details of their sexual relationship, a pattern began to emerge. Sex was always enjoyable and satisfying when Fred initiated. Problems began, however, when Fred waited for Marla to make the first move. Marla knew he was waiting, so in addition to feeling awkward and embarrassed about initiating sex, she also felt pressured to act in a way that was unnatural for her. When Marla made it clear that she enjoyed him initiating sex, Fred was relieved of the feeling that he was constantly placing a sexual burden on her. This freed him to initiate sex more frequently, which was fine with him. He decided that he could adjust to being the sole initiator as long as he knew he wasn't making Marla uncomfortable. However, he did say that he would appreciate any attempts on Marla's part to initiate sex because it enhanced his feeling of being physically attractive and desirable. Marla agreed to practice the Sexual Assertiveness Exercise† and try to initiate sex more often, but welcomed the relief from feeling responsible for their sex life.

## DETERMINING WHAT IS NORMAL

As you observe your sexual relationship and review its history, do you feel that your difficulty is based on an initial difference in sexual interest which has been exacerbated over the years? Would you be happy with your level of sexual interest if you were assured it was perfectly normal, or would you like it to increase?

If you are perfectly content with your level of sexual activity and interest, but your partner is not—or vice versa—the problem may lie in a discrepancy of sexual interest rather than a lack of interest on the part of one of you. In this case, the rest of this chapter may be helpful. It suggests ways for each partner to attain the desired sexual frequency without depriving or coercing the other. If you feel that the problem runs deeper than a mere discrepancy, the next three chapters may address your situation more appropriately.

### The Sexual Interest Evaluation Exercise

To determine your general level of sexual interest, return to keeping records in your journal on a daily basis for at least one week. Carry around a pocket-sized notebook and write in it every time you feel any sexual excitement. Record the date, time of day, what caused you to feel turned on, and the strength of your desire on a scale of 0 to 10—where 0 denotes no excitement and 10 very high excitement. For example:

† See pages 176–77.

*Wednesday March 25*

  6 P.M.   Reading *Playboy* magazine—4

*Thursday March 26*

  8 A.M.   Seeing my husband get out of the shower nude—2
  2 P.M.   Flirting with the office manager—4
  4 P.M.   The physical exertion of jogging—6

Paying attention to your level of sexual arousal on a daily basis may help you to evaluate the frequency and intensity of your sexual interest as well as identify what generates sexual interest for you.

Unfortunately, what happens in most cases is that sexual feelings arise either when your partner is not present or when circumstances make it impossible to act on them. However, if you can ascertain what activities or circumstances *do* stimulate your sexual desire you are in a position to capitalize on these occurrences—or even plan them. Then you can purposefully simmer your sexual feelings‡ so that when you encounter your partner hours later you still feel turned on. Conscious attention, on the part of the less interested partner, to simmering sexual feelings whenever possible can greatly reduce a discrepancy in sexual interests.

## The Ban on Sex Exercise

It is very important for the more interested partner to stop initiating sex for a couple of weeks while the less interested partner learns to simmer sexual feelings. The purpose of this ban on sex is to give the less interested partner nothing to resist, thereby providing an opportunity for self-evaluation of sexual desire.

When this ban on sex is suggested, often both partners resist it. The more interested partner may fear the worst—total sexual deprivation. The less interested partner may experience tremendous guilt or fears of being abandoned. But if a ban on sex is *not* established, the less interested partner will keep avoiding sex in indirect ways. And if the stalemate continues, antagonism will build.

‡ See the Mental Setting, page 160.

Agreeing with your partner to put orgasm-oriented sex off for a few weeks will decrease the need to express power in a negative and depriving way. Meanwhile, through nonsexual touching, you can both concentrate on re-establishing the intimate feelings that were once an important part of your relationship.

When I first saw Janet and Jim, Janet almost never felt like having sex. When they counted up the number of times they had had intercourse in the preceding six months, they came up with a total of three. With tremendous prodding, Janet finally admitted that she didn't want sex, and didn't even want to have to explain why she didn't want sex. She just didn't want it. Jim was horrified. This confirmed his worst fears. However, he realized that, given the sexual frequency of the past six months, a ban on sex really wouldn't constitute a change. Only now, Janet was being honest instead of playing the game: "Maybe I will—if you just do or say the right things"—and then finding everything said or done lacking.

Actually, Janet's ability to say no clearly to Jim, and even more than that, to have him respect her position and agree not to push her, was of crucial importance. For the first time Janet felt as if she really did have some power in the relationship, and stopped expressing her power in a negative, depriving way. Once sex was banned, Janet felt like she had more control in her relationship, which had the effect of freeing her sensual feelings and bringing them to the fore—even though she did not act on these feelings right away.

## The Sexual Readiness Scale Exercise

While the ban on sex is in effect, the Sexual Readiness Scale Exercise[3] is an excellent way to break the persist/resist interaction. It is also useful in determining how great a difference in sexual interest actually exists.

The Sexual Readiness Scale begins at 0 and goes to 10. A zero designates that you have absolutely no sexual interest whatsoever; a 5 means that although you are turned on, you would be equally happy not having sex; while a 10 indicates that you are *very* turned on and are highly desirous of some form of sexual release. All of the other numbers are gradations in between, with those less than 5 indicating a preference not to have sex and numbers above 5 indicating a preference for sex.

Three times a day, every day for a week, trade your sexual readiness numbers. In the beginning, trade numbers at times of the day and under circumstances which will not lead to sex. The best times would be in the morning just before one or the other of you goes off to work, a few times during the day over the telephone, or just before sitting down to dinner. For example, when you call your partner up at three o'clock in the afternoon, you might be a 3 or possibly even a 6. He might be a 2. Just before dinner, he might be a 7 while you're a 5. The reason to share numbers outside of the situations which could develop into sex is to free each of you to focus on your real internal level of sexual desire, rather than reacting to your partner's level of interest instead.

What is often discovered when the Sexual Readiness Scale Exercise is carried out at times when sex is not possible is that the numbers aren't as far apart as expected. One person is not always a 10 and the other is not always a 0. This can be liberating for both people. It makes the less interested partner feel more normal to know that the other is sometimes a 2 or a 3. The more interested partner is relieved to learn that the less interested one can at times be a 5 or a 6.

After you have completed the Sexual Readiness Scale Exercise for a week, start using the scale during times when you could possibly have sex, although actual sexual involvement should still remain off limits. Share your readiness numbers when you wake up in the morning, before you go to sleep at night, after dinner, or at other appropriate times.

When you check out your numbers during potentially sexual times, note whether your numbers are generally higher or lower than they were when sexual interaction was impossible. If you find that you both have relatively consistent numbers over the two exercises, you probably have some realistic picture of just how different your levels of sexual interest are, and the degree of accommodation necessary to satisfy both of you.

If your numbers are a bit higher during the potential sexual encounter times, you are probably exhibiting an appropriate reaction to the circumstances. However, if you note that your numbers are lower when sex is possible, there are probably other issues besides innate sexual drives underlying this discrepancy. Anger expressed in the form of deprivation and rejection, fear of intimacy, or sexual inhibitions are some of the more common causes.

The Sexual Readiness Scale can also be employed if you find yourself confused about your partner's level of sexual interest. Misunderstandings often arise when sexual invitations are not made clearly. Most people don't want to risk being turned down, so if they suspect that their partner will not be responsive, they may try to initiate sex indirectly. On the other hand, some people are just more sexually expressive than others, not intending every sexual remark or gesture as an invitation for sex. If you are not sure whether your partner is just being affectionate or wants sex, ask to trade numbers.

Whenever Harry pushed against Gloria's body or kissed her passionately on the ear, she would worry that she was depriving him if she didn't want more. When Gloria asked for Harry's number at those times and realized that he was only a 4, she was free to respond in kind. She learned that Harry just liked to be sexually demonstrative with her, but was counting on the fact that she would say no most of the time. Now both of them greatly enjoy the pleasure of being seductive while knowing full well that most of the time it isn't likely to evolve into anything more.

Some couples learn the Sexual Readiness Scale and continue to use it years later as a way of letting their partner know that they are turned on. A sexual overture might consist of one person saying, "I'm a 10, what are you?" In this way, the communication is direct and the second partner can reply, "I'm a 7," or, "I'm only a 4 right now, how about waiting until later?" Or, "How about a massage and maybe my number will rise?"*

## The No Exercise

If your partner initiates sex when you are not in' the mood, it is important to be able to say no. Most of us find it difficult to refuse our partner's sexual invitation. Women have trouble saying no because we have been trained that accommodating sexually is our duty. We fear that if we don't participate we may lose our partner

---

* However, do not use the Sexual Readiness Scale to initiate sex during the period when you are ascertaining your levels of sexual interest as this will only confuse matters.

to another who is more willing. Men have difficulty saying no because they have learned that a "real man" should *always* be ready for sex when a willing partner is available.

As a consequence of these cultural sex role scripts, it is difficult for many of us to let our partner know when we are not in the mood for sex, and many of us acquiesce when we are not truly interested. Graciously pleasing your partner on occasion can be a very giving and loving gesture and is unlikely to create problems. However, when it is done frequently and without the motive of giving, it can build resentment and eventually make you averse to having sex. Unless we feel free to say no when our partner initiates sex and we are not interested, we will not feel truly free to respond positively at other times.

The inability to say no is rarely limited to the bedroom. Similar concerns about hurting a partner's feelings or losing love dissuade many of us from saying no to partners in nonsexual areas of our lives. When our partner asks if we'd like to go out to dinner, we might agree when we would actually prefer to eat at home. We might consent to go to the opera when it really bores us, or to have a relative we do not particularly care for live with us for a month. Again, compromising as a conscious and giving gesture is admirable so long as it is intentional and does not create resentment afterward.

The No Exercise has been designed to help people who have difficulty saying no both inside and outside of the bedroom. To complete the No Exercise, say no to three things each day you really don't want to do but would probably agree to if it weren't for this exercise. The no can be said to your partner, a friend, relative, employer, employee, or yourself. Don't try to say no, at least at first, to something that might seriously endanger your job or your relationship. Test the ground with smaller issues, and wait until after you have had more practice before saying no on significant matters. As you build your confidence you can go on to more anxiety-provoking situations. There is an art to saying no without offending the person making the request. This takes time to develop.

One woman who taught music would lend out her music books to her students. One student would always return the borrowed books in a disheveled state. As a result of the No Exercise, when the student requested a loan of another book, the woman politely told her that because of her treatment of the books in the past, she could no longer lend her others. Another woman refused to attend an annual football game which she not only detested going to, but at which she usually caught a cold. One woman informed her husband that he could not borrow her keys. In the past, he had more than once failed to return them, and she had found herself stranded at home unable to use the car.

Many women, although comfortable saying no under most circumstances, are unable to do so in one or two areas of their lives. For example, one woman had no trouble saying no to her children or her boss, but found that she almost never said no when her husband made a request. Another woman could say no to her husband out of the bedroom but not in it. And another woman found that she was able to say no to her husband with ease, but had tremendous difficulty saying no to her parents.

At times the No Exercise is more appropriately fulfilled by saying no to yourself. Many of us respond beyond reason to internal "shoulds" which govern our lives. For example, we may not be able to relax on Saturday until after we have cleaned the house. We may not allow ourselves to leave work until a certain goal has been met, even if it means working all night. These self-imposed "shoulds" can cause as much resentment as unquestioningly fulfilling the needs of others. Learning to say no to these internal "shoulds" can reduce our self-imposed level of stress and tension and, in the process, make us more available to sexual pleasure.

Remember, the exercise is to say no to things that you would normally agree to, but really don't want to do. Some people misunderstand this and think the exercise is to say no to things that they really want to do just to practice saying no. Enough things that you don't want to do will crop up each day so that you will not have to exercise your negative vote on things that you really do want to carry out.

Don't be surprised if, in the beginning, you miss an opportunity to say no to yourself or someone else. Being agreeable and always saying yes may be a well-developed habit that prevents you from recognizing your accommodating behavior until hours or days later. But don't let that discourage you. With practice, you will soon become aware of a missed opportunity to say no just after it has passed, and finally you will become aware of your feelings at the point of decision making.

To build awareness, note when you feel resentful or even just a bit angry. See if those feelings stem from having agreed to do something that you really didn't want to do. One woman found herself in a bad mood while on a dinner date. When she tried to figure out why, it finally occurred to her that she hadn't really wanted to go out with this man at all. For her, saying no and spending the evening alone, curled up with a good book, would have been a far better solution.

### FANTASY REHEARSAL

If you find that even after becoming aware of wanting to say no to something, you still say yes, practice the Fantasy Rehearsal Exercise.† Replay the incident in your mind, but this time imagine yourself saying no. Then imagine the reaction of the person who made the request. First imagine an angry response to your refusal, and fantasize your reaction and your reply. Then replay the scene with the person giving a less negative response. Finally, imagine a quite amicable acceptance of your no. Use the Fantasy Rehearsal Exercise to practice saying no to internal "shoulds" too. For example, imagine going to the beach while the dirty dishes sit in the sink.

Even after the Fantasy Rehearsal, actually carrying out the exercise is likely to be uncomfortable at first. But it does get easier with practice, and the freedom from resentment it provides is well worth the initial discomfort.

## ALTERNATIVES TO SEX

Once you are able to clearly say no to sex, you are free to substitute some other activity that might bring the two of you closer together. Instead of having sex right then you might say, "I would prefer a long walk holding hands." Or, "Let's sit on the couch and cuddle while we watch television together." You could use the Sexual Readiness Scale as a way of suggesting other activities. For example, you might say, "I'm a 2 for intercourse, but I'm an 8 for cuddling and a 9 for a massage."

† See pages 99–100.

The activities which take the place of sex cannot really be considered viable substitutes for sexual interaction, but they can be thought of as the next best thing, given the circumstances. They communicate that you still care and that you find your partner desirable.

In addition to nonsexual activities, there are some explicitly sexual activities that can accommodate both people without depriving the more interested partner or unduly coercing the less interested partner. One of them is to have a sexual encounter in which the more interested partner is the more active participant.

Mary would rarely say no to Dick when it came to sex, but sometimes she would warn him that she wasn't much in the mood, so if he wanted sex, he couldn't expect her to be passionate. By that she meant that she would be a loving companion, but *he* would have to be the assertive one. Dick understood that when Mary said no passion she often meant that she didn't want to expend the amount of energy necessary for an orgasm and that he shouldn't worry about her having one. He should just let go and have a good time. She knew that at some later date the roles would be reversed and she would have the favor returned.[4]

When one of you is turned on but the other is not or when you are both only somewhat turned on, you can use the Sexual Readiness Scale to make the final determination as to whether or not to have sex. One couple decided to have sex whenever their numbers totaled 10. So if one was a 7 and the other a 3, or even if both were 5s, they always made love.

Some women prefer to stimulate their partner orally rather than participate in intercourse when they are not particularly turned on. Some couples have creatively worked it out so that the more interested partner masturbates while the other participates by holding, hugging or kissing.

Couples who overcome the attitude that masturbation is a private, shameful activity and become comfortable stimulating themselves in their partner's presence find that self-stimulation is the single most effective equalizer when it comes to resolving disparities in sexual interest. Self-pleasuring in the presence of a partner allows the couple to feel close and to be intimate. Rather than one person being closeted off in a separate room seeking solitary release, the two people can interact lovingly together while the more interested person exerts the sexual energy and experiences the sexual release. In addition, some people get so turned on watching their partner masturbate, that they end up having sex after all.

If you find that you or your partner resists the exercises in this chapter, or that when you try them one of you forgets the ground rules, or the exercise ends up in a fight, or sexual intimacy is sabotaged in some other way, there is a good chance that more than a normal discrepancy of interest is at the foundation of your sexual problem. In this case, the lack of interest may be caused by relationship problems, individual psychological problems, a strong avoidance habit, or some other factors, all of which will be explored in the next chapter.

*Chapter 12*

# LACK OF SEXUAL INTEREST

While a few women have never in their lives desired sex, the majority of women who suffer from lack of sexual desire have been turned on in the past and have either gradually or suddenly lost their interest in sex. Most commonly, women who generally experience medium to high levels of sexual interest periodically find themselves going through weeks or months when they have no desire.

## CHRONIC LACK OF INTEREST

Chronic and pervasive lack of sexual desire is somewhat rare and usually has very deep roots. A woman who has experienced almost no sexual desire in her adult life was probably traumatized in relation to sex as a child. Either sexual abuse or extremely repressive sexual conditioning is the likely cause.

### Negative Sex Training

Extremely negative parental or religious training about the evils of sex can thoroughly inhibit one's sexual desire as an adult. This is particularly noticeable among those of us who were *very good* as children and tried hard to do what was expected of us. When we were unable to suppress normal childhood or adolescent feelings of sexual arousal or interest, we may have felt sinful and bad. In an attempt to rectify this conflict and please our mothers and fathers or prove we were pure enough to deserve God's love, many of us completely suppressed our sexual feelings.

## Incestuous Experiences

If you had an incestuous experience as a child or adolescent, you may have repressed all of your sexual feelings in an attempt to forget the traumatic event. All children have sexual feelings. When a young girl has a sexual relationship with a father, brother, or other close relative, the experience may be pleasurable, while at the same time she may sense that it is somehow wrong. This can be very confusing. If the sexual relationship is with her father, she may feel particularly special and loved by her father and at the same time guilty and worried about losing the love of her mother —which can create tremendous anxiety. One way to cope with this situation is to cut off all sexual feelings. If you had such an experience, you may have learned to repress your feelings of sexual enjoyment to free yourself from any responsibility or guilt for instigating the sexual activity. Later in life your feelings may remain repressed as a way to avoid being sexually attractive to others and thus reawakening the conflict you experienced as a child.

## Molestation/Rape

A rape or sexual molestation can also be responsible for the loss of sexual interest. Sometimes, for months or even years, the fear associated with the rape or molestation is triggered whenever the woman encounters a sexual or potentially sexual situation.

Undoing extreme sexual repression or a severe sexual trauma will not be an easy task. Uncovering the deeply hidden sexual feelings will take time and should be approached slowly. In this situation, it may be essential to work with a competent psychotherapist. It also helps to have an understanding partner who can patiently support you during this time.

## SPORADIC SEXUAL DESIRE

There are generally good reasons why you find yourself interested in sex on some occasions and not on others. Sporadic sexual interest, like inconsistent orgasmic response, can be ameliorated once the pattern has been tracked down. To determine the conditions that elicit sexual desire and those that block it for you, carry out the Sexual Interest Evaluation Exercise* described in the last chapter.

Pay particularly close attention to those occasions when you feel interested in sex. Many people expend most of their energy scrutinizing the incidents they consider failures—those times when they aren't turned on. But you can often learn more about your sexual requirements by examining the times when you *are* turned on.

When you don't desire sex, and your relationship with your partner is going well, stress, fatigue, boredom, or hormonal swings are some of the likely causes.

### Stress and Fatigue

Work stress is one of the major causes of dampened sexual interest. We have known for years that many physicians and business executives often have little energy left over after work to devote to sex. Now we are becoming aware that stress and fatigue also drain the sexual interest of mothers of small children, women who are competing in the male work force, and women who, as a result of work or family stress, are so chronically fatigued and emotionally depleted that they have no energy left for sex. These people find that when they get away from their normally stress-filled lives their interest in sex begins to resurface. If you find that your sexual interest grows whenever you leave your responsibilities and head off on a vacation, stress or fatigue may be at the root of your problem.

* See pages 217–18.

## Hormonal or Emotional Swings

Does your level of sexual interest fluctuate with the course of your menstrual cycle? Hormonal swings and water retention can have their effect on sexual desire for some women who are particularly sensitive to these changes.

Many women become less interested in sex as they approach the point when they ovulate. Others find their sexual desire diminishing over the period between ovulation and their menses. Birth-control pills can also have an effect on sexual libido. One woman said she felt like a new person after she stopped taking birth-control pills. Although sex had been hassle-free and secure from pregnancy, she felt that her sexual desire had been asleep during the entire time she was taking the pill. Sometimes estrogen deficiencies or progesterone excesses develop after months or even years of taking birth-control pills. Consequently, birth-control pills can be at the root of your current sexual disinterest even if you had been taking them for a period of time before the problem began.

## Boredom

Do you find that the only time you are interested in sex is when you are in what could be called an unusual situation? For example, is your sexual interest heightened when you are out hiking and there is the possibility of being caught if you make love? Or just after seeing a pornographic movie? Or after flirting earlier in the day with a person other than your partner? If so, you might ask yourself if your sexual relationship with your partner is varied enough to maintain your sexual interest.

Some women report that their interest in sex was very high at the beginning of their relationship, and it began to wane after the first year or two. The initial stages of a relationship are filled with the excitement and surprise of getting to know each other which make the sex particularly interesting. However, once you grow familiar with each other, the spontaneity and variety can disappear. Along with the familiarity and comfort, boredom sometimes sets in. After a period of years together, sex can become routine. Even your favorite meal would get boring if you ate it night after night.

# WOMEN WHO ARE NO LONGER INTERESTED IN SEX

If at some point in your life you were turned on to sex, but now have no sexual interest, the severity of the problem will depend somewhat on how long it has existed. Longer standing problems will be more difficult to reverse than recent ones. Also, cases where some degree of sexual interest remains are, in general, more easily treated than those where all sexual feelings have been suppressed.

If you have lost your sexual interest, you can, through some careful detective work, determine the probable cause. To do this, carry out the Sleuthing Exercise† but in regard to lack of interest rather than lack of orgasm. Remember the last times you had a real desire for sex. It might help if you recalled the different places you lived. Imagining yourself in specific surroundings might help you to date when your sexual interest began to decrease or when it stopped altogether. If your lack of interest developed gradually and was accompanied by a history of unsatisfying sex, painful sex, or serious problems in your relationship—these factors may be the cause. If your lack of interest developed suddenly, over the span of a few weeks or a couple of months, and if that time period coincided with some emotional trauma, it is possible that this trauma caused your diminished interest in sex.

## Emotional Trauma

Common traumatic events include extramarital affairs and physical or emotional abandonment by a partner in time of need. For example, Claudia discovered through a friend that her husband had been having an affair. Although she vented her anger and hurt and was quite assured that her husband was no longer involved with the other woman, Claudia remained distant and sexually uninterested. The wound Claudia experienced took almost a year to heal.

Other traumas which can negatively affect sexual interest include, but are not limited to, the birth of a child, the loss of a job, a

† See pages 118–22.

mastectomy, hysterectomy, or the death or illness of a parent, child, sibling, or close friend. Unanticipated marital complications or even the common stresses associated with getting married can cause the loss of sexual interest. Role expectations can be overwhelming and can interfere with sexual desire as early as the wedding night.

Margerie lost interest in sex as a result of her hysterectomy. She had always thought that once a woman reached menopause, she was finished with sex. Margerie's premature encounter with menopause, resulting from the removal of her uterus and ovaries, led her to believe that her sex life was over. This belief, coupled with the fact that she developed extensive medical complications which made sex painful, convinced her that she was no longer an attractive or sexual woman. It wasn't until her distraught husband, who refused to accept such a premature and abrupt ending to their sexual life together, sought therapy, that Margerie had the opportunity to question some of the assumptions she held.

Ann and her husband Paul had been very sexually active during their courtship. However, soon after their wedding day, Ann's interest in sex began to wane. She experienced many changes in her life as a result of marrying Paul, but the one that created the major problem was becoming an instant mother to Paul's two teenagers. It seemed that after the marriage she and Paul were constantly arguing about how the children should be reared. Paul wanted to maintain things as they had always been, and Ann felt she spotted problems that needed to be addressed. Ann also felt Paul sided with the children against her in family arguments. She felt overburdened and unsupported, and her interest in sex decreased until they sought therapy and ironed out some of the problems centering around the children.

## Relationship Problems

The most common cause of lack of sexual interest stems from problems with nonsexual aspects of a relationship. If your sexual interest increases in relation to people other than your partner while it decreases or even drops off completely toward your partner, a problem in the rest of your relationship is a likely cause. Partners who have serious relationship struggles and are constantly undermining and blaming each other cannot expect to feel like making love very often. If years' worth of dissatisfaction and anger have been stored up, it should come as no surprise that you may no longer joyously anticipate the next opportunity to jump into bed.

## RELATIONSHIP DISSATISFACTION

The way that women are scripted in this culture has a great deal to do with why many of us express our negative feelings by withholding sex. We have learned that we should never express unpleasant emotions such as anger or dissatisfaction. Therefore, when we are angry or dissatisfied, we express our feelings indirectly. A lack of sexual interest can be an indirect expression of dissatisfaction with something other than sex. Unless these negative feelings can be voiced more directly, they will continue to block sexual interest. For example, Beth was angry that her husband's parents had overstayed their expected visit by one week. Rather than say anything directly, she silently boiled. When her in-laws finally left and her husband arranged an intimate dinner to celebrate, she found she could not enjoy herself. When he initiated sex later in the evening, she refused. Her unexpressed feelings of anger at her husband for not asking his parents to leave prevented her from being able to joyfully celebrate when they finally did leave.

Sex is one of the ways women in this culture can experience power or control over their lives. Men use success to get what they want; women often use sex. If we see sex as a tool to catch a man or to reward him if he is good to us, then we may also see it as something to withhold when he is inconsiderate or when we're angry at him.

All relationships have ups and downs. Think about whether the ups in your relationship in any way coincide with sex being good, and the downs with times when it isn't. Angela realized that if her partner helped her with their child, with dinner, or with cleaning up afterward, she was more likely to be interested in sex and to have an orgasm when they made love later that evening. When she felt resentful because he was being selfish and she was left with all the work, her sexual desire vanished. There is no relationship that is problem-free. The question is whether the problems experienced in your relationship are at the root of your lack of sexual desire.

Sometimes a lack of interest in sex can be a way to justify terminating an otherwise intolerable relationship. In such cases, the difficulty most likely began long before the lack of sex precipitated the breakup.

## OPTIMAL DISTANCE

Too much distance or too much closeness can create problems in an intimate relationship. The optimal degree of closeness varies from person to person and even from day to day. Lack of interest in sex is sometimes used to create distance when a relationship gets overwhelmingly close. Or it can result from the opposite—not spending enough time together to really connect intimately.

If you are spending too much time together and find that you are getting on each other's nerves, you may want to engineer separate activities; plan a day or weekend apart. Many of us grew up with the idea that if you really loved your mate, you would want to spend every available minute together. But this is not realistic for most people. Too much time together can be suffocating, even in a very intimate and loving relationship. Time apart can revitalize a relationship.

If, on the other hand, you are not together enough, you could set aside a few days or a weekend to spend alone together, possibly away from home. A romantic period of time spent free from the usual cares and crises of daily life can do much to renew and rekindle the spark in a sexual relationship.

## EXTRAMARITAL AFFAIRS

Sometimes an affair is used to gain a partner's attention when certain needs are not being fulfilled at home. If this is your situation and you are unable to communicate your needs directly or your partner is unavailable to hear them, you may find yourself losing interest in sex with your partner and looking for someone else to make you feel loved and desirable.

Donna and Steve came to sex therapy after Steve learned about Donna's affair with her golf instructor. Although he was still in love with his wife, Steve could find no satisfactory way of venting his anger. He was particularly upset because during the months of her affair and prior to that time, Donna had been seemingly disinterested in sex and he had tried to be considerate of her feelings. When he discovered that she had been "screwing around" instead, he felt deceived.

Donna said that for the previous year and a half she had been trying to tell Steve that she required more of his time and attention, but his important executive position seemed to leave little room for her. When Steve recalled the period during which the problems had begun, he realized that he hadn't responded to what Donna had said she needed. He figured that if he made a lot of money, she would be happy. But Donna didn't want money, she wanted Steve. Steve wasn't delighted about the method Donna used to make her point, but he was devoted to her and was grateful to find out about the affair in its early stages, rather than after irreparable damage had been done.

Sometimes an unconscious avoidance of sex is a way to justify an affair when relationship dissatisfaction is not sufficient grounds but lack of sexual intimacy is.

In other cases, sexual disinterest does not occur until after an outside affair has ended and strong feelings of guilt surface. For some women, the burden of guilt is so heavy that only suffering through their partner's anger and retribution will assuage it. Their lack of interest in sex gains their partner's attention and lets them unburden themselves.

## FEAR OF INTIMACY

Some women turn off sexually out of a fear of the intimacy generated by the sexual relationship. This may be true for you if you are highly interested in sex at the beginning of a relationship, but find your interest waning as you become more seriously involved. A fear of excessive dependence, rejection or abandonment as the relationship grows more committed can lead to lack of sexual interest. Avoiding sex whenever possible is one way to maintain a safe level of intimacy and independence. This response, often unconscious, can create distance in the relationship and prevent you from feeling emotionally overwhelmed.

Sometimes the fear of intimacy is a realistic response to a situation where a partner's commitment cannot be trusted, and sometimes it is a neurotic response where the fears are totally unfounded.

A realistic fear might arise when you sense that a problem exists but your partner denies it. For example, when I interviewed Alex and Jody together, Alex professed undying love and affection for Jody. They had wanted to get married for a number of months, but her sexual disinterest had kept them from finally tying the knot. Jody wanted to marry Alex, but she had a nagging sense that he really didn't want to marry her. In all of their discussions he claimed only the opposite.

When I interviewed Alex separately, he admitted that he had tremendous reservations about marriage. Although he loved Jody, he was worried that he would feel tied down and would grow to resent the restrictions that marriage might impose. When I asked why he didn't discuss his reservations with Jody, he replied that he was worried that his ambivalence might cause her to withdraw, and he was afraid he would lose her. Because Alex did not voice his fears, Jody was left with an uncomfortable feeling that something was wrong, though she couldn't put her finger on it. This created distrust, which caused her to hold back sexually.

When Alex was finally able to confess his fears, Jody was relieved. She herself had similar concerns. Now that she could pinpoint the cause of her discomfort, she felt more trusting of Alex and no longer felt the need to withhold sexually. She was confident that he would eventually come to terms with his concern over his loss of freedom.

A neurotic reaction might be exemplified by finding fault with every suitor—for being too short, too tall, too compulsive, too selfish, etc.—or by dating only people who are alcoholic, abusive or otherwise self-defeating. An excessively cautious response to becoming involved in a relationship might stem from a past relationship where you were deceived or rejected. In both of these cases, the fear of intimacy must be overcome in order to achieve a fulfilling relationship.

Making the distinction between a realistic fear of intimacy and an unfounded one is not a simple task. One method is to evaluate patterns in your past intimate relationships. If you have never had a really intimate relationship and you have a pattern of being sexually turned on by partners who are not viable potential mates, and of being turned off by those who would be most appropriate and realistic choices, there is a good chance you are avoiding intimacy.

## LACK OF CHEMISTRY

There are some cases, however, where a close and satisfying intimate relationship exists, but the woman has no strong sexual attraction to her partner and never has had any—even in the early stages of their courtship or marriage. If this is the case, you may find that outside of sex, you have a perfect relationship. You may share the same interests, activities, and friends. You may have totally compatible lifestyles, never fight, and consider yourselves the closest of friends. However, if your sexual interest has *never* been there with this particular partner, and yet has existed in the past with other partners, the problem may lie in a basic lack of physical attraction.

There seems to be some sort of undefinable chemistry that occurs between two people which has to do with the smell, body type, mannerisms, or other elusive characteristics. If that basic chemical attraction is absent, for whatever reasons, the sexual passion can be missing also. If the magic was once there, even for a short period of time early on in the relationship, it is possible to rekindle the feelings once the reasons for the disinterest are identified and eliminated. However, if the passion was *never* there, the prognosis for being able to create lusty feelings is not good.

## SEXUAL DISSATISFACTION

If you have been sexually attracted to your partner, but your sexual experiences together have not been sexually satisfying, this may be the cause of your lack of interest. Think about how you felt about your sexual relationship before you began losing interest. Was sex good for you or did you feel dissatisfied and frustrated? Avoidance is the natural response to an unsatisfying activity. After a long period of negative experiences, you may have begun to anticipate feeling frustrated and, in an attempt to minimize the physical frustration, cut back on your feelings of arousal. The less turned on you felt during sex, the less frustrated you were likely to be in the end. Soon, you may have learned to cut off your sexual feelings altogether.

## Miscellaneous Causes of Lack of Sexual Interest

There are some fears, beliefs, and medical reasons for lack of sexual interest that have not yet been covered.

### PAIN

Like sexual dissatisfaction, painful intercourse can greatly inhibit sexual feelings. If you have had a period of painful sex, you may have learned to avoid the painful experience. One way of doing this is to suppress your sexual interest.‡

### ILLNESS

Most illnesses, disabilities, depressions and other severe psychological conditions have a negative effect on a couple's sexuality. If the illness is transitory, as in the case of flu or a broken leg, the effect on the sexual relationship may be minimal. However, if you or your partner have had a serious illness or disability which has lasted for a protracted period of time, it will almost assuredly lower your sexual frequency and sexual satisfaction. Even after the pain has been relieved, or the illness cured, you may not regain the level of sexual activity experienced prior to the onset of the medical condition without some concerted effort on both your parts.

### MEDICATIONS

Many people don't realize that prescription and nonprescription drugs can affect their sexual interest. Often it is impossible to predict a particular drug's effect on an individual. The same drug may affect one person adversely and another not at all.

Whenever drugs produce undesirable side effects, a competent physician should be consulted. Don't just stop taking a drug that is necessary to your health because you don't like the way it affects your sexual interest or performance. If you discuss the problem with a sympathetic doctor, you might find that you can switch drugs, alter the dosage, or in some cases increase daily exercise or reduce salt intake as a way of ameliorating some of the negative effects.

‡ Chapter 10 is devoted to problems associated with painful intercourse.

## FEAR OF PREGNANCY

Lack of sexual desire is an understandable solution to the fear of becoming a parent, the pain of childbirth, or the possibility of having to get an abortion. If you don't have intercourse, you won't get pregnant. If this is the case for you, your sexual interest is likely to revive once you begin taking birth-control pills or your partner uses condoms to supplement your foam or diaphragm. Keeping a temperature chart or learning the signs of ovulation so that intercourse can be skipped during the most fertile period may also help to ease your fears.

## AGING

A common myth that many women believe is that after menopause a woman is no longer sexually vital, and that older women who are sexually interested and active are undignified. And so, when menopause arrives, many women see themselves as sexually empty or undesirable. This belief can create a problem for women who want to continue being sexual.

On the other hand, a woman who has never enjoyed sex may welcome the change of life as a way to legitimize her lack of sexual interest. Menopause can resolve a long-standing problem by finally providing justification for not having sex.

## FEAR OF SUCCESS AND PLEASURE

Some people believe that if they are too successful or experience too much pleasure in life, they will be punished. If you regard pleasure and success as evil and sinful, and laud suffering as holy and worthy of praise, you may be minimizing your sexual enjoyment or sexual activity in order to escape the imagined consequences.

## A Working Solution

Lack of sexual interest may not be a problem at all, but rather an attempted solution for another problem. Lack of sexual interest may be an appropriate response when there is no suitable sexual partner available. Many women find that when they are not in a relationship, they have very little sexual interest. If this is true for you, celibacy can hardly be considered a pathological response. If anything, it seems to be a mature and responsible reaction. Realistic fears of abandonment or physical harm, or the deepening of a dead-end relationship (for example, with a married man) may also engender an appropriate reaction of limited sexual desire.

Not being turned on sexually could also be a way of protecting your partner. Women whose male partners have erection problems, ejaculate rapidly, or do not ejaculate at all often turn off their sexual interest as a way of preventing their partner from having to face his sexual difficulties.

To determine if your lack of sexual interest has any positive benefits, you might take a moment to consider what negative results might ensue were you to be more turned on to sex. If you decide to make a change, it is important not to throw out the baby with the bath water. What could your lack of sexual interest be protecting you from? If lack of sexual desire is protecting you from something worse, it may be advisable to find another way of resolving the underlying problem before you risk being more sexually interested.

Lack of interest in sex is generally one of the most difficult sexual problems to solve because it can be rooted in so many different and complex issues. The cause of the problem must be understood before the appropriate steps toward a solution can be taken. While some of the causes call for straightforward solutions, for example, doubling up on contraception or changing medications which diminish sex drive, others require the resolution of more serious problems, such as workaholism, fear of intimacy, or marital strife.

Whether or not relationship problems are causing your sexual disinterest, the absence of sexual activity will itself often produce a strain on your ability to relate to your partner. There are very few relationships that remain unaffected by a lack of sexual intimacy. Consequently, it is important that the estrangement created by the sexual disinterest be reversed. There are many ways to do this and we are now ready to discuss a number of them.

*Chapter 13*

# RECONNECTING

In order to pick the best approach for reconnecting with your partner, it is important to determine whether lack of sexual interest is the result of a current and possibly chronic situation, or past circumstances that are no longer relevant. Unfortunately, problems involving a lack of desire can be so amorphous that it may be difficult to know if sexual lethargy is a leftover habit or a response to a difficulty that is still very much alive. Take a moment to ask yourself if you expect you will ever again desire sex with your partner. If your answer to the question is no, you might want to reassess your relationship or seek professional guidance. You may feel your problems are so insurmountable that tackling them on your own would be too difficult. If your answer is yes, ask yourself what would have to change for you to want to have sex with your partner again. If you are aware of what has to change, you can probably best handle the situation by setting up a period of uninterrupted time to discuss your feelings with your partner.\*
You may have practical concerns such as wanting your partner to bathe before sex, or handle you more gently, or not persist sexually when you are clearly preoccupied with other matters. Once

_____

\* Read the Active Listening Exercise on pages 247–50 before carrying out this discussion.

you discuss these issues and agree on ways to deal with them, you may find yourself ready for sex again.

If the problem seems to stem from a breakdown of communication, broken trust, lack of consideration, past hurts, or stored-up resentment, it would be unwise to jump immediately into increased physical contact. Anger, mistrust, or feelings of being a powerless victim may be blocking feelings of sexual warmth and tenderness. In these situations it would be best to begin with the exercises in this chapter aimed at improving communication and restoring loving feelings.

If you have basically good communication and positive feelings toward each other, the lack of sexual activity may be a remnant of some past problem which has since been resolved—an old extramarital affair, past feuds about child rearing, an illness, a power struggle that has since been worked out. Or it is possible that in response to an abundance of work and family pressures, sex has been placed on a back burner while other tasks are attended to. In these cases, the reduced level of sexual activity may be a habit that has developed over time, and the exercises later in this chapter on creating the mood and breaking the avoidance habit may prove to be most useful.†

Use your common sense to determine which exercises to do. All the exercises can work regardless of whether a man or woman is lacking in sexual interest. As with other problems covered in this book, the exercises you choose should be adapted to your unique situation. Do not hesitate to alter an exercise. The more you consider what is best for you, the more success you will experience. My sex-therapy clients always formulate their own homework assignments. With the help of a few suggestions and a little thought, it is possible to design an unending variety of approaches to solving a problem. The best one is the one that suits your needs. If an exercise doesn't facilitate matters, scrap the attempt and begin again. Each exercise is only an experiment. When an exercise fails to elicit the desired response, valuable information can still be gained about what *doesn't* work.

No one exercise is likely to be a panacea. It will probably take

† If the factors inhibiting your sexual interest are more complex, for example entailing physical abuse, or excessive drug or alcohol consumption, you might better benefit from professional counseling.

a number of exercises repeated over a period of time before you see any lasting difference in your sexual interest. Even once improvement has been made, you can expect to backslide. This is all part of the process: two steps forward, one step back. So don't be discouraged if this part of the journey has numerous ups and downs.

## THE MOTIVATION PROBLEM

Lack of motivation is the primary difficulty encountered when trying to increase sexual interest. If you're not particularly interested in sex, it is hard to gather the motivation to do things that would *develop* your sexual interest. You may find it difficult to consistently set aside time for the exercises when you would rather be doing just about anything else. This can result in making a few superficial attempts and then abandoning the task altogether.

Similarly, if you wanted to learn how to ski so you could join your partner in his favorite activity, you would have to be willing to go through the initial awkwardness and resistance that accompanies learning anything new. However, if you hate cold weather and strenuous physical exercise, your initial motivation may not carry you through the difficult learning period to the point where you experience the thrill and joy of skiing down the mountain.

If you decide that you really *do* want to increase your level of sexual interest, be sure that you are doing it for the right reasons. You are very unlikely to succeed if you are motivated solely by the desire to please your partner. If you anticipate no direct benefit to yourself, you are apt to sabotage the process early on, even if you have the best of intentions. However, if you really miss being interested in sex and experiencing the sexual part of your intimate relationship with your partner, you are far more likely to expend the necessary time and energy to bring about a change.

## STORED ANGER AND LACK OF COMMUNICATION

If you have decided that anger and communication problems are at least partially responsible for your lack of sexual desire, you are ready to engage in a series of exercises designed to improve communication, work through past angers, and restore a more joyful and caring attitude toward your partner. These exercises will be most effective for couples who have been together for a short period of time or for whom the problem is fairly recent. They may not be sufficient to reverse strong anger and resentment that has been seething for years.

The necessary ingredient for repairing a troubled relationship is a commitment on the part of both people. Both of you must be willing to make the first steps toward change. Both of you will have to take risks that will make you vulnerable to each other. If you each wait for the other to change first, no progress can be made.

If one of you has a foot out the door, or is waiting for the outcome of the exercises to determine whether you will remain together, you are facing an uphill struggle. If your relationship problems have existed for a long time, and especially if you find yourself contemplating a separation if your sexual relationship is not quickly repaired, it may be difficult for you to resolve the problem without the aid of a therapist. Although many of us can be objective and helpful at solving the problems of others, we often lose perspective when we try to do the same for ourselves. All too often we see only our own point of view and forget that there are other equally valid perspectives on a situation. It is like sitting across from your partner holding a magazine out in front of you so that you are looking at the front cover of the magazine while your partner is looking at the back cover. With each of you looking at only one side, you could argue all day long about what is really on the cover of the magazine. Although you are both looking at the same magazine, your perspectives are quite different. Neither of you could convince the other that one view is correct.

We each have our own perspective and we are each right to a certain degree. The goal of a satisfying relationship, however, is not to win by making our partner lose, but rather to work out problems so that both of us are satisfied. This is not always easy, or even possible under certain circumstances. But it is *more* possible if both people recognize it as the goal.

Anger is bound to occur in any intimate relationship. If there is good there is bad, if there is right there is wrong, and if there is love in a relationship there will be anger. In fact, often the people we feel the strongest anger toward are those we love the most. For they are the people to whom we are the most vulnerable and who can wound us most deeply. Rather than attempting the impossible task of eliminating all anger, we are better off learning to express our anger so that it does not accumulate and in the end displace the love.

To repair a relationship, the stored-up anger must first be dissipated. Then, communication skills must be sharpened so that misunderstandings are prevented or at least kept to a minimum. Finally, good feelings must be restored. Sometimes removing the anger is sufficient, but more often instigating special caring activities is also necessary before the stage can be set for resuming fulfilling sex. Since a sexual problem generally creates anger and frustration for both people, it is necessary that both of you willingly carry out the exercises in this chapter. If you practice the exercises together, you will also develop new skills that you can utilize should other problems arise in the future. For the best results, please read and discuss together the exercises in this section before trying any of them out.

## The Past Hurts Exercise

This exercise has been adapted from an exercise developed by George Bach[1] to help couples express past hurts that accumulate over the years. Thoughtless actions or words, whether intentional or unintentional, can deeply injure one's partner, forming wounds that fester and never quite heal. If a similar hurt is reinflicted on this already tender area, the wound may reopen. For example, when Lydia found out that her husband, Andrew, had been having an affair, she was devastated. Andrew could find no way to relieve her pain so he finally withdrew into himself. Lydia desperately needed contact with him but, at the same time, couldn't forgive him. Even after a year, Lydia continued to be suspicious. Andrew could never understand why they had a fight every time he worked late or had to go away on a business trip. Not discussing the issue and pretending it didn't exist, because both would have preferred that it had never happened, only served to increase Lydia's suspicion.

When they came for therapy, I had each of them make a list of

246    RECONNECTING

hurts the other had perpetrated which still aroused feelings of anger
and pain. It didn't matter how long ago the hurt had occurred, or
how ridiculous it seemed to be still upset by it.

As Lydia read her list, Andrew listened carefully but was not
allowed to reply. When she had completed her list, Andrew began
reading his and Lydia listened. Lydia was then instructed to read
her list again, this time explaining why she was hurt by each of
the items she mentioned: how she had been embarrassed when he
bawled her out in public, how she felt betrayed when he had the
affair, how humiliated she was to learn about the affair from a
friend, and so forth. Andrew then explained how abandoned he
felt when she went away on a trip he begged her not to go on, how
deprived he felt when she wouldn't have sex with him for two
months following the affair, and how worthless he felt when she
stayed at her sister's house for two days and wouldn't talk to him
after a particular fight.

Following this discussion, Lydia began to understand that Andrew
was particularly sensitive to being abandoned. Andrew learned that
Lydia was especially sensitive to being embarrassed in front of
other people. With this newfound knowledge, the two were able to
be more sensitive to the vulnerabilities of their partner and avoid
the kinds of wounds that would be long lasting. They also discussed how they could let go of the past hurts.

To carry out this Past Hurts Exercise yourself, repeat the process
engaged in by Lydia and Andrew. Separately, formulate a list of all
the past hurts each of you still carry around with you. In turn,
share the complete list, one item at a time, without interruption
or comment from the listener. Then go over each item on the list
a second time, this time emphasizing the aspect of the incident that
was particularly painful. See if a pattern develops that can help
delineate your particular areas of vulnerability. Then talk together
about which of the past hurts you are willing to give up or trade,
or what conditions must be met to have sex despite the negative
feelings.

For example, on a few of the items, Lydia and Andrew made a
deal. Lydia would forget the public criticism in trade for Andrew's
dropping the issue of the solo trip. On other subjects they agreed
on a process for future protection. For example, every time Andrew

worked late or went away on business he would reassure Lydia that he was not having an affair and would make a special effort to call her more often. They also chose not to resolve some of the items at that time.

Sometimes a hurt cannot be undone. An affair, for example, happened. It cannot be erased and neither can the bad feelings. Playing the "if only" game is a sure way to lose—if only he hadn't had an affair, if only he hadn't said it takes me too long to have an orgasm, if only I hadn't been raped, if only he hadn't said he liked slim women, etc. There is no "if only"; there is only what is, no matter how disagreeable it may be. If feelings cannot be changed, there are only three options remaining: end the relationship, continue the current pattern of suffering (retaliation or perhaps gloating), or find a way to make sex better even though the hurt feelings remain. When bad feelings cannot be eliminated or diminished, the next best thing is to accept them and get on with life.

Given that what happened happened, what can be done to enable you to enjoy sex? Can you take an hour once a week to ventilate your hurt feelings while maintaining an active sex life? Would you get satisfaction out of making your partner your sexual slave, living just to meet each and every one of your sexual demands? Or can you find some other way to live with your feelings and maintain your sexual relationship?

## The Active Listening Exercise

In addition to dealing with the backlog of stored anger, it is important to learn to express your feelings and effectively resolve issues as they happen. The Active Listening Exercise is particularly useful when one of the sensitive areas discovered through the Past Hurts Exercise has been reinjured.

When it comes to arguments or discussions, we frequently listen to what our partner is saying only long enough to formulate our own rebuttal. After the first few sentences, we assume what the rest of the message will be and begin to prepare our response. Our partner, in turn, listens to only the beginning of our response before busily formulating a retort. As a result, we may be disagreeing with something our partner hasn't really said. No wonder some issues are so difficult to resolve. Most of the time is spent reiterating our own positions louder and longer rather than really understanding our partner's point of view and arriving at some compromise.

The Active Listening Exercise has been adapted from Thomas Gordon's work[2] specifically to address this problem. It is designed to enable you and your partner to concentrate on and really hear what the other is saying, and hence can help you more fully understand each other's position. The exercise can be used whenever you are having a disagreement or when you want to communicate hurt or angry feelings. It can also serve to slow down the action of a full-blown fight and prevent the kind of rapid escalation that obscures and confuses the original issue.

The Active Listening technique requires that one person speak at a time, and the listener feed back the content of the message to assure its correct comprehension. Let's say you begin. After you express your feelings, demands, or point of view (using "I" statements‡) as succinctly as possible, your partner repeats the essence of your position in his or her own words. If your partner's understanding is correct, acknowledge it. If not, clarify your point by re-explaining it in a somewhat different way. The judge of whether the listener has understood the message correctly is the speaker. Even if the listener repeats the exact words the speaker used but with a different tone, the speaker may feel that he or she has not been understood. Subtle misinterpretations can be quite relevant.

Sometimes, a particular point is too long to be fed back in its entirety. In this situation, the point should be broken down into a number of short segments. Each segment should be repeated by the listener before the speaker begins the next segment. This process is continued until you have completed your message and feel that your partner has understood it. (By the way, showing you understand your partner's message in no way implies that you agree with it.) Then it is your partner's turn to present his side of the story, while you feed back his message until he is satisfied that you understand him.

‡ See pages 97–98.

Anita handled her feelings about Harry's coming home late by using the Active Listening Exercise. Anita began: "I was very hurt yesterday when you said you wouldn't be home for dinner. I was disappointed because I had prepared a special meal and was looking forward to an intimate evening at home."

Now, instead of Harry's proceeding to defend himself about his working late and only doing his best to support her anyway, etc., he said, "You are saying that you were hurt yesterday when I didn't come home for dinner because you had planned something special and felt disappointed."

Anita continued, "Yes, and in the future, when this happens, I would appreciate it if you would keep me apprised of your schedule and let me know your plans as early as possible."

To which Harry replied, "So you are saying that you don't ever want me to work late when you have prepared an intimate dinner."

"No, you didn't hear me right," Anita responded. "I'm not saying that I don't want you to work late, I just don't want you to wait until the last minute to tell me about it. I will experience less disappointment, the less I have prepared and the less I have anticipated the closeness. It is the disappointment at the last minute that is difficult for me."

Harry repeated back, "So it is OK if I work late as long as I give you notice earlier in the day."

"Right," said Anita.

"But sometimes I don't know until the last minute."

And Anita repeated, "Sometimes you don't know until the last minute and so you can't tell me ahead of time."

"Correct."

"Well, obviously in that situation I will have to be disappointed. However, it would help if you told me the circumstances: for instance, that you just received certain papers, and they have to be completed by the next day, or something like that."

Harry concluded, "OK, so you want me to tell you why I'm not going to be home on time when I haven't been able to give you sufficient notice."

This example shows how a discussion which could have degenerated into a fight can be slowed down so that each person's point of view is clearly understood and blaming is minimized. Harry now understands that he can ease Anita's disappointment if he tells her about a change in his plans as soon as possible. When circumstances preclude advance notice, she will have to live with being disappointed. Had he not understood her position, Harry might have felt unappreciated, unloved, and blamed for circumstances beyond his control when he was only trying his best to be a good provider. He might have ended up feeling that Anita is never satisfied and that he might as well stop trying.

Initially, you may find the Active Listening Exercise laborious and time consuming, but it is worth the extra time and effort. In the end, it should help you better understand each other's point of view. Practice using active listening a few times during normal conversations before you try to apply it to an argument or heated discussion.

## The Caring Days Exercise

If changes have occurred in your communication process as a result of the previous two exercises, you may already be feeling more loving toward each other. The Caring Days Exercise, adapted from Richard Stuart's work,[3] is designed to capitalize on and nurture this growing affection. It is one way to rejuvenate close and loving feelings that have degenerated as a result of work stress, outside pressures, or relationship problems.

Sit down separately and formulate a list of ten things that your partner does or could do that, in your mind, demonstrate caring. These should be small things, many of which could be carried out on a daily basis, for example: giving you a kiss first thing in the morning, saying "I love you" or leaving love notes for you, putting toothpaste on your toothbrush, bringing home flowers or your favorite ice cream, calling you from work during the day, exercising together, planning weekend excursions, or obtaining theater, symphony, or concert tickets. Avoid picking things that would seem more like a demand or a chore, such as washing the breakfast dishes, cleaning the cat box, walking the dog, or waxing the car.

Once you and your partner have formulated individual lists of at least ten items each, sit down and discuss exactly what each item means. Don't be afraid to ask for your favorite candies, flowers, and special activities. Try to explain to each other how certain acts make you feel cared for. You may be able to list classes of activities rather than just single acts or events. For example, whole days spent outside together could offer a greater variety than simply trips to the beach. The more items you each have on your list, the easier it will be to find things to do for each other on a daily basis without being overly repetitious (although you can probably never say "I love you" too much). As you think of new items, add them to the list.

To carry out the Caring Days Exercise, each of you is to fulfill four of the items on your partner's list every day. To help you remember, post your lists together in a place where you'll both see them, such as on the bathroom mirror or the door to the refrigerator. There are no extra points to be gained from carrying out seven or eight items on the list daily. If one of you goes overboard while the other does only the required amount, the overly conscientious partner is likely to feel resentful and unloved. So stick to the ground rules of only four items each day.

Since most people tend to keep track of their partner's expressions of caring as well as their own, it is a good idea to keep a daily list. At the end of every day, check off the four things you were aware your partner did for you. If either of you failed to notice any of the caring acts of the other, it is up to the one who was not acknowledged to correct the list and apprise the other of the caring act.

Sometimes, well-meant expressions of caring go unnoticed, and this part of the process will help make each of you more aware of what your partner does for you. Also, most people are more likely to respond positively to praise than to punishment. Acknowledging each other's demonstrations of caring gives each of you a pat on the back and reinforces those behaviors.

Rhonda and Patrick sat down together and formulated their individual Caring Days lists. The following are some of the items on each of their lists. The checks mark the items carried out on the particular day. Since these are only partial lists, some days show fewer than the required four items being fulfilled.

*Rhonda's List*

|  | Sept. 8 | Sept. 9 | Sept. 10 | Sept. 11 | Sept. 12 | Sept. 13 |
|---|---|---|---|---|---|---|
| Say "I love you" | √ | √ | √ | √ | √ | √ |
| Kiss me in the morning | √ |  |  | √ | √ |  |
| Suggest exercising together |  | √ |  | √ |  | √ |
| Bring flowers | √ |  | √ |  |  |  |
| Make dinner reservations |  | √ |  |  |  |  |
| etc. |  |  |  |  |  |  |

*Patrick's List*

|  | Sept. 8 | Sept. 9 | Sept. 10 | Sept. 11 | Sept. 12 | Sept. 13 |
|---|---|---|---|---|---|---|
| Have hors d'oeuvres when I come home | √ |  | √ | √ |  |  |
| Say "I love you" | √ | √ | √ | √ | √ | √ |
| Call during the day |  | √ |  | √ | √ |  |
| Put toothpaste on my toothbrush |  | √ |  | √ |  |  |
| Go for long walks together | √ |  |  |  |  | √ |
| etc. |  |  |  |  |  |  |

## CREATING THE MOOD

After you are setting aside intimate time together, doing nice things for each other, and feeling more loving, you may find that you are still not very much in an explicitly sexual mood. In this case, it may be necessary to prime the pump by actively creating sexual interest. The following are some ways to generate sexual feelings. By activating these feelings at different times during the day, you can allow them to simmer and build so that you have a head start when you do get together with your partner.

Some people feel awkward when carrying out these specifically sexual exercises. They worry that they may look foolish in their partner's eyes, or if they do build their sexual anticipation they may be disappointed or their partner may reject their overtures. Try to bear with it. Remember that the progress you have made thus far has been the result of your willingness to risk doing things differently.

## The Sexual Daydream Exercise

Erotic feelings can be created through the use of sexual daydreams or fantasies. To do this, pay attention to attractive people at work or on the street to gather new material for your imagination. Or you might sit quietly and recall extremely pleasurable sexual encounters of the past. Musing about possible or even impossible sexual events can be a way of building sexual energy. Give yourself free rein to let your imagination go. Whether these fantasies could ever actually occur or whether you would even want them to occur is beside the point. The task at hand is to generate more sexual feelings. And thinking about sex is one of the best ways to do that.

Unfortunately, at this point, many people confront the motivation problem. If you have not been interested in sex for a while, your tendency may be to avoid fantasizing. Or you may find yourself postponing it while attending to other things you consider more pressing or important. To help remind yourself to fantasize a few times during the day you could set an alarm clock or timer to ring every few hours. You could paste colored dots on your refrigerator door or on your telephone at work to remind you to imagine a sexy event every time you open the refrigerator door or make a phone call. Or you might take a moment to daydream during coffee breaks, or when you complete some task you attend to every hour or two during the day.

## The Erotica Exercise

Reading erotica can provide new themes for your fantasy life or spark your sexual interest by itself. Even if your relationship has been active sexually, erotica can heighten your sexual desire. Several times during the day, read a few pages from popular novels or such erotic classics as *Fanny Hill* by John Cleland, *My Secret Garden* and *Forbidden Flowers* by Nancy Friday, and *Little Birds* and *Delta of Venus* by Anaïs Nin. To remember to read erotica, use methods similar to those suggested for reminding yourself to fantasize.

### The Erotic Film Exercise

Some women find that viewing erotic films enhances their sexual interest. Many claim that although they don't feel turned on while watching the movies (some even say that they feel turned off or merely amused), they notice that the lovemaking that takes place afterward is more creative or more passionate.

The Erotic Film Exercise consists of watching an erotic film with your partner on a day or evening which you have set aside to be together. If you have your own home projector, you can rent films and watch them in the privacy of your bedroom. If you own a video system, you can rent erotic videotapes. And if your video system includes a camera, you may want to have some fun making your own erotic home movies.

### The Anticipation Exercise

Another way to recharge your sexual batteries is to build anticipation. Call your partner up during the day and make sexual plans for that evening. Even if you are not feeling turned on, pretend you are. You will have to prime yourself in the beginning before you can expect your own natural sexual feelings to flow freely.

By playing a role or pretending you are turned on at various times during the day, you can often trick yourself into really feeling that way. It may seem fake or silly to you, but if this innocent self-deceit produces the desired result and your natural sexual interest blossoms forth, it's worth it. It's similar to planting flowers. While planting the seeds isn't really like enjoying the flowers, if you don't plant seeds, you won't get any flowers. With tending, the flowers will eventually grow of their own accord and begin reproducing themselves. In the same way, you may find that after a period of pretending or acting as if you are excited, your natural sexual feelings will begin to emerge on their own.

You can also practice the Kegel exercises* to generate sexual feelings.

## The Teasing Touch Exercise

Another way to encourage the growth of sexual interest is by frequently touching your partner. Again, don't wait for the urge to overtake you, but do things to actively help create the urge. As you pass each other in the kitchen, take a moment to hug or kiss. Hold hands while walking, sit close together as you watch television, snuggle while you read, and cuddle when you go to bed at night. A pat on the rear end or a stroke of the thigh can be a loving way to demonstrate desire without necessarily meaning that you want to jump into bed at that very moment. In fact, the more displays of physical affection that take place, the less sexually charged each touch will be. And the more that physical and loving attention is exchanged during the day, the easier it will be to make the transition to explicitly sexual contact, so that rather than being a separate isolated activity, sex becomes a natural extension of the physical caring that is expressed throughout the day.

## BREAKING THE AVOIDANCE HABIT

If you have not had sex for an extended period of time, you may find that arousing yourself doesn't alleviate the awkwardness of resuming your sexual relationship. Furthermore, you may have developed a number of ways of avoiding sex that have become a habit. In order for you to break the avoidance habit and reconnect sexually, it will probably be necessary for you to examine the ways you avoid sex.

## The Journal Observation Exercise

To make changes in your sexual pattern, it is important first to determine exactly how you avoid sex. To do this, return to the

* See pages 141–44.

Journal Exercise.† Monitor what occurs on those occasions when sexual interaction is possible and record your observations in a journal. As with the earlier journal exercises, be sure to write in your journal as soon after the observation as possible, and never wait beyond the end of the day to make an entry.

Do you participate in any of the following typical avoidance patterns? Do you work until late at night and then fall into bed too tired to stay awake a moment longer? Have you worked it out so that you and your partner have different schedules and never go to bed or wake up at the same time? Do you notice that you fight regularly at bedtime, or when you are beginning to feel particularly intimate? Is sex initiated only at times which are inopportune— when one of you is cooking dinner, immersed in activities with the children, or focused on completing some difficult-to-interrupt task? As you get close to an opportunity for sex do you find fault with your partner? Do you remember things done to you in the past that made you angry? Do you focus on some physical or emotional flaws —broken promises, mismatched clothes, snoring or teeth-grinding— which wipe out the positive feelings you were beginning to experience?

## Sharing Fears and Vulnerabilities

Once you have determined the ways in which you avoid sex, the next step is for the two of you to discuss your awkwardness, fears, and concerns about making changes in your sexual relationship. For example, you may feel too embarrassed to initiate sex. You may fear that if you did have sex and it didn't go well, one of you might get discouraged and not want to try again. You may fear that you will be too anxious to respond with orgasm, or worry that your partner might no longer find you attractive. You may worry that some unforeseen problem might force you back to square one, causing you to lose the close feelings that have recently developed.

Although sharing these fears and concerns will not make them disappear, it can help reduce them. It may be reassuring to know that you can tell your partner the thoughts that terrify you the

† See pages 80–84.

most and survive it. Knowing that your partner has concerns too can also be comforting. However, concerns won't vanish through talk alone. There are still some hurdles to clear.

## UNBLOCKING THE BLOCKS

In order to re-establish sexual activity, it will be necessary to inhibit the methods you generally use for avoiding sex. Following are some ways to do this. They are meant only as a starting point. Again, it would be best for you to create a procedure for breaking the avoidance habit that exactly fits your situation.

### Creating Time Together

Most of the practical problems can be solved. If working too late depletes you of sufficient time and energy for lovemaking, agree to discontinue work a few hours earlier on specially designated evenings. Don't try for too much—a few good intimate evenings are often better than spending every free moment together and feeling bored.

### Planning Intimate Activities

If the transition between work and intimate time together is strained, you might want to consider taking evening baths or showers together as a part of your bedtime routine. You might like to set aside time to talk or play games together a few nights a week. Scrabble, cards, or some other game that requires relating to each other could substitute for watching television or reading. One woman found it helpful to move their games into the bedroom where they would play once they were already dressed for bed. Being in bed facilitated the transition from playing and talking together to making love.

### Coordinating Bedtimes

Not infrequently, both partners seem to have basic constitutional differences. One person may be a night person, while the other is a morning person. Unless sex can be fit into the middle of the day or early evening (not always easy for working people with children), it is crucial to schedule a few nights a week when you can go to sleep and wake up together. On some evenings, the night owl could go to bed earlier than usual; on others, the early bird could drink a few cups of coffee and live it up.

## Making Dates

If you or your partner avoid initiating sex because you are particularly sensitive about being turned down, you might protect yourself from being hurt by making dates for sex ahead of time. In this way, you can let each other know your interests and needs in advance. Some people feel this kind of initiation is safer because it allows for the refusal of the offer at a time when they are not quite as vulnerable sexually. Furthermore, planning ahead enables you to prepare for those special encounters by simmering your sexual feelings beforehand.

## Avoiding Fights

Fighting at bedtime or at other potentially intimate times is generally more difficult to overcome than other avoidance tactics. With some effort, however, it is possible at least to curtail fighting even if it can't be stopped altogether. Couples have been able to avoid bedtime fights by agreeing not to discuss issues over which they are likely to disagree after a particular hour in the evening. Subjects that are likely to cause a clash are reserved for late morning or early evening discussions. Almost any problem can wait a day to be resolved.

An earthshaking event may warrant breaking the rule. However, if a relatively small matter arises and you insist on fighting over it, perhaps stored-up anger has not been alleviated, in which case the Past Hurts Exercise‡ should probably be repeated. Or you may be experiencing a greater fear of intimacy than you had realized, and may have to work with a therapist before you can feel safe enough with your partner to have close and loving experiences.

‡ See pages 245–47.

## Not Focusing on the Negative

Sometimes thoughts of past injuries or a partner's negative characteristics interfere with sexual intimacy. These thoughts may seem out of your control. You may even find that they arise against your will. While these past hurts or negative characteristics may be founded in fact, for example, your partner may have been inconsiderate or offensive, they may not be useful thoughts to have at that moment. The following Thought Stopping Exercise can be used to help inhibit nonproductive thoughts. However, in order for this exercise to work, you must really want to stop thinking those thoughts.

## The Thought Stopping Exercise[4]

When you focus on some negative trait of your partner's or some past infuriating or hurtful event, close your eyes and say the word "Stop" out loud. If you are not alone you can imagine a voice yelling the word "Stop" instead of saying it aloud. Generally we can think only one thought at a time. If we are listening to someone else talk and our mind wanders to some other subject, we miss a large part of what is being said. In the same way, thinking or saying the word "Stop" interferes with the negative thoughts.

Try it for yourself. Think a nonproductive thought and imagine a voice yelling "Stop," or say "Stop" out loud. Then, with your eyes still closed, take a deep relaxing breath. You might even want to imagine being somewhere that has been especially relaxing and secure for you in the past.

After this moment or two of relaxation, refocus your mind on some other task or activity that requires your full attention. Write a letter, practice a musical instrument, telephone a friend, even balance your checkbook. If the negative thought interferes again, repeat the process, beginning with the word "Stop." As you learn to control your thoughts you may find you can get successful results by softly saying the word "Stop." Or you might prefer to visualize the word or the image of a stop sign.

If your head is filled with negative thoughts because there is nothing more interesting in your life to think about, you might consider seeking more emotional fulfillment. If you have nothing to do all day, your partner cannot possibly begin to meet all of your needs. Most of your partner's needs are in all likelihood being met through work. Unfortunately, a large number of intelligent, creative, and potentially productive women are on antidepressants or other pills when a job, volunteer work, or some other useful activity would give them the sense of self-worth and contribution they need. If your family is grown yet you feel unqualified to be anything other than a housewife, you should realize that many paying jobs are not as difficult as running a family.

## THE FIRST TIME

Once the stage has been set and the methods of avoiding sex curtailed, you may still find that your first sexual experience after a long period of abstinence is awkward. Joe and Sally had been married for seven years. After the second year they stopped having sex. It was a complicated relationship and considerable animosity had built up on both sides over the intervening five years. However, with the help of family therapy, and the exercises suggested earlier in this chapter, the caring in their relationship was re-established. Feeling more positive toward each other made them eager to begin having sex again. But because they had abstained for so long, any sexual approach felt contrived and unnatural. After five years of practice, they had become quite used to the habits of abstention, and they wanted their initial sexual overtures to be as comfortable and anxiety-free as their avoidance pattern had become.

Unfortunately, there is really no way to prevent awkwardness in the beginning. When you are learning to ice skate again after a five-year hiatus, your initial tries may be difficult and ungraceful, and your muscles will probably be sore afterward. But each attempt makes the next one easier until finally a level of ease and comfort has been achieved. If you don't persevere through the first few awkward tries, you might as well forget about being able to skate again. The same is true of sex.

As you approach your first sexual experience following a period of abstinence, a small part of you may urge you to stop making changes and just keep things safe. However, if you want to re-establish sexual activity, it will be necessary to take a few risks. You can do this in one of two ways: by quietly sliding into it and pretending it isn't really happening until after it is over; or by planning ahead and setting up a special event.

## The It's Not Really Happening Exercise

If the two of you have increased your physical touching out of the bedroom and you want more closeness but aren't quite ready for real sex yet, you may find the It's Not Really Happening Exercise a good transition. Before going to sleep or just after waking up, cuddle with your partner. Then put his penis, which doesn't have to be erect, in your vagina and just lie there. Artificial lubrication should be applied and a contraceptive used, just in case. Carefully pick a comfortable position, one that you could fall asleep in if you wanted to. Positions other than that with the man on top are preferable. The goal of the exercise is just to feel close and get ready for sex another day.

Then one day, when you feel ready, touch your partner in a more sexual way and kiss a little longer. Don't wait for your partner's response to go ahead. While women have been role-scripted to expect the man to take the lead when it comes to sex, his awkwardness and vulnerability may cause him to hold back at first. It may be up to you to take some of the sexual risks men have been taking for years. You might recall those times your partner initiated sex and how loved and desirable you felt because he was willing to express his feelings in this way. Then, take a deep breath and as you gently rub his body and his genitals, pretend he is responding in kind. Chances are he will, especially if you have been talking about this problem and working on some of the exercises together. If he doesn't, keep gently loving him—then explicitly ask if he is in the mood for sex. If he is reluctant, you might offer to let him relax while you turn him on, as in the His and Her Exercise.* If he is simply not in the mood, you could ask for a rain check and initiate sex again another day. It is easy to feel hurt if he does turn you down the first time, especially if initiating sex was difficult for you. But don't give up. To renew your courage to try again, you

* See pages 173–75.

might recall those times when you turned your partner down simply because you were not in the mood and not with any ulterior motive.

If you and your partner have not had sex for a period of time, it is quite likely that your partner will also have difficulty reconnecting sexually. As you begin to make some real changes, your partner may seem to subtly resist or not so subtly sabotage your new efforts. This is to be expected. Although your partner may be just as interested as you are in a more active sexual relationship, fears of the unknown and anxiety about your sex life changing often result in unconscious efforts to preserve the status quo.

Both of you will undoubtedly block your progress at various points. As one of you makes a move ahead, there may be a tendency for the other to resist. Rarely do you just breeze through such changes. If this pattern is anticipated, however, it can free you to be more accepting of your own as well as your partner's resistance. Then, when the backsliding takes place, it may slow things down but not bring them to a halt.

It is often possible to break habits or patterns in a relationship even when only one person does things differently. For example, Marie and Mark had not made love for two months. On the rare occasion when one acted sexy, the other would pick a fight over some trivial matter. This, of course, totally dampened the initiator's sexual desire. Marie finally decided that she wanted to change their lovemaking pattern. Despite Mark's behavior, she was not going to play her part in the fighting. So while Mark continued picking fights whenever Marie acted seductive, Marie squelched her tendency to thwart Mark's attempts when he acted at all amorous. Without Marie playing her part in the usual pattern, their interaction had to change. In the beginning, this meant that they only had sex when Mark made the first move. However, Marie's change in behavior altered their pattern of relating enough to allow feelings of warmth and affection to grow. After a while, Mark was less apt to prevent sex when Marie initiated it.

Therefore, don't let your partner's initial resistance deter you. Focus on positively changing those things you can control. Your continued progress will make an impact on your relationship and may inspire your partner to move forward. In the beginning you may have to persevere in your generous behavior without immediate reciprocation from your partner. This may feel like an unfair and lonely stance, but if you truly want your pattern of sexual relating to change, it may be the only thing to do. Waiting for your partner to change first or even to respond positively to your changes may not be realistic. If this approach works, it will have been worth it. If it doesn't, you will be no worse off than you are now.

### The Setup Exercise

To set up the sexual event ahead of time, make a date for a special evening together. Pick an evening when you can sleep in the following day, and do it up right. Go out for an intimate and romantic—but light—dinner. See an erotic film. Bathe or shower together. Light candles in the bathroom and bedroom and take whatever care is necessary to create a sensual environment. Pretend you are making love to this person for the first time. Begin by massaging each other. Take plenty of time and savor the mixture of newness and familiarity.

## MAINTAINING SEXUAL ACTIVITY

When you first resume sex after a long period of abstinence, you will have to continue making an effort to keep your sexual relationship active. The inertia created by the habit of not having sex will naturally tend to pull things back to the way they've been. So don't expect to return to a frequent sex life after the first breakthrough. To fully break the avoidance pattern, you will have to keep creating the mood through the Sexual Daydream, Erotica, and Anticipation Exercises described earlier in this chapter. It is also important not to let more than two days go by without having sex or some other form of intimate physical touching or massage. Frequent physical expressions of caring will be required to offset the avoidance habit and create a feeling of ease with sexual contact. Keep a watchful eye on your sexual frequency for the first month or two, until a new habit of sexual activity has become established. Even after an active sexual relationship has been resumed, you would be well advised to keep your sexual relationship a priority. The next chapter contains suggestions on how to do that.

*Chapter 14*

# ENHANCING YOUR SEXUAL RELATIONSHIP

While people often claim to cherish their intimate relationships, few set aside sufficient time to make them a high priority. After the honeymoon is over, relaxation and intimate contact often get relegated to last place. Keeping an emotional relationship vital requires the same time and care as ensuring the survival of a business. In the beginning, an overwhelming amount of time and energy must be poured into it to create a solid foundation. Even after the foundation is firmly established, constant attention to the details is required. If either partner is taken for granted, the rewards dwindle.

## The Time Exercise

One prerequisite for maintaining a good sexual relationship, particularly for active people, is setting aside sufficient time for intimate, relaxing contact. Busy couples often find that if they don't set aside special evenings or weekends for themselves, all of their available time is scheduled with other things. During any given week they might schedule a dinner with some clients or people who are in from out of town, a PTA meeting, a regular evening class or political meeting, and Sunday with the parents. They then spend the evening or two they have left taking care of household chores and tasks that could not be fit in any other time. The end result is that there is little time left over for themselves.

Sexual contact, when it occurs, is relegated to late at night, without any preceding intimacy.

The Time Exercise is designed to help you set aside more intimate time. Schedule, for the next week, two periods of one hour or longer when the two of you can be together. You can use these special time periods to be sexual, or to be intimate without being sexual. The time set aside, for instance, could be immediately after work to discuss the events of the day over a glass of wine. Or it could be a fifteen-minute walk or some other form of shared exercise before or after work or on weekends. A special long lunch-hour might provide sufficient time for a picnic or erotic matinee. Be as precise as possible in arranging dates and times.

Harold and Mimi would schedule a date together every week to counteract their busy lives. They would write the appointment into their appointment books and consider it as sacred as any of their other meetings. On this special evening they would hire a baby-sitter or take the children to their grandparents. Then, after a romantic dinner together, they would return home, build a fire, drink some cognac, and often make love in front of the fireplace. They looked forward to this weekly ritual and felt that it was, in large part, responsible for their close, loving relationship.

Scheduling weekends or evenings away for the precise purpose of spending sexual time together is another way to rejuvenate romantic and intimate feelings. Weekends don't have to take three full days, nor do they require traveling a long distance. Some couples find that hiring a baby-sitter and going to a local motel fills the bill. When it comes to revitalizing a relationship, time together—away from the telephone, chores, and family responsibilities—is more important than sightseeing.

## The Stress Exercise

Some people find that their job or work with the children is so stressful that when they finally see their partner at the end of the day the stored-up frustration and negative feelings spoil their intimate contact. Tensions of the day find expression through petty fights over trivial issues. If this is true for you, a transition period of separate time between work and intimate time together may be necessary. At first this may appear to take time away from each other, but the quality of the time spent together afterward should be enhanced, making the brief separation well worth it.

To carry out the Stress Exercise, which is adapted from the work of Bernie Zilbergeld,[1] take an hour to read the newspaper, watch television, exercise alone, or do something else you enjoy after a busy day. If you have young children, find a way to occupy them for thirty minutes or so while you allow yourself some private time just to relax.

All too often people are afraid to ask for private time when they need it. They fear that if they don't want to spend every available moment with their partner, they may be considered selfish or unloving, or their partner may be hurt or offended. So they disregard their own needs and try to be attentive to their partner. In so doing, they are only able to give half their attention. Their partner, in turn, often interprets this divided attention as a sign of disinterest. The frustration and resentment experienced by the one partner and the disappointment experienced by the other then creates conflict. An hour of separate time followed by an hour together would be more rewarding than two strained hours spent together.

Sandy and Hank seemed to fight every night. However, by observing their patterns, they realized they almost never fought on the weekends. On weekdays Sandy was home all day taking care of their two children, ages two and four, and she found that as evening drew near she was almost desperate for some nurturing of her own and some adult conversation. Hank was the manager of a small business, and rarely a day went by when some personnel or monetary crisis didn't frustrate him. When he came home in the evening, all he wanted was peace and quiet. Even the noise of the children playing in the next room bothered him when he first came home.

Hank felt that if he could have at least a half hour to himself to work at his hobby of building children's toys, he could hammer and saw away some of his pent-up frustration, and the time spent with Sandy afterward might be more enjoyable. So they experimented. Sandy prepared a snack, and when Hank came home he kissed her hello, took the snack down to his shop, and puttered around for thirty to forty-five minutes before coming upstairs and joining her.

Sandy meanwhile prepared dinner and fed the children. Then all four of them played together until it was the children's bedtime, after which Sandy and Hank enjoyed a quiet, intimate dinner. This was Sandy's time. Hank, having dissipated some of his frustrations in his shop, had plenty of nurturing energy to devote to Sandy. After making this small change in their routine, their fighting ceased and their sex life improved.

## BOREDOM

Many people hold the belief that love, and love alone, makes for good sex. They think that there is something wrong with their relationship if the mere sight of their lover's body does not send them into a passionate frenzy. They believe that lovemaking which requires any planning or incorporates any accouterments is second-rate. This cultural myth dictates that sex should be spontaneous and that the best sex, the sex that is purest and most meaningful, requires no preparation of any kind.

The myth that good sex is spontaneous grows out of distorted memories of the initial exciting lovemaking sessions with a partner. Of course, the novelty of a new sexual relationship and learning about each other creates an excitement all its own. But the spontaneity that occurs during the early stages of the relationship actually results from considerable attention and planning. Dates are often made in advance, providing a period of hours or days during which anticipation can build. Attractive clothing and even sexy underwear are worn and the bedroom or whole house or apartment is often cleaned in anticipation. Then, the evening begins with some intimate activity undisturbed by outside intruders. Finally, somehow, at the end of the evening, you end up in bed together, and this is considered spontaneous.

After years of marriage and particularly once children have entered the scene, the "spontaneous" script undergoes a change. Evening hours are filled with putting the children to sleep, answering telephone calls, and attending to unfinished chores. Then late at night, after an exhausting day of work and family—and with full awareness of having to awake early the next day to start all over again—you fall into bed. Without having spent a moment of intimate time together, you may inadvertently roll over on each other and find yourself making love—that is, if you have the energy. It's no wonder that under these circumstances sex becomes less exhilarating. Your times together have been filled with people and chores. Little energy is left over for an exciting and creative period of lovemaking. Over time this kind of routine and fatigue naturally decrease sexual enjoyment and lead to less and less sex, or perfunctory sex which becomes less and less satisfying.

Good sex requires time, planning, and preparation. The idea that love is the only essential ingredient can result in a relationship's growing stale after a number of years. In this sense, sex is like everything else. You would soon grow tired of walking the same trail, seeing the same movie, or eating the same gourmet meal day after day, even if each of them was the best of its kind. When it comes to sex, minor variations such as changing intercourse positions or the bed you make love in, showering together or massaging each other, going off to a motel occasionally or wearing a sexy negligee may be all that is really needed to enhance your lovemaking.

More importantly, keeping the sexual relationship vital requires paying attention to nonsexual areas as well. All too frequently, we take our partner for granted once we begin living together or get married. We bring our frustrations home and dump them in our lover's lap. We fail to notice how attractive they look, neglect to tell them how wonderful they are. Then we wonder why the sparkle and romance have gone out of the relationship.

Maintaining that romantic and loving aspect of a relationship requires attention. It means giving frequent verbal appreciation rather than assuming our partner knows how we feel. It means boosting each other's egos, saying "I love you," and carrying out thoughtful loving gestures. Maintaining this level of intimacy and caring outside the bedroom does wonders for the sex that is shared inside it.

## Suggestions for Sexual Enhancement

If you are willing to put the kind of time and effort into sex that you put into keeping other areas of your relationship vital, you may find that sex too can take on added dimensions. If you feel it is too late for making those kinds of changes, you might consider the sixty-five-year-old man who read *Shared Intimacies* and said, "I guess it is never too late to teach an old dog new tricks." He felt that the more he learned about sex, the more fulfilling his sexual relationship became.

Of all of the causes of sexual disinterest, sexual boredom is the most fun to remedy. There are innumerable ways to add pleasure and variety to your sexual relationship. The following are some suggestions you may want to experiment with.

## THE SCENE

Expending extra energy creating a sensual scene can enhance your lovemaking. Satin sheets and pillowcases can heighten the erotic sense of touch. Be conscious also of lighting. The soft glow of candles not only enhances physical appearance, but creates a relaxed and erotic frame of mind. If you have a fireplace, making love on a mattress or sheet in front of the warm fire can be a pleasant change. Camping out, even on your deck or in your backyard, can add variety and interest. One couple I talked with almost never made love anywhere except in their own home. However, over the years they had sex in every bed in the house and had initiated every new piece of furniture after they had purchased it. They recalled the washing machine with particular fondness.

## SCENT

The pleasant aroma of soaps, powders, and colognes can do much to stimulate your erotic inclinations. Make certain that the fragrances you choose are also appealing to your partner. Fragrances are very personal and idiosyncratic and one person's favorite scent may be too sweet, overwhelming, or noxious for another.

Many women feel that cleanliness is an important aspect of their sexual turn-on.[2] They like to be clean and they prefer that their partner has bathed also. You can turn the need to be clean into a sensual act by taking baths and showers together. Vitabath, a fragrant and sensual liquid soap that fills the bathtub with bubbles, is highly recommended.

## DRESS

Negligees and sexy underwear can be arousing for both partners. An eighty-six-year-old widowed singing teacher told me, after watching me talk about sexual enhancement on a television program:

"What you say is true, but you left out a very important point. You can't expect your husband to feel in the mood if you wear ugly green pajamas with holes in them to bed at night. You can't wear curlers and a mud pack. You have to wear something slinky and soft so you look attractive and then everything will work out well." I felt well advised and immediately threw out my green pajamas.

Many men and women find being half dressed more enticing than complete nudity. Translucent peignoirs, low-cut negligees, satin teddies, or camisoles can add the finishing touches. It is like a beautiful, carefully wrapped gift. The attractiveness of the package makes the unwrapping a special pleasure in itself. Looking attractive, allowing yourself to feel sexy, and even giving yourself permission to act sexy can add excitement for both of you.

TOYS

Although some people feel that the use of any implements for the purpose of lovemaking is unnatural, many couples find that massage oils, ostrich feathers, rabbit-fur mitts, and other sensual materials help intensify erotic touching. For people who like to play and experiment sexually, there are a variety of sexual toys, from games to vibrators.[3] It is finally becoming as respectable to enjoy sex with a variety of sexual accouterments as it is to obtain the newest gadgets and playthings available to the sports enthusiast or the electronics bug.

FANTASY

Sharing fantasies can add new dimensions to lovemaking for some women. Through fantasy, you can experience all sorts of sexual scenarios—some you've always wanted to try and some you might never want to actually experience, even if you had the opportunity. You may want to enjoy your fantasy silently while making love to your partner, or you may choose to share your fantasies. You could build a fantasy scene together, each elaborating upon the ideas of the other. Or, one of you could spin the fantasized yarn while the other provides the physical stimulation. On occasion, you might want to act out some of your fantasies.

For example, a safe way for a monogamous couple to recapture some of the excitement of making love to someone for the first time is to pretend that you've just met. When out of town, you might arrive separately at a bar, disco, or hotel. After the "unanticipated meeting," you could have the kind of "getting to know you" discussion that generally transpires on first dates: where you live, what you do for work, for relaxation. Then, pretending that you hardly know each other, you could go to a motel room and make love as if it were the first time.

You could tie one person up with scarves or stockings and sexually tease, titillate, and delight them. Being totally helpless can emphasize the pleasure of a passive-receptive role, while being totally in charge allows you to elaborate on feelings of passion and power. Some couples claim this adds a new dimension of trust to their sexual relationship.[4]

## The Oral Sex Exercises

Although some women don't like oral sex, others find it provides variety and heightens their sexual feelings. Women who would like to try oral sex but haven't done so in the past generally have the following major concerns: having vaginal odors which might offend their partner, choking on their partner's penis, or having their partner ejaculate in their mouth.

### CONCERNS ABOUT ODOR

To help alleviate any concerns this antiseptic society may have instilled in you, you might be sure to bathe or shower immediately before your partner has oral sex with you. You could check to see if you have any disagreeable odor by obtaining some lubrication with your finger and smelling it. A slight inoffensive odor is normal; after all, it's not natural to smell like ammonia. If the odor seems excessive or if your partner complains about your scent, it would be wise to make an appointment with a gynecologist. The odor may be a sign of a minor vaginal infection which could easily be treated.

If concern about odor inhibits you, try the following. Tell your partner you want to know explicitly whether or not you have an unpleasant odor. Say that absolute honesty is essential if you are to overcome this concern. That way, if your partner detects an odor, you can wash, and then relax and enjoy yourself. Also, remember that a scent one person finds pleasing can be offensive to another. In the end, it is only important that your partner find your genital odors acceptable, even if your own evaluation is different.

### CONCERNS ABOUT EJACULATING

If having your partner ejaculate in your mouth is a concern, have oral sex while he is wearing a condom. While this doesn't taste particularly good, it can provide security while you practice having him signal you verbally or by tapping your head or shoulder with his hand to indicate he is about to climax. When he signals you, remove your mouth and continue stimulating his penis with your hand. When you feel confident that he will give you sufficient warning before he ejaculates, you can carry out the exercise without the condom.

### CONCERNS ABOUT CHOKING

If you are not concerned with the taste of the semen, but are afraid of choking, you can try the next two exercises. Encircle the base of your partner's penis with your hand while he lies on his back. Your hand will act as a buffer to prevent the penis from thrusting too deeply into your mouth and causing you to choke.

If you are afraid of choking when he ejaculates, teach yourself to close off the back of your mouth. This will ensure that the semen doesn't shoot down your throat. Practice bringing the back of your tongue and posterior wall of your throat together while you squirt a water pistol into the back of your mouth. After some practice, you should be able to figure out how to prevent the water from going down your throat while you are able to breathe comfortably. Then you can do the same thing during oral sex.

## COMMUNICATION AND PLANNING

Ironically, communication, planning, and practice are required for sex to be natural and spontaneous. Through discussion and experimentation, new ideas that appeal to both partners can be generated.

During this process many ideas will probably be tried and discarded. Some activities may be enjoyable one time, because of their newness, but may not be sufficiently interesting to repeat.

Each person's physical and emotional needs must be considered if sex is to be a joyous, unself-conscious experience. If you don't have to worry about how you look or how your partner will evaluate your performance, you can just experience pure pleasure and intimacy—much the way young children can laugh and play together. This kind of fun can add an important dimension to an intimate, loving relationship.

# Section VI

# SEXUALITY:
*An Ongoing Journey*

*Chapter 15*

# WHAT IS PROGRESS?

Almost all people who go through a sex-therapy program experience lapses in their progress. Either they experience setbacks during the course of carrying out the exercises, or after weeks or months of progress, the sexual symptom reappears.

## BACKSLIDING

Very often, an exercise is carried out only once or twice, or a few exercises are carried out one time each and, when immediate progress is not made, the entire project is abandoned. From lack of motivation, ambivalence generated by fear of the unknown, and plain inertia, the subject of the sexual exercises fades into the background and is not brought up again by either partner. Instead, the sexual dissatisfaction smolders, coloring other aspects of the relationship.

It is often easier to avoid the pain of an unsatisfactory relationship than to endure the discomfort required to change it. Caring and constant reminders to continue working on the exercises are necessary if progress is to be made. Generally, the reminding falls largely on the shoulders of the one who most desires the change. The partner who wants most to go to the movies is the one to find the baby-sitter; the one affected most by the breakdown of an appliance locates a repair person; and the one who is most sexually unhappy must persevere with the process of change. It is easy to say, "Well, since I brought up the subject of the exercises two days in a row, I'm not going to initiate anything new until my partner does." This form of self-protection, however, can completely halt all progress.

If you insist that your partner demonstrate love for you by initiating the exercises, you may be setting yourself up for disappointment. It is probable that your partner feels just as awkward about facing your mutual sexual problem as you do and would rather repress the subject (and hence the exercises) than risk feeling like a failure.

The ideal situation would be for you and your partner to each initiate the sexual exercises 50 percent of the time. This, however, is very unlikely. If your partner responds positively to the exercises, even though you have to initiate them, you might just have to accept the role of leader. Your gentle and consistent reminders can keep the process of change in motion, and your continued demonstration of caring and interest may, in time, help your partner to take a more active role.

## RELAPSES

Almost all couples who have successfully reversed a sexual problem experience a relapse at some point. If the same problem that caused the sexual difficulty in the first place reappears at a later date, the sexual symptom may recur. Sometimes, however, a sexual problem reappears in response to other stresses.

We all have our sensitive areas. Some of us develop back problems, headaches, or skin rashes in response to stress. Originally, lifting a heavy piece of furniture may have caused the lower back to go out, a blow to the head may have resulted in serious headaches, or overexposure to the sun may have created lip blisters. Thereafter these areas remain vulnerable to reinjury if care is not taken. And frequently, fatigue, stress, or emotional upset cause the symptom to flare up again in the vulnerable area. Given the amount of physical and emotional stress most of us live with, it is easy to see how lack of sexual interest, inability to reach orgasm, or pain with sex may reappear even after the problem seemed to be completely resolved.

When this happens, as it surely will, don't panic. At this point, most people become depressed or give up, believing that they have made no headway and that the reappearance of the symptom indicates they are beyond help. However, remember that if you could alleviate the problem once, you can do so again. The return of a sexual problem, like the reappearance of other physical problems, can actually be a useful barometer, signaling the existence of an imbalance in its early stages. If used as a warning signal, it can help you alleviate the various stresses in your life before a more serious problem, like an ulcer or a divorce, develops.

When your sexual symptom reappears, use this as an opportunity to re-evaluate your situation. Is it a sign that you and your partner are having relationship problems? Are your lives becoming so hectic that there is no time or energy left over for sex? Is sex becoming routine or dissatisfying? Try to isolate the cause. Discuss the situation with your partner to further your understanding of the problem. Then, begin the appropriate exercises once again. Chances are excellent that after an abbreviated refresher course, and after rectifying the immediate cause of the relapse, you will fairly easily attain sexual satisfaction once again.

## LACK OF IMPROVEMENT

Sometimes people find that they cannot come up with a solution to their particular sexual problem no matter how hard they try, and no matter how many others try to assist them. To every suggestion they seem to have a "yes, but" response. For instance, "I know I should set aside more intimate time, *but* I have two demanding children," or "Buying or wearing a sexy negligee might be nice, *but* it wouldn't make any difference to my partner," or "I tried that once; it didn't work."

If you have been unable to find any exercises in this book which could be of help, you may be expecting your partner to change rather than being willing to make any real changes yourself.

If you are angry with your partner and are withholding sex or orgasm to get your partner to change, you may be putting more energy into changing your partner than you are putting into regaining your own sexual satisfaction. This rarely leads to success. It is difficult enough to change oneself. Changing another, especially someone who does not necessarily want to change, is virtually impossible. Also, by withholding sex or sexual satisfaction, you are not only depriving your partner, but yourself. You might consider working out your differences in other ways so that you can at least have sexual pleasure in the meantime.

Solving your sexual problem may not be possible if the factors which are causing it have not been adequately addressed. If you have completed the relevant exercises in this book and have still experienced no improvement in your sexual problem, you may need professional assistance. Serious inhibitions, relationship problems, or traumatic experiences are often most effectively resolved with the help of a competent psychotherapist. Material in a self-help book, which is designed to provide information and suggestions for a large number of people with very diverse backgrounds, may not be specific enough to deal with your particular situation. This is one of the limitations of a general approach. A psychologist, psychiatrist, social worker, marriage counselor, or spiritual adviser with specific training in sexuality may be better able to help you.

Unfortunately, most people consider psychotherapy as a last resort. They wait to see a therapist until so much ill will has accumulated that therapy becomes the final attempt at reconciliation before separation. Repairing the relationship at this point is extremely difficult, and in some cases, impossible. Psychotherapy and family counseling are far more useful when communication problems and unresolved issues are in their early stages. Like diseases or illnesses, the longer they are left unattended, the more difficult they are to treat. In fact, a preventive approach may be the most effective route to good physical as well as emotional health.

A few sessions with a good therapist trained in family dynamics and sexuality can be the ounce of prevention that is worth the pound of cure. However, not all therapists are equally helpful. Some approaches and methods lumped together under the title of sex therapy get better, faster results than others. Feel free to interview potential therapists about their training in handling sexual problems and their experience solving problems like yours. Beware of a therapist who diverts attention from what you consider to be the problem and focuses *only* on other areas, particularly childhood events. Beware of the therapist whose only method is talking, especially when you do all of it. Successful treatment for sexual problems almost always includes giving advice and homework much like the exercises in this book. Also, you should know that treatment for sexual problems does not usually take a long time, generally not more than a few months of meeting once a week.

You may have to interview a few therapists before you decide which one is best for you. Find out what the therapist's training is and make certain that his or her understanding of your situation makes sense to you. You are entrusting this therapist with a sacred part of yourself, your emotional well-being. Don't let yourself be intimidated. Choose wisely.

## MOVING FORWARD

You can always decide that the effort involved in making a change in your sexual life is not worth it. Nowhere is it written that you must have an orgasmic, sexually active relationship in order to be thoroughly fulfilled and intimately involved with a partner. We are each unique and we each have different priorities. For some, sex is high on the list; for others, it is of relatively little importance. Your analysis of your life, your relationship, and your sexual satisfaction is the only useful guideline.

Beware of comparing your relationship to the unrealistic images portrayed in the television serials, films, and magazines. Our culture seems to be going through a period in which independence and autonomy are more highly prized than mutuality. While these ideals have been beneficial in that they have made people less tolerant of unsatisfying sex and unfulfilling relationships, they have also created an era of somewhat unrealistic expectations, as people jump from one partner to the next in search of the perfect relationship or the perfect orgasm. The "Now" generation won't settle for anything short of total satisfaction, yet it is unwilling to struggle through the hard times and work through the problems inherent in every relationship.

When a current marriage or relationship is not completely satisfying, you may be prematurely willing to end it and seek out another one. If you believe that when the going is rough, it is your partner's fault, you may expect that changing partners will rejuvenate your life. And indeed it may—for a short period of time during the romantic stage of the new relationship. Many people fail to recognize, however, that satisfying relationships require time and attention and that even the best of them go through very difficult periods.

It is perhaps most important of all that you remain true to your values, especially when making changes in a sexual relationship. The sexual liberation movement may advocate getting into swinging, extramarital sex, or homosexual relationships as the route to true liberation, but these activities are not likely to be beneficial for you if they go against your natural disposition. While your preferences may change with time, discomfort and conflict rather than intimacy and satisfaction can result if behaviors are tried which are too divergent from personal values and attitudes.

An active, varied, and orgasmic sexual relationship may or may not be highly valued—certainly close and intimate relationships can survive and sometimes thrive without good sex, or even without any sex at all. However, while satisfying sex can never replace intimacy, it can add depth to an already intimate relationship.

Above all, keep in mind that the devastating aspect of a sexual problem is not the specific problem itself, but the distance created between the two partners when sex doesn't proceed according to expectations. Blaming yourself, feeling inadequate, or blaming your partner only exacerbates the problem. If instead during such times you can hold, talk, or in some other way support one another, you will be taking a significant step in defusing the problem. While it may not resolve the specific sexual difficulty, it will at least prevent some of the buildup of negative feelings that can infect the rest of the relationship and even destroy it.

Best of luck to you on your journey of life, love, and fulfillment. You now have sufficient skills to build a satisfying sexual relationship. There is lots of time, so enjoy the rich road ahead of you as it unfolds.

# Notes

*Introduction*
1. Morton Hunt, *Sexual Behavior in the 1970s* (Playboy Press, 1974). Shere Hite, *The Hite Report* (Macmillan, 1976).
2. Ellen Frank, Carol Anderson, and Debra Rubenstein, "Frequency of Sexual Dysfunction in 'Normal' Couples," *New England Journal of Medicine* 299 (1978): 111–15.
3. Lonnie Barbach and Linda Levine, *Shared Intimacies: Women's Sexual Experiences* (Anchor/Doubleday, 1981).

*Chapter 1*
1. Julia Heiman, "Physiology of Erotica: Women's Sexual Arousal," *Psychology Today* 8 (1975): 91–92.
2. Aaron Haas, *Teenage Sexuality* (Macmillan, 1979), p. 61.
3. Aaron Haas, *Teenage Sexuality*, p. 84.
4. Clifford Penner and Joyce Penner, *The Gift of Sex: A Christian Guide to Sexual Fulfillment* (Word Books, 1981), pp. 232–33.
5. *The Holy Bible*, King James Version (The World Publishing Co., 1964), Genesis 38:8–10.
6. Alfred C. Kinsey, Wardell Pomeroy, Clyde Martin, and Paul Gebhard, *Sexual Behavior in the Human Female* (Pocket Books, Simon & Schuster, 1953), pp. 390–91.
7. Lonnie Barbach, "Group Treatment of Preorgasmic Women," *Journal of Sex and Marital Therapy* 1 (Winter 1974): 139–45.
8. Alfred C. Kinsey, et al., *Sexual Behavior in the Human Female*, p. 170.
9. Aaron Haas, *Teenage Sexuality*, p. 98.
10. Bernie Zilbergeld, *Male Sexuality* (Little, Brown, 1978).
11. Harold Robbins, *The Betsy* (Pocket Books, 1971), pp. 101–3.

12. Arvalea Nelson, *Personality Attributes of Female Orgasmic Consistency (Or Romance Makes You Frigid)* (University of California, Berkeley, 1974).
13. Merle Shane, *Some Men Are More Perfect Than Others* (Bantam, 1976), p. 76.
14. Aaron Haas, *Teenage Sexuality*, p. 181.
15. Aaron Haas, *Teenage Sexuality*, p. 109.
16. Aaron Haas, *Teenage Sexuality*, p. 76.

*Chapter 2*
1. Personal communication with Brandy and Lewis Engel, psychotherapists in San Francisco, California.
2. Susan Campbell, *A Couple's Journey: Intimacy as a Path to Wholeness* (Impact Publishers, 1980).

*Chapter 3*
1. See Betty Dodson, *Liberating Masturbation* (Body Sex Designs, 1974). Tee Corinne, *Labia Flowers* (Naiad Press, 1981).
2. Joanie Blank, *The Woman's Sex Playbook* (Down There Press, 1979).
3. Shere Hite, *The Hite Report*.
4. Gerda de Bruijn, "From Masturbation to Orgasm with a Partner: How Some Women Bridge the Gap—And How Others Don't," paper presented at the International Congress of Sexology (Tel Aviv, Israel, 1981), p. 9.
5. Dan Tulchinsky and Kenneth Ryan, *Maternal-Fetal Endocrinology* (W. B. Saunders Co., 1980).
6. The Federation of Feminist Women's Health Centers, *A New View of Woman's Body* (Simon and Schuster, 1981).
7. Arnold H. Kegel, "Sexual Functions of the Pubococcygens Muscle," *Western Journal of Surgery* 60 (1952): 521–24.
8. Georgia Kline-Graber and Benjamin Graber, *Women's Orgasm* (Bobbs-Merrill, 1975).
9. John Perry and Beverly Whipple, "Pelvic Muscle Strength of Female Ejaculators: Evidence in Support of a New Theory of Orgasm," *Journal of Sex Research* 17 (1981): 22–39.
10. F. E. Sultan, T. S. Chambless, A. Williams, J. L. Lifschitz, M. Hazard, and L. Kelly, "The Relationship of the Pubococcygeal Condition to Female Sexual Responsiveness in a Normal Population," paper presented at the Association of the Advancement of Behavior Therapy (New York, November, 1980).
11. E. E. Levitt, M. Konovsky, M. P. Freese, and J. F. Thompson, "Intravaginal Pressure Assessed by the Kegel Perineometer," *Archives of Sexual Behavior* 8 (1979): 425–30.
12. Named after E. Grafenberg, who discovered and wrote about the area in 1950 in an article entitled "The Role of Urethra in Female Orgasm," *The International Journal of Sexology* 3 (1950): 145–48.

13. Morton Hunt, *Sexual Behavior in the 1970s*, p. 191.
14. William Masters and Virginia Johnson, *Human Sexual Response* (Little, Brown and Company, 1966).
15. Personal communication with Beverly Whipple.
16. Personal communication with Beverly Whipple.
17. Josephine Singer, "Seven Patterns of Orgasm in Women," submitted manuscript (1981).
18. Shere Hite, *The Hite Report*, p. 73.
19. Shere Hite, *The Hite Report*, p. 73.
20. Shere Hite, *The Hite Report*, p. 101.
21. Shere Hite, *The Hite Report*, p. 103.
22. Frank Addiego, Edwin G. Belzer, Jr., Jill Corroll, William Moger, John D. Perry, and Beverly Whipple, "Female Ejaculation: A Case Study," *Journal of Sex Research* 27 (1981): 13–21.
23. R. Birch, quoted in "Female Ejaculation: Discovering What Was Always There," *Sexuality Today* 3 (1980): 1.
24. William Hartman, Marilyn Fithian, and Barry Campbell, "The Polygraphic Survey of Human Sexual Response," paper presented at the International Congress of Sexology (Rome, Italy, 1978).
25. Alfred C. Kinsey, et al., *Sexual Behavior in the Human Female*, pp. 390–91.
    Morton Hunt, *Sexual Behavior in the 1970s*, p. 191.
    Shere Hite, *The Hite Report*.
26. Gerda de Bruijn, "From Masturbation to Orgasm with a Partner: How Some Women Bridge the Gap—And How Others Don't."
27. Lonnie Barbach and Linda Levine, *Shared Intimacies: Women's Sexual Experiences*.
28. Alfred C. Kinsey, et al., *Sexual Behavior in the Human Female*, pp. 172, 173.
29. Alfred C. Kinsey, et al., *Sexual Behavior in the Human Female*, p. 173.
30. Alfred C. Kinsey, et al., *Sexual Behavior in the Human Female*, p. 142.
31. Alfred C. Kinsey, et al., *Sexual Behavior in the Human Female*, p. 132.
32. Alfred C. Kinsey, et al., *Sexual Behavior in the Human Female*, p. 158.
33. Shere Hite, *The Hite Report*, p. 19.
34. Alfred C. Kinsey, et al., *Sexual Behavior in the Human Female*, p. 161.
35. Shere Hite, *The Hite Report*, my computation of Hite's data.

*Chapter 4*
1. Linda Levine and Lonnie Barbach, *The New Supermen* (to be published in 1983).
2. Richard Bach, *Illusions* (Delacorte Press, 1977).

*Chapter 5*
1. Phillip Sarrel and Lorna Sarrel, "The Redbook Report on Sexual Relationships," *Redbook* (October 1980), p. 77.

2. Lonnie Barbach and Linda Levine, *Shared Intimacies: Women's Sexual Experiences*, p. 146.
3. Lonnie Barbach and Linda Levine, *Shared Intimacies: Women's Sexual Experiences*, p. 156.
4. Linda Levine and Lonnie Barbach, *The New Supermen*.

*Chapter 6*
1. Gerda de Bruijn, "From Masturbation to Orgasm with a Partner: How Some Women Bridge the Gap—And How Others Don't," p. 6.
2. Barbara Hariton and Jerome L. Singer, "Women's Fantasies During Marital Intercourse: Normative and Theoretical Implications," *Journal of Counseling and Clinical Psychology* 42 (1974), p. 322.
3. Gerda de Bruijn, "From Masturbation to Orgasm with a Partner: How Some Women Bridge the Gap—And How Others Don't," p. 6.

*Chapter 7*
1. Some bioenergetic techniques for increasing sexual pleasure can be found in Jack Rosenberg's book, *Total Orgasm* (Random House, 1973).
2. Alfred C. Kinsey, et al., *Sexual Behavior in the Human Female*, p. 50.
3. Shere Hite, *The Hite Report*.

*Chapter 8*
1. Donald Marshall, "Too Much in Mangaia," in *Human Sexual Behavior* (Basic Books, 1971), edited by D. S. Marshall and R. C. Suggs.
2. R. Bakwin and H. Bakwin, *Psychologic Care During Infancy and Childhood* (Appleton Century, 1942).
3. H. F. Harlow, "Love in Infant Monkeys," *Scientific American* (June, 1959): 68–74.
4. The Body Rub Exercise is adapted from William Masters and Virginia Johnson, *Human Sexual Inadequacy* (Little, Brown, 1970).
5. Two good books on massage are *The Massage Book* by George Downing (Random House and Berkeley: The Book Works, 1972) and *The Art of Sensuous Massage* by Gordon Inkeles (Simon and Schuster, 1975).
6. Lonnie Barbach and Linda Levine, *Shared Intimacies: Women's Sexual Experiences*, p. 148.

*Chapter 9*
1. Personal communication with Carol Rinkleib Ellison, a therapist in Berkeley, California, who is a leading proponent of the importance of mental stimulation for vaginal response.
2. P. H. Gebhard, "Factors in Marital Orgasm," *The Journal of Social Issues* 22 (1966): 95.
3. Morton Hunt, *Sexual Behavior in the 1970s*, p. 201.
4. An excellent self-help book for men with sexual problems is *Male Sexuality* by Bernie Zilbergeld.

5. Lonnie Barbach and Linda Levine, *Shared Intimacies: Women's Sexual Experiences*, p. 87.

## Chapter 10

1. Personal communication with Mark Glasser, M.D.

## Chapter 11

1. Morton Hunt, *Sexual Behavior in the 1970s*, p. 190.
2. Bernie Zilbergeld and Carol Rinkleib Ellison were instrumental in distinguishing discrepancies in desire from lack of desire.
3. The Sexual Readiness Scale was designed by Lewis Engel and Brandy Engel.
4. Lonnie Barbach and Linda Levine, *Shared Intimacies: Women's Sexual Experiences*, p. 170.

## Chapter 13

1. The Past Hurts Exercise is adapted from George Bach and Herb Goldberg, *Creative Aggression: The Art of Assertive Living* (Avon, 1975).
2. The Active Listening Exercise is adapted from Thomas Gordon, *PET: Parent Effectiveness Training* (Wyden, 1960).
3. The Caring Days Exercise is adapted from Richard B. Stuart, *Helping Couples Change* (Guilford Press, 1978).
4. The Thought Stopping Exercise is adapted from Joseph Wolpe, *Psychotherapy by Reciprocal Inhibition* (Stanford University Press, 1958).

## Chapter 14

1. The Stress Exercise is adapted from Bernie Zilbergeld, *Male Sexuality*.
2. Lonnie Barbach and Linda Levine, *Shared Intimacies: Women's Sexual Experiences*, p. 39.
3. A tasteful selection of vibrators, bath oils, and other pleasurable products chosen specifically for women can be obtained through *Eve's Garden*, 103 South Street, Boston, Massachusetts 02116. A large selection of new age games and toys including some designed to enhance sexual pleasure are available through *Uniquity*, 215 4th Street, P. O. Box 6, Galt, California 95632.
4. Lonnie Barbach and Linda Levine, *Shared Intimacies: Women's Sexual Experiences*, p. 90.

# INDEX

# Index

Male genitals, sensitivity of,
    compared to female genitals,
    55–56
*Male Sexuality* (Zilbergeld), 69n
Mangaia, sexual initiation in, 151–52
Manual stimulation, 112, 115, 126
  of clitoris, 54, 56, 74, 82, 93, 96,
    126, 134, 186, 187, 197
  as nonintercourse sex, 157
Marijuana, lack of vaginal
    lubrication due to, 200
Marital unhappiness, blocked
    orgasms due to, 190
Marriage counselors, 88, 191, 280
Massage oils, 160, 270
Massages, 115, 162–63, 263
  stomach, 179
Mastectomy, loss of sexual interest
    due to, 231–32
Masters, William H., 27, 60, 63, 157,
    161, 211
  on orgasm, 27
Master's and Johnson's sensate
    focus exercise, 161
Masturbation, 2, 5, 65, 69–76
  during adolescence, 16–17
  biblical references to, 15–16
  body movement and, 138–39
  body stimulation and, 130
  changing hands during, 137
  clitoris and, 132, 134, 137, 138, 140
  determining orgasm problems by,
    70–73
  Enlarging Options Exercise, 134–36
  expanding sensitivity, 136–39
  experimenting with, 133–36
  frequency among teenage girls
    and boys, 15
  Hite on, 140
  as indirect expression of anger, 182
  Kinsey on, 16–17, 69, 72, 73, 74n,
    140
  men and
    frequency, 69
    premature ejaculation, 184–85
  mental arousal and, 130–31, 135
  negative societal feelings about,
    72, 73
  nineteenth-century attitude toward,
    16
  orgasm by, 2, 5, 16, 107
    first time, 108–9

  but never with partner, 107–15
  to intensify feeling, 139–40
  partner sex and, 110–11, 133,
    134–36, 137, 148–49, 181–82,
    225–26
  phallic-shaped objects used for,
    145–46, 203, 204
  positions for, 134–35
  religious condemnation of, 15–16, 72
  as safest way to learn about sex,
    16, 69–70
  slowing down process of, 131–32
  without using hands, 134
  vagina and, 134, 140
  vibrators for, 109, 133, 134, 136,
    145, 270
Masturbation Exercise, 73–76
Masturbation Observation Exercise,
    110–11
Mature vaginal orgasm, 27, 28
Media, the
  images of beauty provided by,
    128–29
  sexually permissive messages of,
    30, 31–32, 34–35
  unrealistic sex fantasy model
    provided by, 18–19, 23, 212, 281
Medications, 211
  sexual disinterest due to, 238
Men
  acquiring knowledge of female
    genitals, 155–56
  concern about penis size and
    erection problems, 6, 19, 27, 32,
    101, 240
  cultural role scripting for, 9
  fantasy model of, 18–20, 46
  foreplay and, 184–85
  frequency of masturbation among
    teenage boys, 15
  genital sensitivity of, 55–56
  importance of communicating with
    women about her sexual
    preferences, 95–96, 101, 151–56
  masturbation and
    frequency, 69
    premature ejaculation, 184–85
  nonintercourse sex and, 27
  physical touching and, 56–57
  as powerful and dominating, 14
  premature ejaculation, 6, 69,
    184–85, 240

Men (*continued*)
  response to partner's
    self-stimulation of clitoris,
    178–79
  responsibility for sexual
    problems, 5
  as sexual experts, 17–18, 21, 28,
    151–52
  the sexual revolution and, 32–33
Menstrual cycle, 60, 84
  vaginal pain due to deep
    thrusting and, 106
Mental arousal, 130–31, 135
  for nonintercourse exercises, 160
Missionary position, 27
Misunderstandings, 39–40, 103
Mittens, use in body rubs of, 163, 270
Mixed messages about sex, 12–15
Moans while having sex, 154
Molestation
  blocked orgasm due to, 189
  sexual disinterest due to, 228
Monkeys, tests proving desire for
    bodily contact, 157
Monogamy, sexual liberation
    movement and, 43
Mouth, use in body rubs of, 163
Movie stars, 32
Multiple orgasms, 32, 65, 68, 126
Muscle tension, 61–62, 139
Music, sensual, 159
Myotonia, 61–62
*My Secret Garden* (Friday) , 253

Nails, use in body rubs of, 163
Negative feelings, 265
  not focusing on, 259
Negative power, 36–38
Negative sex training, sexual
    disinterest due to, 227–28
Negligees, 269, 270, 279
Nelson, Arvalea, 20
New relationships, initiating
    communication in, 94–96
Newspapers, 30, 34
Nin, Anaïs, 254
Nipples, 130
  erection of, 62
  oral stimulation of, 153
Nocturnal emissions (wet dreams) ,
    15

No Exercise, 221–24
Nonintercourse exercises, 158–75
  Body Rub Exercise, 161–66, 171,
    172, 174
  His and Her Exercise, 173–75, 261
  mental setting, 160
  setting the scene, 159–60
  Sexual Request Exercise, 171–73
  Yes Exercise, 168–71
Nonverbal communications, 92–93
"Now" generation, 282
Nude pictures, 131
Nurturers, cultural role script as,
    25–26

Oils, 72, 186
  use in body rubs of, 160, 163, 270
  sensual, 159–60
Old relationships, initiating
    communication in, 96–97
Onanism, *see* Masturbation
Oral sex, 26, 69, 70, 82, 96, 125, 126,
    133, 153, 154
  concerns about, 271–72
  enjoyment of, 176, 177
  as foreplay, 186, 204
Oral Sex Exercises, 4, 271–72
Oral stimulation, 112, 115, 124, 153,
    225
  of clitoris, 153, 183, 197
  as nonintercourse sex, 157
  of penis, 204
Orgasm, 2–3, 9, 51, 101
  blocks to, 107–27, 187–91
    dissatisfaction with orgasm,
      125–26
    Fantasy Enhancement Exercises,
      187–88
    inconsistently orgasmic with
      partner, 122–24
    orgasmic with masturbation but
      not with partner, 107–15
    orgasmic with previous partner
      but not current partner, 116–18
    psychological blocks, 188–91
    relationship problems, 121–22,
      191
    Sleuthing Exercise for removing,
      113–22, 231
    used to be orgasmic with current
      partner, 118–22
  breast stimulation and, 28, 65

Role scripting, *see* Culture, role
  scripting
Romantic/realistic dichotomy, 20
Rubbing, 115
  of genitals to produce orgasm, 108–9

Saliva, 146, 197
  as vaginal lubricant, 199–200
Sarrel, Lorna, 92
Sarrel, Philip, 92
Satin sheets, 269
Satin teddies, 270
Satisfaction as part of the sexual
  process, 68–69
Scars, 128
Scented oils, 160
Scents, 269
Scratching genitals to produce
  orgasm, 108–9
Scrotum, 55
  stimulation of, 155
Self-awareness, 25–26
Self Clitoral Stimulation Exercise,
  179–81
Self-evaluation, 87–88
Self-help books, 280
Selfishness, accepting pleasure and,
  167–68
Self-stimulation, *see* Masturbation
Self-Stimulation Exercise, 130–31
Semen, 272
Seminal fluid, cramping pains due
  to, 207
Sensual environment, creating, 159–60,
  269
Sensual oils, 159–60
Setup Exercise, 263
Sexual Assertiveness Exercise, 176–77,
  217
Sexual contact, explicit,
  recording, 81–83
Sexual Daydream Exercise, 253, 263
Sexual disinterest, *see* Sexual
  interest, lack of
Sexual dissatisfaction, loss of
  sexual interest due to, 237
Sexual dysfunction, 207–8
Sexual initiation, 215–17
Sexual interest, 5, 211–26
  alternatives to sex, 224–26
  breaking avoidance habit, 255–57

creating mood for, 252–55
dangerous circumstances and, 211
determining normal level of, 212,
  217–24
enhancement of, 264–73
expectations and the media, 212
first experience after abstinence
  period, 260–63
lack of, 227–28
  boredom and, 267–68
  causes for, 238–40
  lack of communication, 243–52
  motivational need, 243
  stored anger and, 243–52
loss of, 231–37
  emotional trauma, 231–32
  relationship problems, 232–38
maintaining, 263
sporadic desire, 229–30
unblocking blocks to, 257–60
Sexual Interest Evaluation Exercise,
  217–18, 229
Sexuality, 30–31
  conflict and, 31
  peak age of, 18
  written material on, 33
Sexual Olympics, 32–33, 125
Sexual process, 59–69
  arousal, 60–61
  desire, 60
  orgasm, 64–68
  physiological readiness, 61–64
  satisfaction, 68–69
Sexual Readiness Scale Exercise,
  218–21, 224, 225
Sexual Request Exercise, 171–73
Sexual revolution, 282
  monogamy and, 43
  problems arising from, 30–33
Sexual toys, 270
Shain, Merle, 24
*Shared Intimacies: Women's Sexual
  Experience* (Barbach and
  Levine), 5n, 88n, 97, 268
Sheets, satin, 269
Showering together, 257, 263, 269
Simultaneous Stimulation Exercise,
  146
Singer, Josephine, 65, 114
Situationally orgasmic women, 71
Skin as erogenous zone, 158
Sleuthing Exercise, 118–22, 231